✳

HOW PEARY REACHED THE POLE

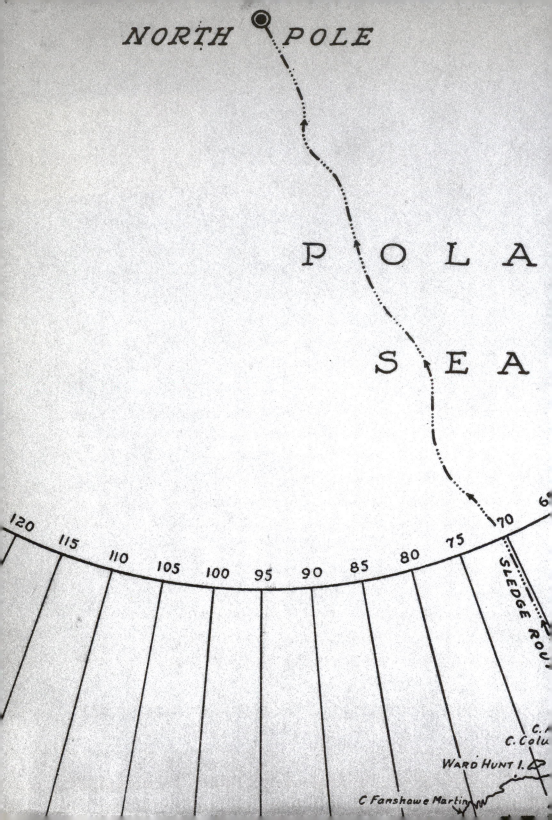

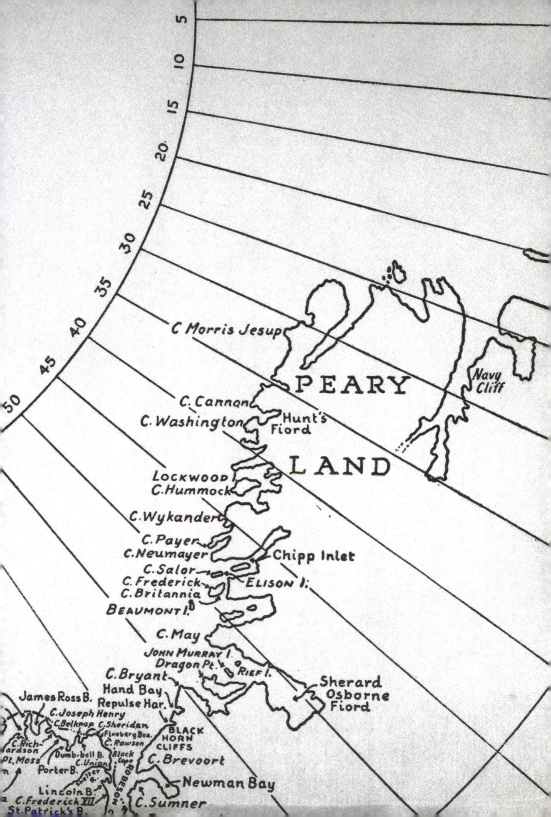

HOW
PEARY
REACHED
THE
POLE

The Personal Story of His Assistant

by

DONALD B. MACMILLAN

Introduction by
Genevieve M. LeMoine, Susan A. Kaplan, and Anne Witty

McGILL-QUEEN'S UNIVERSITY PRESS

Montreal & Kingston • London • Ithaca

© McGill-Queen's University Press 2008

ISBN 978-0-7735-3450-6

Legal deposit fourth quarter 2008
Bibliothèque nationale du Québec

Printed in Canada on acid-free paper that is 100% ancient forest free
(100% post-consumer recycled), processed chlorine free.

Originally published in 1934 by Houghton Mifflin.

This book has been published with the help of a grant from Kane Lodge Foundation, Inc.

McGill-Queen's University Press acknowledges the support of the Canada Council for
the Arts for our publishing program. We also acknowledge the financial support of the
Government of Canada through the Book Publishing Industry Development Program
(BPIDP) for our publishing activities.

Library and Archives Canada Cataloguing in Publication

MacMillan, Donald Baxter, 1874–1970
How Peary Reached the Pole : the personal story of his assistant / Donald B. MacMillan,
introduction by Genevieve M. LeMoine, Susan A. Kaplan, and Anne Witty.

Includes index.
ISBN 978-0-7735-3450-6

1. MacMillan, Donald Baxter, 1874–1970–Travel–Arctic regions. 2. Peary, Robert E.
(Robert Edwin), 1856–1920–Travel–Arctic regions. 3. Arctic regions–Discovery and
exploration. 4. North Pole–Discovery and exploration. 5. Explorers–United States–
Biography. I. Title.

G670.1909.M33 2008   910.9163'2   C2008-903903-3

This book was designed and typeset by studio oneonone in Sabon 10.5/14

Frontispiece: The *Roosevelt*, taking on water from the Cape York Glacier. Photograph
by Donald B. MacMillan, Peary-MacMillan Arctic Museum, Bowdoin College,
3000.33.279

TO

THE MEMORY OF

Rear-Admiral ROBERT E. PEARY, U.S.N.

The true explorer does his work not for any hopes of
reward or honor, but because the thing which he has
set himself to do is a part of his being and must be
accomplished for the sake of its accomplishment.

CONTENTS

PREFACE

How Peary Reached the Pole was written by Donald B. MacMillan in 1928 and published in 1934, marking the twenty-fifth anniversary of Robert E. Peary's 1908–09 North Pole Expedition. This re-issue of *How Peary Reached the Pole* commemorates both the hundredth anniversary of Robert E. Peary's 1908–09 North Pole Expedition and the 2007–09 International Polar Year. The book's republication occurs at a time of increased concern about the effects of climate change on northern ecosystems and communities, and increasingly vexing geopolitical issues about access to the Northwest Passage and the Arctic Ocean.

It is worth noting that one hundred years ago a number of countries were vying to be the first to plant their flag at the North Pole in order to claim whatever lands and resources might be there. When explorers determined that there was no exposed land at or near the North Pole, people turned their attention elsewhere. One century later, nations are again competing for access to the resources of the region, this time with a focus on what might be found below the ocean floor. This re-issue of Donald B. MacMillan's *How Peary Reached the Pole*, long out of print, will allow a new generation to read the book, providing an opportunity to reflect on our relationships to a challenging and fragile ecosystem and the people who call the Arctic home.

This edition of the work includes a new introduction with a biography of MacMillan and photographs drawn from the hand-tinted glass lantern slide collection he used to illustrate his popular lectures. MacMillan's papers (including his North Pole journal) are housed in the George J. Mitchell Department of Special Collections and Archives at Bowdoin College in Brunswick, Maine, and his photographs are housed in the Peary-MacMillan Arctic Museum and Arctic Studies Center, also part of Bowdoin College.

Work on this publication began in 2005 when we reread *How Peary Reached the Pole* and were reminded both how delightful it is and that it provides a perspective on the North Pole Expedition that cannot be found elsewhere. Kane Lodge Foundation, Inc., awarded the Arctic Museum a grant that allowed staff to begin background work. Audrey Amidon, a Bowdoin graduate (class of 2003), had the task of sorting through typescripts of various versions of Donald B. MacMillan's North Pole lecture housed in Special Collections. She successfully correlated individual North Pole lantern slides in the Arctic Museum's collection with MacMillan's notes on his 1910 lecture script and began digitizing the images for ease of use.

Zoë Eddy, class of 2010, completed the task of digitizing the North Pole lantern slide collection, further facilitating its study. Portland Color, of Portland, Maine, painstakingly generated clean, high-resolution digital versions of many of the photographs. The Museum's Charles L. Hildreth Fund made this preservation and access work possible. In 2007 Kane Lodge Foundation, Inc., provided additional support in the form of a publication subvention that has allowed us to include color images in this publication. The Museum's Russell and Janet Doubleday Fund underwrote staff research and writing.

We want to thank Audrey Amidon and Zoë Eddy for their hard work, and the staff of Bowdoin College's George J. Mitchell Department of Special Collections and Archives, Hawthorne-Longfellow Library, for providing easy access to MacMillan's lecture notes. We are grateful to Mildred Jones, a longstanding Arctic Museum volunteer, who rescanned the photographs that MacMillan included in the original publication to ensure the high quality reproductions in this new version. We also want to express our gratitude to the directors of Kane Lodge Foundation, Inc., for their ongoing support of this endeavor and our appreciation to the staff members of McGill-Queen's University Press for their efforts to bring this project to fruition.

Susan A. Kaplan and Genevieve M. LeMoine

INTRODUCTION

Genevieve M. LeMoine, Susan A. Kaplan, and Anne Witty

How Peary Reached the Pole was Donald B. MacMillan's fourth and last book. In it, MacMillan describes the beginning of his career in the Arctic, as a member of Robert E. Peary's 1908–09 North Pole Expedition. Written some twenty years after the fact and from the perspective of a seasoned Arctic traveler, the book is, however, more than a simple retelling of the memorable events of the expedition, although it is also that. *How Peary Reached the Pole* is an extended argument about the value of Peary's methods, equipment, and leadership, a response to the writings of Peary's many detractors, and an unparalleled window onto the day-to-day ups and downs experienced by the men on the expedition.

The basic outline of the events of the expedition and its aftermath are well known. On 6 April 1909 American Arctic explorer Robert E. Peary, his African American assistant Matthew Henson, and northwest Greenland Inughuit[1] Ootah, Ooqueah, Seegloo, and Egingwah reached the North Pole by dog sledge. They marked the event by planting a silk American flag, made for Peary by his wife, Josephine, atop a mound of ice. For Peary, this was the culmination of eighteen years of planning, experimenting, and traveling in the far north. Reaching the Pole was an achievement he sought for himself and for his country. For Henson, who had been at Peary's side during every expedition except the first, this was a thrilling time: he understood how much hard work, sacrifice, and courage had been needed to get to this point and he was filled with patriotic pride. For the

Inughuit, however, it was just another day on a curious and sometimes dangerous excursion to a region nearly devoid of life.

On 6 September 1909 the Associated Press received a cable from Peary, sent from Indian Harbour in southern Labrador, announcing that he had reached the North Pole on 6 April 1909. During the following days Peary and crew members sent additional communications from the Marconi station at Battle Harbour, Labrador. The press converged on Battle Harbour where, on 16 September, Peary held a news conference (Figs. 1 and 2). He immediately became embroiled in controversy as in the first week of September Frederick A. Cook had announced that he and two Inughuit companions had reached the North Pole on 21 April 1908. While telegrams were sent to and from Battle Harbour, Cook was being credited with "discovering" the North Pole. Peary quickly challenged Cook's claim, and both men's accounts, as well as the dispute between them, became headline news.

Both Cook and Peary reported flying the American flag at the northernmost point in the world and leaving records of their accomplishments at the Pole. However, as the North Pole is located in the Arctic Ocean, those records were left on ice, floating on the open ocean. Currents immediately pulled the ice south and east, where warmer waters and the sun melted it, sending any records to the bottom of the sea. The men's reputations and whatever documentation they kept with them were the only basis by which the veracity of their accounts could be judged.

Eventually Peary was declared the "winner" of the race to reach the North Pole and geographic societies, universities, and governments, including the United States Congress, bestowed honors upon him. The members of the Peary scientific parties, who had all participated in support sledging activities, were honored for their efforts as well. Initially, Henson received honors only from African American organizations and it was not until decades later that his country acknowledged his achievements. The Inughuit, without whom the Americans would not have reached the Pole, received no official recognition whatsoever, though Peary acknowledged their contributions in his accounts.

Figure 1. Robert E. Peary as photographed by a reporter, Battle Harbour,
Labrador, September 1909.

In *How Peary Reached the Pole* MacMillan describes the expedition,
the subsequent controversy, and the honors from the perspective of a seasoned Arctic explorer (modestly skirting the issue of honors he received as
a result of his participation in the expedition). In doing so he significantly
increases the value of the book to historians. As a first-hand account,
How Peary Reached the Pole is an important primary source. And, unlike
the other first-hand accounts, it is also an analytical study of Peary's methods, career, and place in the history of Arctic exploration.

Figure 2. A group of reporters huddled on the deck of SS *Roosevelt* at Battle Harbour, Labrador, in September 1909.

WRITING ABOUT PEARY'S NORTH POLE EXPEDITION

First Person Accounts

Peary's 1908–09 North Pole Expedition is among the most thoroughly published of all Arctic voyages. Peary published the first reports, which were serialized in *Hampton's Magazine* in 1910 (Fig. 3) and then appeared in the book, *The North Pole: Its Discovery in 1909 Under the Auspices of the Peary Arctic Club*, published that same year. First-person accounts by other expedition members soon followed, despite the initial ban on publishing and lecturing about the expedition stipulated in the men's contracts and enforced by Peary. George Borup, the youngest member of the sledging/scientific party, wrote a lively if boyish account, titled *A Tenderfoot with Peary*, in 1911. Matthew Henson's book, *A Negro Explorer at the North Pole*, appeared in 1912 and included an introduction by Peary. John Goodsell, the expedition surgeon, completed a manuscript in 1915 but never published it due to an extended dispute with Peary. An edited version of it was published posthumously in 1983 by the Mercer County Historical Society as *On Polar Trails: The Peary Expedition to the North Pole, 1908–09*.

The last first-hand accounts of the expedition appeared years later. Robert A. Bartlett, the captain of SS *Roosevelt* and the last member of the sledging/scientific party to turn back before Peary, Henson, and the four Inughuit proceeded towards the North Pole, included a brief description of his role in the expedition in his 1928 book *The Log of Bob Bartlett*. Donald MacMillan, also a member of the sledging/scientific party, who had lectured on the topic beginning in 1910 and had published a few related articles, did not write his book-length account, *How Peary Reached the Pole*, until 1928 and did not publish it until 1934. By that time he was the only surviving member of the scientific staff who had not written an account of the expedition and was also an accomplished explorer in his own right.

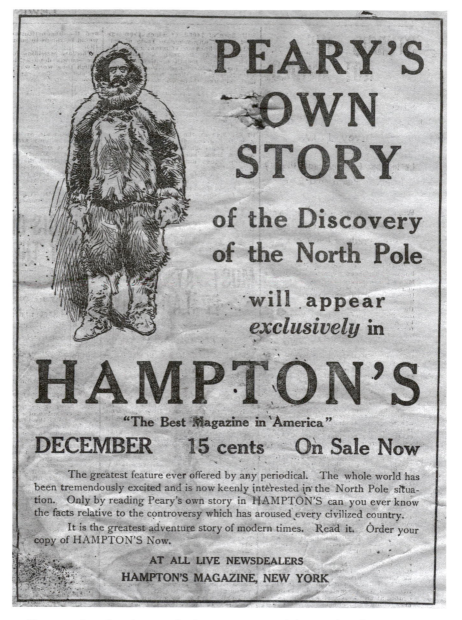

Figure 3. An advertisement for Peary's account of the North Pole Expedition serialized in *Hampton's Magazine* in 1910.

Subsequent Literature

These first-hand accounts were by no means the only books written about the expedition. Driven largely by the controversy, books about Cook and Peary's North Pole expeditions began appearing soon after the explorers made their competing claims, including Charles Morris' edited 1909 work *Finding the North Pole*, George Bryce's 1910 work *The Siege and Conquest of the North Pole*, W. Henry Lewin's 1911 book *Did Peary Reach the Pole?*, Edwin Swift Balch's 1913 work *The North Pole and Bradley Land*, and Thomas Hall's 1917 publication *Has the North Pole Been Discovered?*

Much of the writing about the discovery of the North Pole published in the last forty years has continued these discussions of the North Pole controversy and the characters of the two men. John Weems wrote a biography of Peary that appeared in 1967, titled *Peary: The Explorer and the Man*, and Cook was the focus of Howard Abramson's efforts that resulted in the 1991 publication *Hero in Disgrace: The Life of Arctic Explorer Frederick A. Cook*. Barry Lopez dealt with both Peary and Cook in his 1986 work *Arctic Dreams*, as did Pierre Berton in his 1988 work *The Arctic Grail*. Polar explorers and adventurers attempting to replicate Peary's marches joined the debate, including Will Steger and Paul Schurke with their 1987 book *North to the Pole* and Wally Herbert with his 1989 book *The Noose of Laurels*. (See also the web site for the 2005 Barclays Capital "Ultimate North" expedition led by Tom Avery). Many authors continue to focus on the character of both men, including Robert Bryce in his 1997 book *Cook and Peary: A Controversy Resolved* and Bruce Henderson in his *True North: Peary, Cook, and the Race to the Pole*, published in 2005. Allen Counter shifted the focus slightly in 1991 when he published *North Pole Legacy: Black, White, and Eskimo*, in which he made the case that Henson was the first man to reach the North Pole (see William Mills 2003, *Exploring Polar Frontiers,* for a list of other North Pole "first" contenders). Parts of the explorers' journals, accounts, calculations, and photographs have been examined by many of these authors in efforts to establish whether the men had the time, energy, and navigational skills to travel the distances claimed. Thomas Davies and his colleagues at the

Navigation Foundation scrutinized Peary's expedition records, instruments, and photographs to try to determine his farthest north and published their findings in the 1989 work *Robert E. Peary at the North Pole*. In 1996 William Molett published *Robert Peary and Matthew Henson at the North Pole*, in which he analyzed Peary's navigation techniques as well as the techniques employed by other explorers. A steady stream of newspaper and magazine articles and cartoons focused on various facets of this controversy have also appeared.

Another body of literature dealing with Peary, Cook, Henson, and the North Pole controversy adopts a broader view of these men's efforts and their expeditions. *Arctic Exploration and International Relations, 1900–1932: A Period of Expanding National Interests*, the 1992 work by Nancy Fogelson, provides insights into the political and economic motivations that drove various nations, including the United States, to invest in the Polar race. Lisa Bloom reviews popular literature written mostly by explorers and discusses what the works reveal about issues of gender, race, and class in her 1993 book *Gender on Ice: American Ideologies of Polar Expeditions*. Lyle Dick has written an insightful analysis of Peary and interactions between the explorer's men and the Inughuit in his 2001 book *Muskox Land: Ellesmere Island in the Age of Contact*. Most recently, Michael F. Robinson's 2006 publication *The Coldest Crucible: Arctic Exploration and American Culture* uses archival documents and published works to discuss individual American explorers' relationships to the scientific and political establishments, as well as the public's changing attitudes and expectations about explorers.

Most of the popular publications leave the impression that the effort to reach the North Pole was solely Peary's idea and a personal goal. The broader perspective reveals that he was working for a government eager to expand its horizons in a world in search of new exploitable resources. In the early 1900s, the known High Arctic islands, Baffin Island, Ellesmere Island, and even islands yet to be discovered had been claimed by the Dominion of Canada and much of Greenland was under Danish colonial rule. Both countries were concerned that the United States would claim northern Greenland and Ellesmere Island by citing Americans' long history of exploration of these lands, beginning with Elisha Kent Kane in 1853. New sources of natural resources were on everyone's mind, and Peary's extended stays in these lands, beginning in 1891, were seen by other nations as threatening. At the same time, the United States government and American businessmen eagerly awaited Peary's reports. It is not surprising that Peary's expedition funding came from American industrialists, nor that he had the backing of the president of the United States and used his career as a US Navy civil engineer with naval officer rank to enhance his visibility and status. When Peary ventured north, carrying associations with powerful sectors of the nation, and returned home claiming attainment of the Pole, he became an emblem of what the country aspired to be.

HOW PEARY REACHED THE POLE

Bert went to the traps but found nothing, but did see tracks of rabbits.
Made a table tennis set and played Miriam and Bert. Began the account
of Peary's North Pole trip.   Thursday, Jan. 19, 1928

Donald B. MacMillan composed this rather sketchy journal entry in Anetalak Bay, Labrador, in the winter of 1928. He was there as the leader of a ten-member scientific expedition, sponsored by the Field Museum of Natural History in Chicago, that was to spend a year in Labrador conducting research. When not busy with expedition-related tasks, MacMillan worked on a variety of projects, including a Labrador Inuit dictionary and this book. MacMillan's situation in Anetalak Bay differed in many ways from his first winter in the Arctic nineteen years earlier, when he was one of Robert E. Peary's assistants on the 1908–09 North Pole Expedition, but it was firmly rooted in that early experience. In the intervening years MacMillan had developed his own career as an Arctic explorer, with twenty years of leading his own expeditions, and had become an innovator, researcher, and educator. He was a well-known expert on Arctic issues, with a broad knowledge of northern work that gave him an important perspective on his early experience. It is this perspective that makes his book stand out from those published shortly after the North Pole Expedition members returned to the United States.

By the time MacMillan began working on *How Peary Reached the Pole*, he had already published a variety of scholarly and popular articles as well as two books describing his own expeditions: *Four Years in the White North*, which appeared in 1918, and *Etah and Beyond*, published in 1927. As in those books, the text of *How Peary Reached the Pole* is largely based on the journal he kept at the time, augmented by a detailed knowledge of both recent and older accounts of Arctic exploration, with the story presented as a chronological narrative of the events of 1908–09. Despite the years that had passed, many of the events MacMillan describes come across as fresh – his sense of wonder at first encountering the Polar Eskimo, his exhilaration at going to the northernmost tip of Greenland, and his indignation at the subdued reception the expedition members received on their return to New York. However, as the title suggests, MacMillan's intent is not only to demonstrate his conviction that Peary did reach the Pole in April 1909 but also to argue that Peary's methods, perfected over many years of trial and error, made such a journey, if not easy, at least possible.

More than any of the other members of the expeditions (with the possible exception of Bartlett), MacMillan took Peary's methods and built on them, making him uniquely well placed to evaluate Peary's accomplishments. His own long sledge journeys, particularly on the 1913–17 Crocker Land Expedition, made good use of the Peary methods. He modified these methods, sometimes in useful ways, but more often than not he returned either to Peary's techniques or to the older, Inughuit ways. In 1914, for example, MacMillan experimented with a light-framed sledge similar to those used in Alaska. It proved too fragile for the rough sea ice and he soon went back to the sturdier Inughuit-type sledge Peary had favored. Similarly, although MacMillan's trips did not generally warrant laying out the series of supply caches that the trip to the Pole had required, he was meticulous about planning and supplies and was intolerant of the more laid-back approach taken by Peter Freuchen, for example, that he experienced on an aborted trip across Melville Bay during the Crocker Land Expedition.

Perhaps influenced by the attacks on Peary's character during the controversy that raged after their return from the North Pole Expedition, MacMillan describes a Peary rarely seen in other books, a man very concerned about the welfare of his men and one who paid meticulous attention to every detail of the training and safety of the crew, as well as to the fine-tuning of equipment and techniques. MacMillan's appreciation of Peary's actions is colored by his own experiences as an expedition member and then as a leader, but it is not simply the result of after-the-fact reflections: most of the incidents MacMillan describes and many of his opinions on them appeared first in his 1908–09 journal, written while the events he describes were happening. On 30 May he wrote:

> It is hard to believe that this stretch of country so inhospitable to this gallant band of men[2] is the same over which we are now passing two weeks earlier in the year; a country from which we have taken fifty-two musk-oxen, a large number of hare and ptarmigan, enjoying almost every minute of our forty-two days. Our happiness and our health are not to be ascribed to a change in local conditions, but to a perfect equipment even to the smallest details as worked out by Commander Peary during his twenty years of arctic service.

Similarly, in his 1910 lecture he reports, "Borup and myself, two inexperienced men, but with Commander's perfect equipment were passing old world records and having the time of our lives." The book expands upon the journal, of course, but MacMillan's admiration of Peary and his techniques comes across as clearly in his earlier writings as it does in this later publication.

The picture MacMillan paints of Peary is more nuanced than those that have appeared in recent years, showing sides of Peary that are often overlooked. Kind gestures and thoughtfulness are not usually associated with Peary's gruff image, but MacMillan reports a number of instances in which Peary's concern for the well-being of his men went beyond what one would expect. In *How Peary Reached the Pole* (p. 92) he reports, for example, that during a period when MacMillan was ill and confined to bed, "Commander, always considerate and ever kind, never failed nightly to open his door and play for me my favorite pianola record 'The Wedding of the Winds.'" He also describes how Peary personally warmed MacMillan's frostbitten feet against his stomach on the trip to the Pole (pp. 166–67).

More important than these small kindnesses, MacMillan describes at some length Peary's intense focus on all aspects of the expedition. MacMillan had gotten an initial hint of this when he was summoned to Peary's hotel room in New York to sign his contract. There he found Peary testing countless varieties of equipment in his quest to find the lightest and most efficient articles for use on the Polar Sea (p. 12). Throughout the book, MacMillan describes in some detail the efforts that Peary made to ensure he used the best equipment. When commercial models proved inadequate he resorted to designing his own, creating a stove that turned snow into boiling water in nine minutes and then extinguished itself! (p. 153). Peary wanted a stove that would balance the need to travel as lightly as possible by reducing the amount of fuel required with his conviction that a warm and happy crew worked more efficiently and that hot tea was therefore an absolute necessity.

MacMillan makes it clear that Peary's planning for success did not stop with perfecting his equipment. "Commander Peary was a good physical director" too, according to MacMillan (p. 99). To prepare the new members of his team, referred to as the "Tenderfeet," for relay work across snow- and ice-covered terrain, Peary assigned them and their Inughuit companions scientific and hunting duties so the newcomers could learn to function in this challenging environment and the small groups would become efficient teams. This not only allowed them to develop important skills but also got them into top physical shape and kept them busy during the dark winter months. MacMillan describes these early experiences in detail. For instance, he explains how he learned to effectively aim his long dog whip by assembling a "team" of dogs that had died and covering their coats with snow. He then stood on his "sledge," placed the appropriate distance from the dogs, and cracked his whip. If he inadvertently hit a dog (the whip is snapped above or next to a dog to encourage and direct it but is not supposed to strike the animal) a puff of snow would appear and he would know he had not yet perfected his technique.

MacMillan also describes the relay system Peary developed to move parties of men driving dog-drawn sledges laden with equipment and food north across the Arctic Ocean and discusses how Peary constantly adjusted the make-up of parties. He explains the thinking that went into Peary's design of the rawhide-lashed, twelve-foot long sledges used on this expedition, how Peary determined the weight each sledge should carry, and why no one carried a sleeping bag.

More than any of the other first-hand accounts, *How Peary Reached the Pole* highlights the important role that Inughuit men and women played on the expedition. Foreshadowing his life-long interest in their culture, MacMillan's description of his first encounter with the Inughuit is a mixture of wonder and admiration, tinged with inevitable confusion and even distaste for their unfamiliar ways. He is impressed by their ingenuity and the suitability of their tents for the harsh weather they must withstand but put off (initially at least) by the unfamiliar odor of people who dress in skin clothing and have little reason or opportunity to bathe. As he gets to know the Inughuit better, MacMillan describes individual personalities and tells stories of cultural miscommunications in both directions. In so doing he provides a sense of the truly difficult – as well as amusing – situations men and women from dramatically different cultures encountered while working together.

WHO WAS DONALD B. MACMILLAN?

Donald Baxter MacMillan was thirty-three years old when he agreed to accompany Peary as a member of the 1908–09 expedition. MacMillan had long had an interest in the north, although with no real expectation of traveling there himself. However his upbringing, his love of the outdoors – especially the sea – and his legendary physical strength and agility prepared him well for what lay ahead.

As the youngest of five children growing up in a seafaring family in Provincetown, Massachusetts, MacMillan was mischievous and daring. Not even a near-drowning accident in the icy waters of Provincetown Harbor slowed him down, according to his biographer Everett Allen. A summer voyage to the Bras d'Or Lakes, near Sydney, Nova Scotia, to visit his father's family gave him an early taste for travel and for the sea. As a fishing schooner captain, MacMillan's father, Neil, regularly sailed the North Atlantic, visiting Labrador, Newfoundland, and Greenland, bringing his children sealskin *kamik*s and tales of sea ice and the midnight sun. As a child (Fig. 4), MacMillan anticipated following his father's career and seeing these wonders himself. The tragic death of his father at sea in 1883 when MacMillan was nine, followed only a few years later by the death of his mother, Sarah Gardner MacMillan, led to dramatic changes in young MacMillan's life. He spent a few years living with the Provincetown family of Captain Murdick McDonald, a Grand Banks fisherman, before moving to Freeport, Maine, to live with his older sister, Letitia, and her husband, Winthrop Fogg. Characteristically, though, he remained close friends with many people in Provincetown for the rest of his life.

In Freeport, MacMillan was quick to take advantage of any opportunities that presented themselves. He worked at many jobs through his high school years (Fig. 5), including operating a gymnastics school, where he began to develop a life-long affinity for teaching as well as his remarkable strength. His hard work paid off when he was admitted to Bowdoin College in Brunswick, Maine. There he worked diligently, graduating in 1898 with a degree in geology in spite of a year off due to illness (Fig. 6). MacMillan's years in Freeport and then at Bowdoin set him on some of the paths he was to follow for the rest of his life, although he had no expectation at that point of being an Arctic explorer.

When he left Bowdoin, MacMillan began his professional life as a teacher, initially as principal of the Levi Hall school in North Gorham, Maine, and later as a teacher at elite private schools, first Swarthmore

Figure 4. Donald MacMillan, age 10.

Preparatory School and later Worcester Academy (Fig. 7). During summers, he operated a camp for boys on Bustin's Island in Casco Bay just off Freeport, Maine (Fig. 8). It was there that he first attracted the attention of Peary, also an alumnus of Bowdoin College and equally devoted to outdoor activities and summers in Casco Bay. MacMillan made the news when he rescued nine people in two separate boating accidents. These

Figure 5. Donald MacMillan's
high school graduation portrait.

Figure 6. Bowdoin College Indian Club team.
MacMillan is in the second row, far left.

Figure 7. Donald MacMillan as a physical education instructor at Swarthmore Preparatory School, 1901.

Figure 8. Donald MacMillan at his summer camp for boys on Bustin's Island, Maine.

actions impressed Peary, who invited MacMillan to join the 1905–06 North Pole expedition. Much to his dismay, MacMillan found himself unable to accept Peary's offer: he had just signed a new contract with Worcester Academy and felt bound by that.

His keen disappointment at not being able to go to the Arctic comes across in this book, as it did in later interviews with biographer Everett Allen when he confessed that he had attended the departure of Peary's ship SS *Roosevelt* from Portland, longing to be aboard but unwilling to announce his presence to the lucky members of the voyage. Imagine his excitement, then, when he learned that Peary had not been successful and was determined to try again. That Peary offered MacMillan a position on the 1908–09 expedition is evidence of the strong impression MacMillan had made on him. MacMillan was, in many ways, Peary's ideal candidate for the position – physically strong (the strongest man he knew, according to Peary's assistant Matthew Henson), experienced at sea and in outdoor activities, and well educated.

The opportunity to accompany Peary was a major turning point for MacMillan. He was granted a leave of absence from Worcester Academy but, although he maintained a strong commitment to education, never returned to take up his appointment there. His excitement at going north, and his thorough enjoyment of the time he spent there, come across clearly in the book, so it comes as no surprise that he abandoned his teaching career to take up the life of Arctic explorer.

MacMillan's decision to embark on this new path came at a crucial time. Peary had, with the 1908–09 North Pole expedition, attained what in many lectures he characterized as the "last great geographical prize." What was there left for an Arctic explorer to do? With characteristic determination and adaptability, MacMillan set out to demonstrate that there was much left to be accomplished and spent the rest of his long life doing just that.

In fact, in the early years of the twentieth century, despite the "discovery" of the North Pole, there was still much that was unknown about the Arctic. Early on MacMillan worked in many areas – he focused on geographical exploration, naturally, but also on scientific and anthropological research. He began graduate work in anthropology at Harvard and continued his Arctic career, completing three summer trips to Labrador in 1910, 1911, and 1912. Ultimately, however, he had his sights set on bigger things. With George Borup, his friend from the North Pole Expedition, he planned a major expedition to the far north with the goal of reaching Crocker Land, a place Peary had sighted in 1906, far across the ice to the northwest of Cape Thomas Hubbard. Raising money for such an undertaking was difficult for two essentially untried young men, but Borup was working as a curator at the American Museum of Natural History in New York City and managed to secure the museum's support for an expedition in 1912. Sadly, before the arrangements could be completed he drowned in a boating accident, leaving MacMillan to argue for the museum's continued sponsorship. He was eventually successful, although the expedition was delayed by a year, leaving New York in the summer of 1913.

The Crocker Land Expedition, which lasted from 1913 to 1917, was the second major turning point in MacMillan's Arctic career. The lessons he learned in those four years shaped his approach to the north for the next forty years. Once the North Pole had been reached, there were few remaining geographic unknowns in the Arctic. Crocker Land, thought to be an island to the northwest of Ellesmere Island, was a last, faint hope for new land. However, after a grueling sledge journey over the sea ice in the spring of 1914, MacMillan demonstrated that, as some had suspected, it was a mirage, the *fata morgana* seen by many Arctic travelers. With no major exploration left, and a strong desire to continue working in the north, MacMillan had to turn his energies in other directions: if no new land was out there waiting to found, there certainly remained much to learn about the Arctic (Fig. 9). In the early part of the expedition, MacMillan had struggled to work well with the Inughuit. He had not shown himself to have Peary's depth of experience and the Inughuit saw no reason to respect him. He had to both earn their respect and learn to listen to their more experienced voices, something he accomplished only after some hard lessons on the sea ice.

Over the next years MacMillan, rather than trying to discover new lands, supported the zoological and geological work of Maurice C. Tan-

Figure 9. Borup Lodge, MacMillan's northwest Greenland base of operations during the Crocker Land Expedition, 1913–17.

quary and W. Elmer Ekblaw, two University of Illinois scientists on his team. He busied himself collecting ethnographic objects, expending great care and thought shooting still photographs and motion picture films of Arctic animals and Inughuit life and compiling an extensive Inughuit vocabulary list.

Like Peary, MacMillan was also interested in extending technology. During the Crocker Land Expedition, he had taken some of the earliest surviving motion picture film of the Arctic. He had also brought a radio operator and radio equipment but, despite tremendous effort, no broad-

Figure 10. Schooner *Bowdoin* anchored off Baffin Island, 1929.

casts were successfully sent to or received from the south. As he waited for a relief ship to appear (his return was delayed by two years), he began to envision a better way to conduct northern research. As Peary had needed the *Roosevelt*, so MacMillan decided he needed a vessel, although of a different sort.

After his return from northwest Greenland and a stint in the US Navy in World War I, MacMillan was eager to go north again. By then he had the experience, and the reputation, to allow him to do this on his own terms. He raised money to build a schooner that he had designed expressly for sailing the ice-choked uncharted waters of the far north. That vessel, the schooner *Bowdoin* (Fig. 10), was launched in 1921 and still sails today. Unlike the *Roosevelt*, which Peary envisioned as an icebreaker, MacMillan wanted a strong, nimble vessel that could sail into and maneuver through the pack ice. The *Bowdoin* was strong enough to withstand being frozen into the sea ice for the winter, with a shallow draught that allowed her to avoid many of the uncharted rocks along the Labrador, Baffin Island, and Greenland coasts (Fig. 11).

Figure 11. Schooner *Bowdoin* in winter quarters in northwest Greenland, 1924.

With the *Bowdoin* as his base of operations, MacMillan embarked on the third stage of his career, in which research and technological experimentation were the two driving forces. In the summer of 1921, when his vessel was launched, he sailed with a small crew to southern Baffin Island to test her capabilities. There he tried again to make a radio work in the far north, filmed, photographed, and, with scientists from the Carnegie Institution, studied magnetic variation, natural history, and anthropology of the region. Returning to the United States in 1922, he embarked on a lecture tour, one of his main sources of income at the time. After a lecture in Chicago he was asked what he found most difficult about working in the dark Arctic winter. Having learnt from Peary and the Inughiut that the winter itself is no great hurdle if you are properly prepared, MacMillan responded that for him the most difficult thing was the isolation, the lack of communication from family and friends. He told how, despite the best efforts on two expeditions, they had been unable to establish radio contact with anyone. In the audience that night, as recounted by John Bryant and Harold Cones in the 2000 publication *Dangerous Crossings: The First Modern Polar Expedition, 1925*, was Eugene McDonald, president of Zenith Corporation. McDonald approached MacMillan to tell him that new technology his company was developing should make radio communication possible. This fortunate encounter began a fruitful collaboration between the two men. Tests over the winter of 1923–24, when MacMillan froze the *Bowdoin* into Refuge Harbor in northwest Greenland, proved that the Zenith shortwave radio could indeed penetrate the electromagnetic disturbance of the auroral band, which had prevented longer radio waves from traveling south. This gave rise to a Navy-sponsored expedition in the summer of 1925, led jointly by MacMillan, McDonald, and Richard Byrd, to test the potential of radio communication and flight in the Arctic. Weather and ice conditions, combined with untried amphibious airplanes, prevented a flight over the Pole, but the men demonstrated the possibility of such a flight in principle. More significantly, the radio tests were a resounding success, with broadcasts from northwest Greenland heard by naval radio operators as far away as Tasmania (Fig. 12).

Increasingly, MacMillan's expeditions focused on testing equipment and supporting the scientific research of others. For example, on the 1927–28 trip, during which he wrote *How Peary Reached the Pole*, he introduced Labrador residents to motorized travel over the sea ice in a modified Model T Ford. This was his last over-wintering expedition, but throughout the 1930s and early 1940s he continued to take scientists north. Miriam Look MacMillan, whom he married in 1935 (Fig. 13), soon became a member of those expeditions as well. Over the years he included more and more young men – students – on these expeditions, making a slow transition to the final stage of his career, during which the training and education of young people were his main objectives. Often the young men who accompanied him were assistants to scientists from

Figure 12. Inughuit broadcasting from Etah, 1925.

sponsoring institutions, but over the years they came to take the place of the researchers, collecting data on their behalf.

During World War II, MacMillan was called to Washington, D.C., and worked with the Navy on a variety of Arctic-related intelligence and reconnaissance projects. The *Bowdoin* was requisitioned for Arctic work by the Navy, with Lieutenant Stuart Hotchkiss in command of the schooner. Following the war MacMillan purchased the *Bowdoin* back from the Navy and he and his wife resumed their trips north. By this time, MacMillan's expedition crews were made up almost entirely of young men who paid for the privilege of sailing with him. There was always a physician along, who provided medical care not only to the crew but also to people in the remote communities the schooner visited. The MacMillans also provided school and medical supplies and other forms of support to northern com-

Figure 13. Donald and Miriam MacMillan at the
wheel of the *Bowdoin*.

munities. These voyages continued every summer until 1950, with a last
trip in 1954 when MacMillan was eighty years old (Fig. 14).

MacMillan's observations about the Inughuit in *How Peary Reached the
Pole* are best understood in relation to his subsequent experiences. Following his first encounter with the Inughuit in 1908–09, he went on to
work extensively with them and grew to understand facets of their culture
he had not understood during his first visit. By the time this book was published, he had spent many years living among these people and had developed long-lasting friendships with many of them. MacMillan's affection

Figure 14. Donald MacMillan, age eighty, at the wheel of the *Bowdoin* departing on his last Arctic expedition, 1954.

for the people he worked closely with is evident, although some stories did not make it from the journal to the book. For instance, as the *Roosevelt* steamed south in August 1909, dropping off families on the way, he wrote in his journal (Aug. 22):

Our next stopping place was Itti-bloo. There we lost three more Esquimaux, two my special favorites – Inn-u-gee-to and Tu-cum-ak whom I loaded with things. They were the youngest married couple on board. When I was shot on the 11th, Tu-cummek, thinking I was going to die, remained outside my door for three or four hours. As soon as I heard it I sent for her to come in to see me. She brightened up when I began to laugh and joke [with] her.

Some forty years later MacMillan was still in contact with Tukummeq and other Inughuit who had worked on the 1908–09 expedition (Fig. 15).

MacMillan's portrayal of the Inughuit members of the team is complex. He includes humorous stories, gently poking fun at cross-cultural misunderstandings, from his own attempts to learn the language (pp. 135–36) to Kood-look-to's attempts to learn to write (p. 202). Scattered throughout he describes practical jokes the Inughuit and Westerners played on one another and their laughter at each other's mistakes, highlighting the generally good relations that men and women from two very different cultures had established. Like Peary, MacMillan is quick to give the Inughuit credit for their strength, courage, and many skills. And although a condescending tone, born of a deeply ingrained racism characteristic of the time, creeps into the prose sometimes, for the most part MacMillan writes of the Inughuit as equals, doling out praise or criticism for individuals according to the situation.

PHOTOGRAPHY IN THE NORTH

Like most members of the North Pole Expedition scientific staff in 1908–09, MacMillan had a camera with him. This comes as no surprise – it is evident that every member of the staff was expected to take (and process) photographs. Peary had all of his staff sign agreements giving him the rights to any photographs that they took, and in some cases he directed them to take photographs of specific things (Borup seems to have been designated the "official" photographer for these purposes). When they returned from the north, Peary requested all of the men's photographs and selected those he wanted to use in his own publications before returning them. It is also clear that many of the expedition members shared or exchanged pictures, with some images appearing in multiple collections, often with no photographer identified.

There is little evidence that MacMillan was anything more than an occasional amateur photographer prior to 1908, but he took over 200 photographs in 1908–09, marking the beginning of a long-term interest in photography. MacMillan used a small selection of these images to illustrate the original edition of *How Peary Reached the Pole*, augmented by a few photographs taken by others. These images convey the basic work of the expedition, but they only scratch the surface of MacMillan's work as a photographer.

By 1910, MacMillan, with Peary's blessing, was presenting illustrated lectures about his role in the expedition. He used "magic lantern" slides, black and white images printed on glass and then hand-tinted by professional colorists, meant to be projected before an audience. The quality of such slides varies considerably, but those that MacMillan used, now housed in the Peary-MacMillan Arctic Museum, were hand-tinted by skilled artists, following MacMillan's precise directions as to which parts of the image to color and what colors to use. Considering that the colorists had probably never been to the far north, the results were spectacular, capturing the remarkable intense blues and pastel greens of the Arctic land and seascapes. A number of these images are reproduced here, some published for the first time.

To modern eyes accustomed to the saturated colors of Kodachrome and even digital prints, hand-tinted images appear simultaneously archaic, beautiful, and somewhat other-worldly. On close inspection, the genius of the colorists is evident. Wherever possible, for example, they did not apply a tint. In Plate 3 color has been used very sparingly for the sky, MacMillan's *kamiks* and the ruff of his hood, the dog's harness, and a few highlights in the snow. Everything else has been left in its original monochrome, subtly reinforcing the key elements of the image and its sharpness. The colorists also made the best use of the tints available to them. In Plate 6 the blue-green of the open water is hinted at in the tinting of the water-saturated snow left on the surface of the remaining ice, giving the image a natural look impossible to achieve otherwise.

MacMillan used his lantern slides to great effect. He eventually built up a repertoire of talks based on the North Pole Expedition and his later expeditions. Notes, scripts, and typescripts of his various North Pole talks are housed in the George J. Mitchell Department of Special Collections and Archives at Bowdoin College. He illustrated his talks with lantern

Figure 15. MacMillan with three women who worked as seamstresses on the North Pole Expedition, Tookie (Tukummeq), Evaloo (Ivaloo), and Inawaho (Inugaarsuk), 1950.

slides until the 1940s, when 35mm Kodachrome slides replaced them as the medium of choice in lecture halls and classrooms. Since that time, his beautiful slides have sat virtually undisturbed, a fragile archive. With the advent of improved scanning technology, it has become affordable to scan these slides, rendering them accessible once again. It seems fitting then, that a selection of these slides, newly digitized, accompany the reprint of this long-unavailable publication.

✳

REFERENCES CITED

Abramson, Howard S. 1991. *Hero in Disgrace: The Life of Arctic Explorer Frederick A. Cook*. New York: Paragon House

Allen, Everett S. 1962. *Arctic Odyssey: The Life of Rear Admiral Donald B. MacMillan*. New York: Dodd Mead

Balch, Edwin Swift. 1913. *The North Pole and Bradley Land*. Philadelphia: Campion

Bartlett, Robert A. 1928. *The Log of Bob Bartlett: The True Story of Forty Years of Seafaring and Exploration*. New York: Blue Ribbon Books

Berton, Pierre. 1988. *The Arctic Grail: The Quest for the North West Passage and the North Pole, 1818–1909*. New York: Viking

Bloom, Lisa. 1993. *Gender on Ice: American Ideologies of Polar Expeditions*. Minneapolis: University of Minnesota

Borup, George. 1911. *A Tenderfoot with Peary*. New York: Frederick A. Stokes

Bryant, John H. and Harold N. Cones. 2000. *Dangerous Crossings: The First Modern Polar Expedition, 1925*. Annapolis: Naval Institute Press

Bryce, George. 1910. *The Siege and Conquest of the North Pole*. London: Gibbins

Bryce, Robert M. 1997. *Cook and Peary: The Polar Controversy Resolved*. Pennsylvania: Stackpole Books

Cook, Dr. Frederick A. 1911. *My Attainment of the Pole: Being the Record of the Expedition that First Reached the Boreal Center, 1907–1909: With the final summary of the polar controversy*. New York: Polar

Counter, Allen. 1991. *North Pole Legacy: Black, White, and Eskimo*. Massachusetts: The University of Massachusetts Press

Davies, Thomas D. 1989. *Robert E. Peary at the North Pole. A Report to the National Geographic Society by The Foundation for the Promotion of the Art of Navigation*. Maryland: The Navigation Foundation

Dick, Lyle. 2001. *Muskox Land: Ellesmere Island in the Age of Contact*. Calgary: The University of Calgary Press

Fogelson, Nancy. 1992. *Arctic Exploration and International Relations, 1900–1932: A Period of Expanding National Interests*. Fairbanks: University of Alaska Press

Goodsell, John W. 1983. *On Polar Trails: The Peary Expedition to the North Pole, 1908–09*. Revised and edited by Donald W. Whisenhunt. Austin: Eakin Press

Hall, Thomas F. 1917. *Has the North Pole Been Discovered?* Boston: Richard G. Badger

Henderson, Bruce. 2005. *True North: Peary, Cook, and the Race to the Pole*. New York and London: W.W. Norton

Henson, Matthew. 1912. *A Negro Explorer at the North Pole*. New York: Frederick A. Stokes

Herbert, Wally. 1989. *The Noose of Laurels: Robert E. Peary and the Race to the North Pole*. New York: Macmillan Publishing Company

Lewin, W. Henry. 1911. *Did Peary Reach the Pole?* London: Simpkin, Marshall, Hamilton, Kent and Co.

Lopez, Barry. 1986. *Arctic Dreams*. New York: Scribner

MacMillan, Donald B. 1934. *How Peary Reached the Pole*. Boston and New York: Houghton Mifflin

–1927. *Etah and Beyond; or Life Within Twelve Degrees of the Pole*. Boston: Houghton Mifflin

–1918. *Four Years in the White North*. New York: Harper & Brothers

Mills, William J. 2003. *Exploring Polar Frontiers: A Historical Encyclopedia*. Santa Barbara: ABC-CLIO

Molett, William E. 1996. *Robert E. Peary and Matthew Henson at the North Pole*. Kentucky: Elkhorn Press

Morris, Charles, editor. 1909. *Finding the North Pole*. Springfield: Hampden

Peary, Robert E. 1910. The Discovery of the North Pole. *Hampton's Magazine* 24

–1910. *The North Pole: Its Discovery in 1909 Under the Auspices of the Peary Arctic Club*. New York: Frederick A. Stokes

Robinson, Michael F. 2006. *The Coldest Crucible: Arctic Exploration and American Culture*. Chicago and London: University of Chicago Press

Steger, Will with Paul Schurke. 1987. *North to the Pole*. New York: Times Books

Weems, John E. 1967. *Peary: The Explorer and the Man*. Boston: Houghton Mifflin

ENDNOTES

1   Inughuit is the name for the Inuit living in northwest Greenland. Explorers often referred to them as the Polar Eskimos or Smith Sound Eskimos.
2   MacMillan is referring to members of L.A. Beaumont's party, of the Nares Expedition of 1875–76. Two of his men died, others suffered from scurvy, all experienced great hardship.

PLATE 1. Robert "Bob" Bartlett, captain of SS *Roosevelt*, was known for his ability to navigate vessels through ice-laden waters.

PLATE 2.
During the late spring and into summer teams used tents, such as these on Littleton Island, for shelter when traveling.

PLATE 3. Dogs worked hard and eagerly awaited feeding times.

PLATE 4. Inughuit seam-stresses, including "Bill" (Eqariiusaq), would chew a boot sole to soften it prior to sewing.

PLATE 5. SS *Roosevelt* was built to push, ram, and crush her way through sea ice.

PLATE 6. In the spring, puddles developed on the ice and leads opened, signaling that it was time to prepare to move the *Roosevelt* from her winter harbor.

PLATE 7. Sledging parties used ingenuity to overcome obstacles. Here, a group is crossing a lead using a piece of floating ice as a raft.

PLATE 8. American flag and sledges in Peary's camp at the North Pole.

PLATE 9.
In June, when much of the snow cover was melting off the land, the men helped the dogs drag the sledges over bare ground. Here Kood-look-to is traveling from Fort Conger with a dog team.

PLATE 10. When men stopped to camp, essential tasks included tending to their sore feet and caring for their skin boots.

PLATE 11. Peary looked confident while talking to the press at Battle Harbour, Labrador. His hopes for a triumphant return from the North Pole were dashed by the controversy resulting from Frederick A. Cook's competing claim.

✳

HOW PEARY REACHED THE POLE

✳

FOREWORD

The discovery of the North Pole on April 6, 1909, by Rear-Admiral Robert Edwin Peary was the culmination of a three hundred years' quest, an achievement which the world should not and cannot forget. Repeatedly declared impossible, the greatest nations had striven for centuries, at the cost of many lives and the expenditure of millions, to cross the hundreds of miles of ice and reach the northern apex of the globe. The man who accomplishes often is even greater than the task accomplished, so it is in part my purpose to explain this great leader who succeeded where so many had failed – gloriously, it is true, but failed. I shall try to tell the manner of man who persuaded the Polar Eskimos to penetrate the interior of the great Ser-mik-suah, the abode of evil spirits; who induced them to leave their homes and journey seven hundred miles due north and to travel out over the drift ice of the Polar Sea so far that they declared that they would never again see their wives and children. And I shall try to explain the secret of the power which he possessed over his white men, who, had he wished, would have followed him through broken ice, crossed treacherous thin leads, surmounted pressure ridges, and clung to him until the last ounce of food was gone and the last dog eaten. In short, I shall attempt to portray a great character who has been little understood and, at times, grossly misunderstood.

It will also be my purpose to answer many of the questions which have persisted down the years, such as: 'Did Peary really reach the Pole?' 'Did he know when he reached it?' 'Why did he send his white men back to land?' 'Why did he prefer to travel with a Negro?' 'How far north did Dr. Cook really go?' 'Did he think he was there and did he deceive himself?' 'Was it his intention when he left the United States to make an honest effort to reach the Pole, or was it a deliberate fraud?'

Much of the controversy which has arisen over this great discovery has been due to a lack of understanding of the problems of Polar work. Few critics know what it means to sledge over the rough ice of the Polar Sea; they are ignorant of Arctic history, of what Peary had done in his northern work; of what had been done with two, three, or five sledges; of how sledges must be built to withstand the shock of traveling through and over the rough sea ice north of Grant Land and Greenland; how heavily sledges should be loaded for the work in hand; how many dogs should be used for each sledge; how much food these dogs require; how and what kind of clothes must be worn to withstand the bitter temperatures of sixty and seventy below zero: ignorant of a hundred and one things to be learned only in actual work. Lack of knowledge and understanding of these points was and is responsible for the misplaced criticism which followed Peary's success.

To us who had the honor of serving under this great leader and who knew the perfection of his equipment after years of overcoming difficulties, there was never a question at any time as to who discovered the Pole. We knew what was demanded of a man physically and mentally to combat successfully the hostile elements of the Northland. First, and above all others, was experience. Too little has been made of this and too much of facts and incidents which have no bearing on the main question. After his years of hard, honest work, Peary deserved a better fate than to have men doubt his word or the complete success of his achievement. In him we have the finest example of determination and persistency in all Arctic and Antarctic history. His name will stand for all time as the Discoverer of the North Pole.

✳

FARTHEST NORTH IN 1906

What has proved to be my life's ambition was first aroused by my reading, early in my boyhood, of that masterpiece of Arctic adventure, 'Arctic Explorations,' by Dr. Elisha Kane. What real boy ever read it without yearning to see Eskimos, snow houses, polar bears, and stretching ice fields, despite the hardships and suffering and death so vividly portrayed? Tracking in Melville Bay, meeting the Smith Sound Eskimos, landing on Littleton Island, fighting the pack beyond Refuge Harbor, winter quarters in Rensselaer Harbor, the sledge trip to Humboldt Glacier and the death of Pierre and Baker, the long winter night and then again the long winter night, followed by the retreat southward in open boats subsisting largely upon the country, the dramatic incident at Godhavn as Kane and his men rowed out in the battered *Faith* to meet Captain Hartstene's squadron – all written graphically and beautifully – what a story that was!

My interest once aroused, I followed on with Captain Isaac Israel Hayes, in his one hundred and thirty-three ton *United States,* sailing through the leads of Melville Bay and failing to reach his objective. Kedge anchor gone, stern boat smashed, bulwarks stove in, bowsprit and foretopmast sprung, mainsail blown to pieces, iron sheathing torn, deck planks opened, and rudder split, the once staunch little schooner crept into the sheltered waters of Hartstene Bay to remain frozen in for a year. Then came the story of Captain Charles Francis Hall, who in 1871 pushed his ship, the *Polaris,* farther north than ship had ever sailed or steamed before. His grave is a rough pile of rocks in a lonely valley swept by cold winds and drifting snows – the most northern in Greenland, almost within the shadow of the Pole. Then I came to know the story of the *Jeannette* under Lieutenant George Washington De Long and that of the Greely Expedition, both ill-fated, distinguished alike for suffering and heroic struggle against tremendous odds. I followed with absorbed and ever-increasing interest the career of adventure, achievement, and vicissitude, but I hardly dared dream that I too should some day listen to the roar of the demons of the North and assist in the last campaign which reached the summits of the citadel. So my feelings may be imagined when one day early in the spring of 1905 I received the following telegram:

Have a place for you on North Pole trip. When can you meet me in Portland?
PEARY

'Do you want to send an answer, sir?' the boy inquired as I signed the yellow pad.

I stood for a few seconds pondering just what to do.

'Not today. I'll take it down later,' I finally replied.

After all these years of boyish fancy and imagination, of vain hopes, my opportunity had come! For the next few hours I was lost in another world, oblivious of school, dormitory duties, classes and gymnasium work. But why my delay? A few days before I had renewed my contract to teach another year at Worcester Academy. Should I plead off, or, if necessary, break the contract? I walked and walked again the quarter-mile track. There could be but one decision. I walked down the hill to the Union Station and sent my regretful answer:

Sorry, but unable to accompany you this year.
MACMILLAN

When the *Roosevelt* sailed from Portland on her trial trip in June, neither Peary nor Captain Bob Bartlett knew that I cast off her lines from the dock and sat there long after everyone had gone, watching her steam out past the breakwater and on past Portland Head out to sea. My one opportunity – and I had refused it! The door was closed. Would it ever open again? It seemed more than doubtful.

Still puzzled at the workings of Fate, I went back to another year of work. At last, after months of waiting the news came:

Peary Fails to Reach the Pole. Breaks World's Record. Reaches 87° 6′ North Latitude. Party land starving on northern shores of Greenland.

With the stocky, sturdy little *Roosevelt* he had steamed through the ice-beset waters of Kane Basin, up through Kennedy and Robeson Channels to the Polar Sea, where he had established winter quarters on the northern shores of Grant Land just beyond the camp of the British expedition of 1875–76. By sledging ninety miles westward to Cape Columbia, he would be within striking distance of the Pole. A terrific gale which drove the pack eastward thwarted all of his carefully laid plans. His caches of food, placed upon the trail by his supporting parties against his return with empty sledges, were scattered to the winds. The disrupted pack carried him sixty miles to the east.

The trail was broken. He realized that the food between him and home could never be reclaimed. Still he heads north. Here faith and courage bordered on rashness. He goes beyond the Italian record of Captain Cagni, surpasses that of the great Nansen, and 'places his country's flag at Farthest North,' one hundred and seventy-four miles from the Pole!

With food nearly gone and additional leads forming, Peary might never be able to reach land; in fact the conditions were far more against him than in his favor. They fight their way through rough ice and over the tops of pressure ridges, ever twisting, turning, and groping for better sledging. Cautiously they pick their way over thin ice and work toward the end of open leads. Snow-covered hills are slowly mounting above the southern horizon. There is slight hope, but it is quickly shattered at sight of the 'Big Lead.' If it does not freeze over, it spells death by starvation. It is absolutely impassable. No one virtue is more demanded of an explorer than patience, but how hard to be patient with land and home and safety in sight, with food and life dwindling away, while each day with its increasing warmth adds to the certainty of the end!

After a long series of adventures and hairbreadth escapes, this is the one time in Peary's life when he feels that all is over. He walks to the edge of the lead for another examination. It is frozen, but the pressure of his foot breaks it. But here is their one chance of life, a slim one, it is true, but a chance. The thin ice might hold if snowshoes are used. It is one of the great dramatic moments in all Arctic and Antarctic work: a line of five men, some fifty feet apart, carefully advancing over a film of ice that bends and cracks beneath their weight, not daring to lift their snowshoes, but cautiously sliding one out a few inches beyond the other. No man could help another if in danger, and each man knew this. Twice Peary hears a cry and says to himself, 'Some poor fellow has gone!'

He steps up on to firm ice a quarter of a mile distant. He counts his Eskimos. They are all there! They reach the northern shore of Greenland through a chaos of shattered ice. They kill more of their dogs for food and use their last sledge for fuel. The wobbly tracks of a starving party are seen clearly outlined in the snow. One of the supporting parties is lost and walking away from the ship! Little Sig-loo is found on hands and knees hunting hare with a bow and arrow made from his snowshoes and an old spoon! No man is more resourceful than an Eskimo. Finally, they stagger on to the ship, followed by one dog. Peary had failed, but he had won, too.

With rudder post wrenched and torn, rudder hanging by a thread, heavy timbers cut away for fuel for the boilers, two and three feet of water sloshing back and forth in her hold, the *Roosevelt* careened and reeled like a drunken man across Baffin Bay, begged for fuel along the Labrador, and finally reached Sydney, where most of her crew left her. They had had enough of Arctic work. Shipping new men, she came on dizzily through the Bras d'Or Lakes, headed for Cape Cod, worked her uncertain way through Long Island Sound, and crept into New York Harbor the night before Christmas, where amid the din and confusion, unable, in her weakened condition to respond readily to her helm, she smashed into a ferryboat.

If ever a ship was duly christened for her life-work, the *Roosevelt* was on this her first trip into the Arctic regions. She could never have a more difficult test and return to civilization. She had done the thing for which she was designed, and had placed Peary at his objective on the northern shore of Grant Land. He had failed to reach the Pole. Would he ever go again? was the all-important question for me.

✳

HEADING NORTH IN 1908

The answer to my question was not long deferred. In his first important speech after his return, Peary laid down his credo as follows:

> To me the final and complete solution of the Polar mystery which has engaged the best thought and interest of some of the best men of the most vigorous and enlightened nations of the world for more than three centuries, and today quickens the pulse of every man or woman whose veins hold red blood, is the thing which should be done for the honor and credit of this country, the thing which it is intended that I should do, and the thing I must do.
>
> The result of the last expedition of the Peary Arctic Club has been to simplify the attainment of the Pole fifty per cent, to accentuate the fact that man and the Eskimo dog are the only two mechanisms capable of meeting all the varying contingencies of Arctic work, and that the American route to the Pole and the methods and equipment which have been brought to a high state of perfection during the past fifteen years, still remain the most practicable means of attaining that object.
>
> Had the past winter been a normal season in the Arctic region, and not, as it was, a particularly open one throughout the northern hemisphere, I should have won the prize. And even if I had known before leaving the land what actual conditions were to the northward, as I

know now, I could have so modified my route and my disposition of sledges that I could have reached the Pole in spite of the open season.

But these ringing words answered only half of my personal question. Winter had gone. Spring days were here. School days were nearly over and then the beautiful blue waters of the Maine Coast, a good boat, a cracking good breeze! The white-tiled swimming-pool at Worcester Academy was alive with boys. There was the constant rebound of the springboard, the splash of bodies. White figures darted here and there.

As I swam down the pool, a messenger boy entered the door. Sitting on the edge of the tank with my feet in the water, I read this telegram:

If you are still interested in Arctic exploration, come to see me at once Grand Union Hotel, New York City.
PEARY

The gong sounded. The boys looked surprised, but they never knew why they lost their last five minutes of recreation.

Late that night I was in New York – too late to catch Peary. A note awaited me, 'I'll see you at breakfast in the morning.'

That breakfast will ever be remembered. Peary's deeply lined face can never be forgotten. He spoke modestly of what he had done, regretfully of what he hadn't, and hopefully of what he planned to do.

'MacMillan,' he said, 'I am fifty-two years old. This is probably the last attempt of my life. I want you to be in command of one of my supporting parties. We may go beyond the limit and never come back. This nearly happened on my last trip. Now you go back to school and think it over and let me know your decision at the end of two weeks.'

Two weeks' time to arrive at a decision which I had arrived at twenty years before! I signed the contract there and then at the breakfast table. But before I signed, in order that there should be no misunderstanding whatsoever, he emphatically asserted, and repeated: '*Remember, you are not to go to the Pole!*'

After my years of Arctic work and fourteen Arctic and sub-Arctic trips, how well I can understand why at the very beginning he wanted this point clearly understood. Biting winds, stinging drift, extreme cold are but trifles compared with the endurance and patience called for in dealing with the ambition of the average first-year assistant. Commander Peary had seen too many of his men bitterly disappointed and bitterly resentful on their return home, because *their* ambition had not been realized. It developed that their real purpose in going North was not to be loyal assistants to their commander, but to gain personal glory, compared to which the success of the whole expedition was but a minor detail. Kane, Hayes, Hall, Greely, Peary, Nansen, Sverdrup, Amundsen, Shackleton, Scott – each might have written an interesting and illuminating chapter upon this strange working of the mind of man – but it would not be believed.

Here Commander Peary's honesty and squareness were evidenced as they were many times later. He might take us with him to the end of the last mile, or he might leave us. Let every man prove his worth. Notwithstanding the reiterations of the Press upon our return to America, *every man understood this before he sailed from home.* The headlines, 'Men bitterly disappointed upon being sent back by Peary,' were utterly untrue. There were no misunderstandings; there were no disappointments; there were no regrets. Peary was as square as a brick from start to finish.

The success of an Arctic expedition depends upon former experience in the field and adequate preparations to meet varying conditions. Failure is often registered long before the actual start of the expedition. Peary fully realized this and paid infinite attention to every detail, the little things which mean so much when one is fighting in the last ditch against the so-called Evil Spirits of the North: winds, cold, drift, pressure ridges, open water, thin ice, darkness, and 'piblock-to' among the dogs. His room at the Grand Union was a veritable curiosity shop – sledge stoves of every conceivable pattern, designed for economy of fuel, lightness, strength, compactness, samples of dog traces, webbing for harnesses, wood for sledges, thermometers, instruments of precision, clothing, and on and on, *ad infinitum.* He was plainly tired of it and wanted to leave as soon as possible for his little island home, Eagle Island, on the Maine Coast.

'When can you report?' he inquired eagerly; adding: 'I want you to come here to New York and continue this work while I am away. I will furnish you with a list of supplies and equipment which you are to buy.'

'I will return to Worcester, finish up my school work, and be back within two weeks,' I told him.

Within the promised time, I was back buying five-gallon milk cans for water, swing bunks for our staterooms, cameras, films, rifles, shotguns, sheepskins, snow knives, sledge hatchets. It was interesting work, but hot! Read the papers for the week of July 1–6, 1908. Heat prostrations and deaths! The very thought of the North, of the ice fields and icebergs was a comforting one. But in setting down this date of so long ago, the realization is forced upon me of how necessary it is, for a just appreciation of the problems facing the expedition, to emphasize the difference of viewpoint of those days and the present toward the North Pole, Arctic exploration, and all concerned with it.

In these days when improving methods of communication make the ends of the earth our nextdoor neighbors, it is difficult completely to picture the times when the Pole was NEWS in capital letters. And it is the more important to do so, for the detractors of Peary have made a concerted attempt to belittle the importance of his discovery. But in those hot days of July, 1908, every word about the Far North was devoured by avid readers, their appetites whetted by the adventurous deed of Peary, the tragic fate of Andrée and his balloon, the efforts of that scion of a Royal House, the Duke of the Abruzzi, the expeditions of Wellman with balloons, too, the marvelous drift of the *Fram* and Nansen's dashing attempt at the Pole; all this was headline stuff in the great newspapers of the world. Even as far back as the De Long expedition of the *Jeannette* in 1879, James Gordon Bennett of the New York *Herald* had furnished the sinews of war. The Jackson Expedition of the middle nineties owed much to Harmsworth. And as expedition followed expedition throughout the last decade of the nineteenth century and the first of the twentieth, account after account was given to a public enthused by the pertinacity, resourcefulness, and heroism of these gallant men.

Among these pioneers of the North, Peary, through his long and per-

sistent efforts, stood at the top in popular esteem. His first interest in the
Arctic had been awakened as far back as 1886 by reading an account of
the Greenland Ice Cap, then unexplored. He found that no knowledge
existed of the character, area, or formation of this vast stretch of frozen
waste. A lesser man might have been deterred from any Arctic work by the
tragic fate and fearful sufferings of the Greely Expedition which was only
two years back, but with only one companion he started on his first pio-
neering expedition. It was only a summer voyage, but for the first time the
great ice cap was penetrated for a distance of a hundred miles when the
two men with their meager facilities were forced back by incessant storms
and blizzards. But this first meeting with the problems of the North fired
Peary with an enthusiasm for exploration which was the keynote of the
rest of his life. Far up on the white back of the Greenland Ice Cap, buried
beneath drifting snows, he listened to the roar of the Demons of the
North, who for centuries, jealous of their domain, had been guarding
every avenue of approach. They gave this tall, sinewy, raw-boned young
lieutenant of the United States Navy a savage welcome. Their premoni-
tions that this man might batter down door after door, wall after wall, and
wrest away secret after secret were well grounded. Their challenge was
accepted. Thereafter the desire to conquer the North was Peary's very
breath of life.

In 1891 Peary returned on what was his first serious expedition; that of
1886 had been but little more than a reconnaissance. He was landed on
the shores of McCormick Bay, strapped to a board with a broken leg.
Pleadings of wife and friends that he return home were of no avail. He
would remain. Now we find him plodding up over the great Greenland Ice
Cap to learn the secret of that great Ice Sahara. Weeks later he returned at
the end of a remarkable journey. He had reached Navy Cliff in latitude
81° 37' 5", longitude 34° 5'. Northern Greenland had been crossed for the
first time. But perhaps the greatest gain of this and the subsequent expedition was his acquaintance with and knowledge of the Eskimos on which
so much of his future success was to depend.

He was not satisfied. In 1893 we find him in Greenland again. But from
the very start this expedition was followed by persistent bad luck. Sup-

plies for the next year's trip were cached upon the ice cap where they were soon buried in the worst of blizzards. All hope for the contemplated expedition necessarily was abandoned, but Peary insisted on going on himself with such supplies as he could gather from the ship and the Eskimos. One cache was eventually found, but the main base, including the vital supply of oil so necessary for fuel, was never located. Peary's detractors have pointed to this loss of supplies as an instance of his faulty navigation, but when it is realized that the pole which marked the site of the discovered cache only protruded a few *inches* above the snow, the unfairness of this criticism becomes obvious. The most skilled scientist in the world, with the most elaborate apparatus of the greatest precision, could only locate such a needle point in that great white waste through the greatest good luck. And there is no sound reason for believing that the mark was actually above the snow.

Most of his party had returned to America, but not Peary. With the absolute minimum of supplies he forced eastward, undaunted, with the Negro Matthew Henson and his loyal assistant Hugh J. Lee. What a thrilling moment when, with supplies nearly exhausted, strength failing, they looked backward over the trail toward home and comfort, and declared that they wanted to go on and take the one chance of finding sustenance among the rolling hills beyond the ice cap! The Gods of the Brave walked with these men. They found the musk oxen. Again the ascent and the long, long trail southward, strength failing, dogs dropping, until one alone remained. Miles apart but still plugging on, they finally reached their northern home on Bowdoin Bay.

In 1897 we again see Peary returning to the struggle, this time to make his first attempt at the Pole itself. His ship, the *Windward*, was locked in the ice of Kane Basin in a vain endeavor to reach Kennedy and Robeson Channels and, possibly, the edge of the Polar Sea. In sledging through the Arctic night in an effort to establish an advance base, he froze his feet to the ankles and all his toes had to be amputated. But he would not return on the relief ship the next spring; crippled as he was he insisted on remaining for three years more. With headquarters at Etah he failed in his main quest. At Cape Sabine he failed again. At Fort Conger he failed again. He had, however, reached the northernmost point of Greenland, Cape Jesup, and surveyed farther down the eastern coast of this northern continent. His first attack on the real Polar ice was blocked at latitude 83° 50′ north by pressure ice of ferocious formidability. His farthest north was reached on April 21, 1902, at 84° 17′ 27″. He had failed and failed again, but he knew why he had failed. His base must be nearer his objective. To do this he must have the staunchest ship and the most powerful ship possible – his *Windward* had been hopelessly under-engined. So the *Roosevelt* was built, and I have told of her christening trip – which I had missed.

She now lay, in July, 1908, at the Recreation Pier at the foot of East Twenty-Third Street, preparing to set out on what must certainly be her commander's last effort for the Pole. Repeated failures had only spurred him on to perfect his plans, his equipment, his personnel. His years of experience were now to have their due reward. It was here that I met the other members of the expedition. George Borup, my roommate, a graduate of Yale, had spent one year as an apprentice in the Altoona Machine Shops. He was not especially interested in any one branch of Arctic work. He simply wanted to go. He was young, strong, clean, energetic, and one of the finest fellows I have ever known.

Captain Robert A. Bartlett was from Brigus, Newfoundland, a descendant of a long line of seafaring men. Thirty-three years old, 'built on the ground,' he looked as hard as nails, and was. None but a real sailor could have brought that ship home from the Arctic in 1906. We had a good captain in Bob.

J.W. Goodsell, of New Kensington, Pennsylvania, was our physician and surgeon. Dr. Goodsell was born in Leechburg, Pennsylvania, in 1873. He received his medical degree from Pulte Medical College, Cincinnati, Ohio, specializing in clinical microscopy. Goodsell was of old fighting stock of Revolutionary and Civil War days. He was a bit too heavy and slow for sledging, but a bulldog in determination and stoical to the last degree when suffering from low temperatures, as he certainly did on the Polar Sea.

Matthew A. Henson, Peary's colored assistant, was a veteran in Arctic work; experienced, capable, strong physically, and courageous in the face of danger. I had read so much about him that naturally I studied him with interest. Although he was forty years old he was the best field man aboard ship. Peary said that 'Henson can handle a sledge better, and is probably a better dog driver than any man living, except some of the best of the Eskimo hunters themselves.'

Ross G. Marvin, secretary and assistant to Peary, had served in a similar capacity on the 1905–06 trip. Marvin was a graduate of the New York State Nautical School, St. Mary's and also of Cornell University. At the time of our departure he was an instructor in civil engineering at Cornell. Marvin had not intended to go on this trip. How strange a fate that it should happen as it did! The day before we sailed he came to the East Twenty-Third Street Pier to see Peary, Bartlett, and other good friends. A casual remark revealed that he would like to accompany us. Satisfactory arrangements were soon made. Marvin was to hurry home, pack his things, say good-bye and catch the first train for Sydney. Little did he realize that he was hurrying to his death. Marvin was lost on the Polar Sea.

Our chief engineer, George Wardwell, had watched the *Roosevelt* take shape and grow in a large shipyard in his own home town, Bucksport, Maine, and felt that he must be a part of her and of the Peary Expedition. Big, jovial, companionable, congenial, he was loved by everyone on board.

Tom Gushue was our mate, a man from Captain Bob's home town, Brigus. Quiet, mild-mannered, deliberate in action and words, we all respected him. There never would be trouble on an Arctic expedition if all men were as fine in character as Tom Gushue.

Charlie Percy, the cook, was also from Brigus. Commander Peary never had a more devoted follower or a greater admirer than Charlie. Rarely have I ever found such loyalty as he showed to the Commander. Charlie died some years ago at Peary's island home in Casco Bay, and is buried within sight and sound of the sea he loved so well.

John Murphy was our boatswain; Banks Scott, second engineer; William Pritchard, cabin boy; John Connors, John Coady, John Barnes, Dennis Murphy, George Percy, seamen; James Bently, Patrick Joyce, Patrick Skeans, John Wiseman, firemen.

The day of our departure will be long remembered—for its heat. On that July 6th we were roasting to death at the foot of Twenty-Third Street.

'Peary, I believe in you'

Who wouldn't go North on a day when there were seventy-two heat prostrations and twelve deaths! But as if Nature had not done her best, our big
chief was contributing a hundred and more degrees of heat from his boilers,
knowing that he would be called upon to furnish the noise for our departure, and also to answer scores of salutes all the way up the East River.
Charlie's lunch was untouched. It was too hot to eat.

At last we backed away from a crowded pier. There were a few scattered cheers. A few good-byes. 'Good luck!' One man in his cups leaned
far over the cap log, swayed dangerously back and forth, waved a very
limp arm and wrist, and yelled: 'I'll see you – up there.' Many in the crowd
undoubtedly thought that his chances of getting there were fully as good as
ours. Perhaps they remembered the crowds who had thronged Telegraph
Hill in San Francisco to watch the crew of the ill-fated *Jeannette* sail for
their doom.

But such thoughts could not remain for long. Every captain of every
steam thing afloat pulled his whistle cord that day. It was one long toot
from East Twenty-Third Street to our anchorage at City Island where we
were to land our guests. We were under orders to remain there for the night
and to proceed to Oyster Bay the next morning to meet the President and
his family.

'Teddy,' as he was called by the world, was delighted with and interested
in everything – ship, men, dogs, equipment. It was 'By Jove!' time and
again, and 'How I should like to go!' Young Theodore and Kermit were
all over the ship, fully as interested as their dad. The Eskimo dogs especially
claimed their attention. With 'I believe in you, Peary! Good luck!' Roosevelt was gone, and his namesake headed north on her long journey.

✳

GOOD-BYES AT SYDNEY

While the *Roosevelt* was steaming on to Sydney, Nova Scotia, I was still busy ordering various items necessary for the work in hand with instructions to ship everything to that port. There I joined the ship, having gone overland by train, as did Ross Marvin. The days at Sydney were busy ones putting on the finishing touches of our equipment. All things forgotten must be purchased here if possible, for Sydney is known to the Arctic man as the Jumping-Off Place from Civilization.

An Arctic expedition is never ready. One who has never been on such an expedition can have but the vaguest idea of the tremendous amount of work called upon properly to equip a ship and men going beyond the confines of civilization, to say nothing of preparing for the possibility of a retreat southward in open boats, or even on an ice pan, as has happened several times in the history of the work. The omission of a single article of importance might seriously endanger the lives of the whole party. A mistake in the order or a blunder in the packing could easily spell failure. It is reported that one expedition sailed with thousands of cartridges which would not fit the calibre of a single rifle aboard! Since fresh meat is absolutely necessary for the maintenance of good health, which is necessary for good work, because of this omission one would be compelled to resort to the most primitive methods of capturing game, I fear with ill success in a country where even the natives starve. The man who talks glibly of living on the country and boasts that he can go to the North Pole with nothing on his sledge but his rifle is chuckling in his sleeve at how easily people are fooled – but not those who go into the North.

Peary was a master explorer. Several times he had returned from his farthest point staggering from starvation, and he appreciated to the full the value of a loaded sledge. This was the reason why he ordered 30,000 pounds of pemmican; 16,000 pounds of flour; 10,000 pounds of sugar; 10,000 pounds of biscuit; 7000 pounds of bacon; 3500 gallons of kerosene; 3000 pounds of dried fish; 1000 pounds of coffee; 800 pounds of tea; 100 cases of condensed milk – to name but a small part of the total list of supplies. Peary's starvation periods, however, were due in no instance to ignorance of conditions, inexperience, or lack of skill in hunting. In some places in the North a child could live through some years if told in June or July that he must gather sufficient food for the following winter. In one day, for example, we gathered four thousand fresh eggs of the eider duck. But there are many places where the best Eskimo hunter would starve, and many have starved.

As we packed the last of our stores, we were naturally the object of interest to all Americans in the vicinity. Among them were Gilbert and Mrs. Grosvenor, of Washington, D.C. Dr. Grosvenor, now the President of the National Geographic Society, was at that time its managing editor, and deeply interested in all matters pertaining to exploration. He and his wife had been waiting for more than a week to greet Commander Peary and wish him Godspeed. They accompanied us on the *Roosevelt* on the first stage of our journey from Sydney to North Sydney.

Not all Americans, however, were so loyal or so hopeful as Dr. and Mrs. Grosvenor. I was highly amused one day as I was standing on the piazza of the old Sydney Hotel to hear a conversation between a man and a woman, obviously 'from the States.'

'Where is she?' she inquired, her eyes searching all over the harbor.

'There – that black one with the three masts,' he replied, pointing to the *Roosevelt* steaming up the harbor.

'Do you mean to tell me that that thing is going to the North Pole?' she queried, with scorn and contempt emphasizing every word.

'So they say,' he meekly answered.

Captain Bob Bartlett on the *Roosevelt*

The *Roosevelt*'s Clearance from Sydney
She was the only ship that ever cleared for the North Pole

'Never!' she declared with tightly closed lips.

She was fully prepared to see a battleship or an ocean liner as large as the *Great Eastern*, successfully to accomplish such an undertaking.

At last all was ready. With bunkers bulging with coal the *Roosevelt* was ready for sea on July 17th. Beautiful weather and a fair wind prompted Captain Bartlett to sail at once. When going into the North with objective uncertain, real destination unknown, it is customary to clear the ship for 'Points at Sea,' a roving license issued at the nearest custom house. Bob cleared the *Roosevelt* for the North Pole, probably the first and only ship's papers which will ever be issued with that point as the destination. I believe that old Sir John Knight of England did receive orders from the King to sail to the Pole, but not to remain – he must return at once!

Late in the afternoon, we steamed out to sea, accompanied by a tug which was to carry back to port those who were to bid us the last good-bye. The lighthouse on Flat Point on our starboard hand recognized the *Roosevelt*. HPZ – TDL, 'Good-bye, we wish you a pleasant voyage,' was fluttering from the signal mast, a touch of friendliness always appreciated by the sailor outward bound.

When we were well out clear of the land, the little tug puffed up alongside to take on board Mrs. Peary, daughter Marie, young Robert, Colonel Borup, father of George Borup, and a Mr. Warren. Our last word was from young Robert, who called up from the tug to Charlie Percy, the cook, 'Charlie, take good care of Dad.'

We were now alone and on our way to the big job ahead. No one who has not experienced it knows what a feeling of relief comes when crowds, flags, whistle blasts are left behind and the land drops below the horizon. It is like a Sunday morning following the rush of a busy week. Nothing but the chug of the engines, the vibration of the propellers, the swash of waters along the sides. Captain Bob was headed toward Point Amour where we were to send our last messages home by land wire. From then on nothing would be heard from us for over a year.

CHAPTER 4

✳

FROM PARRY TO PEARY

But what exactly was our big job? Fully to appreciate the magnitude of the task before us, and furthermore to gain an understanding fairly to weigh the evidence in the controversy that arose from Peary's successful enterprise, it is necessary to become more or less familiar with the efforts made to reach the Pole and the methods adopted in the search. Nothing can be more instructive than a comparison of the means of transport, food supplies, clothing, sledges, equipment, and so on of the various expeditions whose deeds make up the history of Arctic navigation.

The first explorers who reached high northern latitudes were Davis and Baffin in the sixteenth and early seventeenth centuries, but in the course of time their discoveries came to be regarded as legendary and almost apocryphal, so that it was not until the work of Ross and Franklin in the early years of the nineteenth century that their surveys were confirmed and extended. The first expedition of modern times concerned with the Pole is considered to be that of Captain William Edward Parry of England. In 1817 Captain Scoresby had reported that on a whaling expedition he had reached latitude 81° 30′ North, and urged the Government to continue the work of exploration which had been virtually in abeyance for years. Accordingly two expeditions were sent out in 1818, but the first, which was intended to go as far as possible on the way to the Pole, was crushed in the ice and had to return home. But in 1826 a new start was made. The plans were based on the reports of whalers that as far as they could see to the north the ice was so smooth that a coach and four could be driven over it. How far from reality this proved! It should be remembered, in addition, that until Nansen's great expedition in the *Fram* an open Polar sea was presumed through all the computations of geographers and physicists, so that water transport was considered an essential. Parry, therefore, proposed 'to attempt to reach the North Pole, by means of traveling with sledge boats over the ice, or through any spaces of open water that might occur.' For this journey over the ice two boats were constructed, having great flatness of floor, with the extreme breadth carried well forward and aft, and possessing the utmost buoyancy, as well as capacity for stowage. These boats were twenty feet long and seven feet wide. The timbers were made of tough ash and hickory, one inch to half an inch square, and a foot apart, with a half timber of smaller size beneath the two. On the outside of the frame was laid a covering of Macintosh's waterproof canvas, coated with tar. Over this was placed a plank of fir, then a stout piece of felt, and over all, an oak plank of the same thickness as the fir. This whole coating was firmly secured to the timbers by iron screws from the outside. On each side of the keel, and projecting considerably below it, was attached a strong runner shod with smooth steel in the manner of a sledge. The boats rested entirely on these runners when on the ice.

We also applied to each boat [continues Parry] two wheels of five feet diameter, and a small one abaft, having a swivel for steering by, like that of a Bath chair; but these, owing to the irregularities of the ice, did not prove of service, and were subsequently relinquished. A span of hide rope was attached to the fore part of the runners, and to this were affixed two strong ropes of horsehair, for dragging the boat; each individual being furnished with a broad leathern shoulder-belt, which could readily be fastened to or detached from the drag ropes. The boats weighed 1539 lb. and 1542 lb. respectively.

The expedition sailed from Hammersmith on the eighteenth of April. They had taken aboard eight reindeer as draught animals, but these proved no more successful for northern work than did the ponies, mules, and burros tried by later expeditions. They left their ship, the *Hecla*, on the twenty-first of June in their boat sledges, and they proceeded through open water until they reached latitude 81° 12′ 51″, the highest latitude which had ever been reached. The ice journey was begun on the twenty-fourth, but they found the ice very irregular and the going difficult. Sleeping in their boats at night, and hauling them by standing pulls by day, their progress was very slow. They were compelled to make three and sometimes four trips over the same strip with their boats and baggage. Then the boats had to be launched several times to cross narrow ponds of water. After a hard day's work they frequently found that they had not progressed two miles – they had counted on twenty. They reached a latitude – of 82° 45′ – a record that stood as the Farthest North for forty-eight years and turned back, exhausted and discouraged, firmly convinced that man could never reach the Pole.

The loss of Sir John Franklin and his men sent many expeditions into the Arctic, about forty in all, but the most important in the history of the Pole was that of Dr. Elisha Kane. His plan was based on the presence of probable land masses of Greenland to the Far North, which was only deduced at that time. He left New York on the little hermaphrodite brig the *Advance,* of one hundred and forty-four tons, on the thirtieth of May, 1853. Rensselaer Harbor, in latitude 78° 37′, was reached and dépôt parties were sent out. One of these parties was nearly lost, scurvy developed, and through two frightful years of sickness and suffering the expedition held out, only to be forced in the end to abandon the *Advance* and retreat southward in boats. Of course this dire tale of suffering and heroism startled the world, but the expedition was of real importance in the development of Arctic work. Morton reached a latitude of 81° 22′ north, the highest which had been attained on the American side of Greenland. For the first time the Eskimo dog was used in the work, and critics of Peary's sledging speeds would be well advised to consider the following note from Dr. Kane's book:

I find by my notes that these six dogs, well worn by previous travel, carried me with a fully-burdened sledge, between seven and eight hundred miles during the first fortnight after leaving the brig – *a mean travel of fifty-seven miles a day.*

Dr. Kane did not add that he himself was nearly worn down from illness, anxiety, and lack of food at the time, and so in no fit condition to make such an effort. He also emphasized again and again the necessity of fresh meat as a preventive or curative of the dreaded scurvy. And he was the first to avail himself of the friendship of the Eskimos and, in part, to live the same life. Failure to grasp these lessons so powerfully presented in Dr. Kane's narrative cost succeeding expeditions heavily, both in men and suffering.

After leaving the brig and hauling their sick men and boats over miles of ice, the party was welcomed by the Eskimos at Etah, where in a measure they were refitted and certainly invigorated by the supply of food, mostly in the form of seal meat. Their trials seemed more or less at an end, and for the first few days farther on to the settlements of Southern Greenland all went well. Birds' eggs made up their provisions in part. But gales set in, they failed to find eggs, they were driven into the sea ice, and it seemed as though all their efforts had been in vain and that they were to disappear almost in sight of safety. There could be no more dramatic moment than when these starving heroes at last sighted a seal asleep on the ice. Dr. Kane writes in his own vivid way:

> It was an ussuk, and so large that I at first mistook it for a walrus. Signal was made for the *Hope* to follow astern, and, trembling with anxiety, we prepared to crawl down upon him.
>
> Petersen, with his large English rifle, was stationed in the bow, and stockings were drawn over the oars as mufflers. As we neared the animal, our excitement became so intense that the men could hardly keep stroke. I had a set of signals for such occasions which spared us the noise of the voice; and when about three hundred yards off, the oars were taken in, and we moved in deep silence with a single scull astern.
>
> He was not asleep, for he reared his head when we were almost

within rifle shot; and to this day I can remember the hard, careworn, almost despairing expression of the men's thin faces as they saw him move: their lives depended on his capture.

I depressed my hand nervously, as a signal for Petersen to fire. McGary hung upon his oar, and the boat, slowly but noiselessly sagging ahead, seemed to be within certain range. Looking at Petersen, I saw that the poor fellow was paralyzed by his anxiety, trying vainly to obtain a rest for his gun against the cutwater of the boat. The seal rose on its fore flippers, gazed at us for a moment with frightened curiosity for a plunge. At that moment, simultaneously with the crack of our rifle, he relaxed his long length on the ice, and at the very brink of the water, his head fell helpless on one side.

I would have ordered another shot, but no discipline could have controlled the men. With a wild yell, each vociferating according to his own impulse, they urged both boats upon the floes. A crowd of hands seized the seal and bore him up to safer ice. The men seemed half crazy; I had not realized how much we were reduced by absolute famine. They ran over the floes, crying and laughing, and brandishing their knives. It was not over five minutes before every man was sucking his bloody fingers or mouthing long strips of blubber.

It is good to know that after their long ordeal this was the final test. Other seals were captured, and soon the pitiful relics of the years in the Arctic were picked up by Captain Hartstene's squadron.

In 1860 Dr. Isaac Israel Hayes sailed for the North on the fore-and-aft schooner *United States*, of one hundred and thirty-three tons burden, little more than a fishing schooner. Sailing through the leads of Melville Bay, failing to reach his objective, the east coast of Ellesmere Land, he found shelter in Hartstene Bay, where he was frozen in for a year. Dr. Hayes had been the surgeon on the Kane Expedition and had suffered with the rest, a striking example of how the North holds and grips. His programme of work shows plainly the limitations of geographical knowledge, and how thoroughly he had profited by the lessons of his previous experience. Dr. Hayes wrote:

Accepting the deductions of many learned physicists that the sea about the North Pole cannot be frozen, that an open area of varying extent must be found within the ice-belt which is known to invest it, I desired to add to the proofs which had already been accumulated by the early Dutch and English voyagers, and, more recently, by the researches of Scoresby, Wrangel, and Parry, and still later by Dr. Kane's expedition.

It is well known that the great difficulty which has been encountered, in the various attempts that have been made to solve this important physical problem, has been the inability of the explorer to penetrate the ice-belt with his ship, or to travel over it with sledges sufficiently far to obtain indisputable proof. My former experience led me to the conclusion that the chances of success were greater by Smith Sound than by any other route, and my hopes of success were based upon the expectation which I entertained of being able to push a vessel into the ice-belt, to about the 80th degree of latitude, and thence to transport a boat over the ice to the open sea, which I hoped to find beyond. Reaching this open sea, if such fortune awaited me, I proposed to launch my boat and to push off northward. For the ice transportation, I expected to rely, mainly, upon the dog of the Esquimaux.

Equipped with a boat which he shortly abandoned, Hayes crossed to the west coast the next spring – a fearful journey which took thirty-one days – and reached Lady Franklin Bay. His ship was in such condition from her experience with the ice that he felt compelled to return home to refit, but the Civil War had broken out, so that further Arctic work was impossible for him.

In 1871 Charles Francis Hall, blacksmith, publisher, dreamer, visionary, the greatest Arctic enthusiast the world has yet seen, pushed his ship, the *Polaris,* an old river gunboat of three hundred and eighty-seven tons, to latitude 82° 11′, much the farthest north a ship had ever sailed or steamed. Insane, perhaps, abnormal certainly, Hall was obsessed with the ambition to reach the Pole. A new land, a new race of people – one might find anything there! After one short trip he died, believing at the end that he had been poisoned. The retreat of the crew of the *Polaris* is another epic of Polar work.

England had held the record of Farthest North since the sledge-boat journey of Captain Parry, and now in 1875 the Government decided to fit out an expedition, 'regardless of expense,' at least to reach the Polar Sea. The two ships of the party under Captain Nares were driven almost to the ice of the Polar Basin, and in the work of the first autumn Aldrich traveling west from the ship attained the Farthest North, latitude 82° 48′. Although a few dogs had been taken, they failed to find favor with the expedition, so that when the spring work began we find these heroic, gritty men hauling their boats and supplies by standing pulls through snow and ice which often reached their hips. Two parties were sent out – one along the northern edge of Grant Land, the other out over the ice toward the North Pole. The latter soon abandoned one of their boats, but this was only to make room for their sick who came down one after another with scurvy. They reached latitude 83° 20′ 26″, where they were forced to return by the appalling physical breakdown of nearly all the men. The western party had to return from the same cause. In fact, if Nares had not sent out relief parties to both divisions, it would have been impossible for them to survive. The northern party had three sledges and three boats, all hauled by men, almost the same methods used by Parry half a century before. There was an immense outcry when the expedition reached England. The exact cause of the disease was never determined, but it was presumed to be due to inferior packing of provisions.

In his report Captain Nares wrote:

Whether or not land exists within the 360 miles which stretch from the limit of our view to the northern axis of the globe is, so far as sledge traveling is concerned, immaterial. Sixty miles of such pack as we now knew to extend north of Cape Joseph Henry is an insuperable obstacle to traveling in that direction with our present appliances; and I unhesitatingly affirm that it is impracticable to reach the North Pole by the Smith Sound route.

It was left to Peary to prove how mistaken this view was.

In July, 1879, Lieutenant George Washington De Long sailed from San Francisco, in the ship *Jeannette,* in an expedition fitted out by James Gordon Bennett. It was planned to sail through Behring Strait and to take advantage of a current which was supposed to exist to drive as far north toward the Pole as possible. All San Francisco turned out to wish them success, little realizing that it was a farewell to most of that crew. Telegraph Hill was black with people, and gay with flags, steam whistles, cheers, and a salute of twenty-one guns. What was once the old *Pandora* disappeared over the northern horizon. Two long years of silence followed. The world wondered and waited, and searched and then waited again. At last from the desolate shores of Siberia the report filtered through that ten Americans had landed, that the *Jeannette* had been crushed, that Lieutenant Chipp had been lost with all his men, that Nindemann and Noros alone of the De Long party of twelve had staggered through to safety. The next spring a frozen hand projecting from a snow bank revealed the fate of the leader. The *Jeannette* had been beset within a week of leaving the Siberian coast and was never afterward released from the ice. Her position was 71° 35′ and by the sixth of March, 1880, she had reached 72° 12′. She drifted on until she was crushed on June 12, 1881, in latitude 77° 14′ 57″. The crew had taken to the ice with three boats and with such supplies as they could carry. It was weeks, however, before they could launch the boats and sail toward the Siberian coast. One of the boats was undoubtedly lost in a storm during which the three were separated. De Long's reached the shore with almost no provisions, the beginning of a losing fight against hunger. Gulls, decayed fish, boots, anything was eaten, but only two, the strongest, who had been sent on ahead to bring relief, escaped. They had failed to reach the Pole; but associated with all such failures in the North there are facts recorded and discoveries made which are of more real value than the attainment of a mathematical microscopic point. De Long had proved the Siberian Ocean to be a shallow basin dotted with islands, and exploded the theory of a great continent to the north of Asia.

But the day of the adventurer in the North was drawing to a close and the scientist was entering the field. The realization had come that the

North holds locked up in its snow-clad hills secrets of inestimable value. By international agreement it was arranged to establish seven circumpolar stations to make simultaneous observations. The United States decided to establish two – one at Point Barrow, Alaska, and the other at Lady Franklin Bay, Grant Land, four hundred and ninety-six miles from the Pole. In 1881 Lieutenant Adolphus W. Greely was landed at Discovery Harbor, not far from the headquarters of the Nares Expedition of 1875. For two years there was nothing but success. The *Proteus* had sailed away, promising to return every year. Then came the long night, the bitter cold of January and February, and the remarkable sledge trip of Lockwood and Brainard along the northern shores of Greenland, establishing the world's record of Farthest North as 83° 24′.

Then the delightful days of summer, and as the ice field splits into sections, the men stand watch at the end of the point looking southward toward home. Another winter night follows, and again they take turns at the end of the point. Again the ship fails. They read their orders:

> In case no vessel reaches the *permanent* camp in 1882, the vessel sent in 1883 will remain in Smith Sound until there is danger of its closing by ice, and, on leaving, will land all her supplies and a party at Littleton Island, which party will be prepared for a winter's stay, and will be instructed to send sledge parties up the east side of *Grinnell Land* to meet this party. If not visited in 1882, Lieutenant Greely will abandon his station not later than September 1, 1883, and will retreat southward by boat, following closely the *east coast of* Grinnell Land until the relieving vessel is met or Littleton Island is reached.

In view of the tragedy which followed, it is sad to note that, when Greely and his men started their retreat in pursuance of these instructions, the party was in excellent health and that they had sufficient provisions of all kinds to have carried them over another year. But orders are orders! In open boats they fought their way through the pack ice of Hall Basin, Kennedy Channel, and Kane Basin, every day expecting to meet the ship which the Government had promised to send. Nipped by floes, squeezed out bodily, the five boats continued on their way, with impossible ice here, open water there, now carried east, now west, but ever south, today encouraged, tomorrow discouraged.

Wearily they plodded over the ice to Wade Point. At Cape Sabine they found a cairn which stated, in brief, that the relief ship *Proteus* had been crushed, that the crew had gone home. Despite desperate attempts to recover stores left by the Nares Expedition, despite all expedients to live on seaweed and their own fur clothes, the inevitable happened. No party, not even Eskimos, can live for ten months on forty days' food. When the sun returned in the spring of 1884, it found them dying one by one, wrapping up their little bundles and writing their letters home.

In June, 1884, Commander W.S. Schley, U.S.N., broke all records for early navigation in these waters, smashed through the ice of Melville Bay, and on the twenty-second rounded Cape Sabine, every man on deck searching for signs of life. Off in the distance, standing on the top of a little ridge, they saw a man feebly waving a flag. He fell, rose to his feet again, and fell again. Only seven were left out of twenty-five, and one of the seven succumbed later – a pathetic story of a struggle to live until help came.

America had now given lives and treasure to achieve Farthest North. Now Norway under the great Nansen secured the record. Bits of wreckage from the *Jeannette,* which, as we know, was sunk off the northeastern coast of Siberia, had been found on the coast of Greenland. Logs of Siberian pine had been found in the same locality. Nansen deduced from this evidence the existence of a current across the Polar Sea which would drive a ship frozen in the ice north of Siberia somewhere near the North Pole and eventually out of the ice toward Southern Greenland. The *Fram* was especially built for this task, the first ship built with the idea of standing the continuous pressure of the ice pack. The expedition sailed in 1893, and, as the world knows, the *Fram* emerged from the pack after a drift of four years across the Polar Sea. Gone now was all idea of an open Polar Sea which had so long obsessed scientists, also the belief in land to the north, and it was now known that, instead of being a shallow basin, the Arctic Ocean was of tremendous depth. The supposed current, however, was proved to be without basis of fact, for the prevailing winds were

entirely responsible for the drift. But after a year or so of the monotony of
the drift, varied only by constantly repeated observations and the appearance of a very occasional bear, Nansen decided to attempt a dash to the
Pole with sledges. At the last port of call he had purchased a number of
what he himself describes as rather inferior Siberian dogs to be used in
case the *Fram* were wrecked and the crew had to take to the ice. He had
built a number of sledges, and with them and the dogs, he started out in
the spring of 1895, with only one companion. Each man had to drive several sledges, and the only experience they had in driving dogs had been
gained around the ship after she had been frozen in. The result was that in
practice one man had to lead the way while the other drove the several
sledges. In this connection, thoroughly to appreciate the situation, it may
be of interest to recall the fundamental principle of using dogs so clearly
stated by Dr. Hayes in 1861: 'In order to obtain the best results which the
Eskimo dog is capable of yielding, it is essential that he shall be able to trot
away with his load. To walk as a dead drag is as distressing to his spirits
as the hauling of a dray would be to a blooded horse.'

But Nansen's dash was brilliant in the extreme, and just as extreme in
the hazards that he took. He had cut loose from his base; he had but one
companion, and if anything had happened to either, the result would have
been more than disastrous; he had too scanty provisions – he relied on
killing the dogs for food, and he wished he had taken more – but his success was as brilliant as his daring. On April 7, 1895, he attained Farthest
North in latitude 86° 13'. The return is a stirring adventure story. After a
much longer time than they had foreseen and after traveling a much longer
distance than they had estimated, Nansen and his companion landed on an
island, where they were forced to spend the winter, subsisting on bear
meat. By some coincidence of fate Nansen and the *Fram* reached Norway
within a few days of each other, thus bringing to Norway not only the
record of the Farthest North, but data of inestimable scientific value.

Next it was the turn of Italy to get the record. In 1899 the Duke of the
Abruzzi led one of the most elaborately fitted out expeditions that ever
attempted the conquest of the North, with the islands north of Spitzbergen as a base. None of the party had had experience in Polar work, but

many had been tried on mountain ice, and the Duke had climbed Mount Saint Elias in Alaska. Unfortunately during the preparatory work the Duke was so badly frostbitten that he could not make the final journey, and the command devolved upon Captain Cagni, himself so badly injured by frostbites that a lesser man would have abandoned the trip. The northern party started off in three detachments, one of four men, the other two of three each. The dogs had been acquired in Vienna. Twelve sledges were used, so that it was impossible for each team to have a driver. The camp equipment alone weighed nearly half a ton, and the total weight of the loads reached 6718 pounds. It was designed that as the supplies were lowered, one detachment was to return, then the second, and finally the main body would proceed alone. Unfortunately one of the returning parties was lost, either through being driven so far to the west as to render it impossible to find the land or through breaking through a lead. The former is the more likely solution, as Cagni himself on his return drifted out of his course so far that he had to change his direction drastically. In spite of all obstacles, in spite of hands which were a constantly open wound – on his return he had to have his fingers amputated – Cagni succeeded brilliantly. On April 24, 1900, he reached latitude 86° 34', the Farthest North until Peary reached 87° 6' on April 21, 1906.

It was our task to surpass even that figure, but on that first night out from Sydney, I feel sure there was no fear in the heart of anyone that we should fail. We knew that our leader had the experience that his predecessors had lacked; that our equipment and our organization were adapted to the work in hand to the last degree, and despite the sufferings and horrors which other expeditions had undergone, such was our confidence in the Commander that we turned in without a qualm as to the future. Our greatest fear was that we might fail him.

✳

LABRADOR

In spite of the calm of our departure, what a night that first out from Sydney, July 18th, was! There was a 'kick-up,' as a sailor would say, coming from somewhere, caused probably by the tides of the Gulf of St. Lawrence working up against the wind. Everything was moving on board ship which could possibly move, and a few things which were supposed not to move. Wind and weather should be kind to an Arctic ship leaving home, for she is always frightfully loaded, even dangerously so. The *Roosevelt* with her sharp bilges was not a carrier; she was an ice-breaker, and yet an excellent sea boat. She was designed and built for a definite purpose – to force her way through heavy ice fields up through the dangerous waters of Smith Sound, Kennedy and Robeson Channels, to the edge of the Polar Sea, but not beyond. Peary knew the Polar Sea too well for that.

That the staunch *Fram* ever came back was almost a miracle. That the reconstructed *Jeannette* withstood the terrible strain for almost two years was a tribute to her builders. Finally she was crushed as flat as the proverbial pancake. The *Race Horse* was turned completely inside out, her keel bursting up through her deck. And this in the comparatively smooth waters of Melville Bay! So, when a well-known explorer advocates the use of the submarine in the Polar Sea we naturally question the wisdom of his plan – although not his vision, his faith, and his courage – and hold the results in grave doubt.

To withstand the ice pressure, the *Fram* was necessarily so constructed that on her first night at sea she rolled her quarter boats under. Admirably adapted to withstand the ice which she would be called on to meet for years, she was not planned to be steady in a seaway. Every sailor knows a ship, to be called a good ship, must be designed and built for a certain purpose; she is not expected successfully to meet requirements outside that purpose. The *Roosevelt* was an improvement over the *Fram* as a good sea boat, but she could certainly roll. Later on during the trip our stateroom was known to the other members of the expedition as 'The Chamber of Horrors' – not complimentary, perhaps, but one which undoubtedly had its beginning from the condition of the room on the morning after. Cups, water pitcher, toothbrushes, ink, toothpowder, pictures, rifles, shotguns, knives, clothing – all were in a horrible mess washing back and forth in water which covered our floor to a depth of two or three inches. The opening act began with an astounding acrobatic feat by our stateroom lamp, which jumped from the bracket and landed chimney down in the water pitcher! Borup, who had never been to sea before, could not get over it for some minutes.

With porthole screwed up tightly, where the water came from I could not imagine, unless the bottom was out of the ship completely. In the morning we learned that the coal piled on the main and after decks had clogged the scuppers, forcing the wash over the doorsills into the cabins.

After such a night only one call to coffee and toast at five o'clock was necessary. We were up and having our first sight of the west coast of Newfoundland on the starboard bow. At six o'clock we were off Cape George, wondering why the red in Red Island. It looks like a huge mass of hematite. It was thick with fog on the morning of the nineteenth, and it was well that it lifted just when it did, for we were headed right in on Point Rich, just north of which is a dangerous mass of small islands, reefs, and shoals, where many a good ship has ended her days. It is no disgrace for a captain to lose his ship in the Straits of Belle Isle. Strong tides, prevailing fogs, ice, and a strong magnetic influence on the compass of a ship make it one of the worst places on the Atlantic Coast. In fact it is known as 'The Graveyard of Ships.'

Captain Bob now headed toward Point Amour. To our great surprise, upon rowing into a small cove under the lighthouse, we found the water literally filled with capelin (*Mallotus villosus*), a new species of fish to us from the New England coast. They resemble a smelt, but are smaller. At first we scooped them into the boat with our hands, but then, remembering that our dogs liked fish, we utilized our hats, landing about fifteen hundred in all. Fried for supper, they proved delicious. Later I learned why the arrival of capelin on the Labrador Coast is so eagerly awaited. They are the lure, the food, of the great schools of codfish which annually visit the shores during the months of July, August, and September. The cod is the great harvest of the Newfoundland and Labrador fishermen. In their vocabularies only the cod is 'fish.' Salmon, trout, and herring are not 'fish.'

The next morning we saw our first iceberg, the most impressive sight of the whole Northland, with the possible exception of the parent of them all, the great Greenland Ice Cap, five hundred thousand square miles in area, and attaining a height of ten thousand feet. A most interesting phenomenon, going on and on into the great white silence, it makes us wonder as to the whys, and hows, and when. For centuries the iceberg was a real enigma to the mariners of the North Atlantic. It was by general consent conceded to be a detached portion of an enormous snow bank formed on the shores of a northern land. It is not, as many still believe, formed in salt water, nor of salt water, but is composed of tiny snowflakes which fall upon the land, even hundreds of miles from the coast. In the course of time these flakes are pressed down and solidified by their own weight into ice.

Ice under the influence of gravity will move or 'flow,' but how no one really knows. It is fortunate that ice, apparently as brittle as glass, has this property closely related to viscosity, for it enables northern lands to be relieved of the weight of the annual precipitation. When the melting powers of the sun and rate of flow of the glaciers both fail to diminish the ice supply, the result is an Ice Age, of which the world has known at least five. The accumulated snowflakes of centuries move down and out toward the coast at rates varying, according to time, locality, and the angle of the slope, from the fractional part of an inch to one hundred feet in a day, during the month of August. The last observation was made by scientists in the Bay of Augpadlartok, near Upernivik. Greenland, latitude 73°. Eventually the frontal edge of the glacier extends well out into the water; it is then broken off by flotation power and becomes an iceberg. Think of its age! The Greenland Ice Cap is some seven hundred miles wide at its broadest part. Let us assume that this ice has been creeping from a point one hundred miles inland slowly toward the coast at the rate of one inch per day. That mass of detached ice, an iceberg, is made of snowflakes which fell more than seventeen thousand years ago!

Although we were supplied with thirty thousand pounds of man and dog pemmican, Peary, in anticipation of every need, decided to add to our commissary department some thirty thousand pounds of whale meat, fresh or otherwise. Eskimo dogs are not unduly particular as to the age of their food, and whale meat is certainly good food – for dogs. There are a number of so-called whaling stations along the Labrador Coast, one of which is located at Cape Charles, just south of Battle Harbor. There we counted seven whales on the beach, all finbacks (*Balænoptera physalus*). Two had been killed recently, and one was promptly purchased and cut up for our use.

We were away again in the early evening with our after deck buried beneath seventeen thousand pounds of meat. When it dawned upon one of our Eskimo dogs that we had such a stupendous amount of meat on board, he immediately went into a fit, whether or not from sheer joy or the excitement of the moment, I do not know. He lay on his side quivering from nose to tail. After the sun had shone upon this mass for three weeks, I am surprised that we didn't all do this! The dog slowly recovered, looked a bit dazed, ran aft nearer the meat, sniffed, and dropped again! As the months went by I learned more and more about this malady, which is known to the Smith Sound Eskimo as 'piblock-to.' It is undoubtedly a type of rabies which may at any time attack a whole team, and completely destroy it.

Guided by our sense of smell, we now headed for Hawks Harbor, the site of another 'whaling factory,' where we were to meet our consort the *Erik*, which had been chartered to accompany us as far as Etah. She was to load twenty-five tons of very, very old meat. Our three wealthy tourists, Larned, Whitney, and Norton, all fine fellows who had engaged passage on the *Erik*, had never dreamed of such a cargo.

The Arctic is full of surprises, and one came to the immaculately white-clad ladies and gentlemen of the steam yacht *Wakiva* of New York. She was anchored in Hawks Harbor, and her party came aboard the *Roosevelt* to pay their respects to our Commander. As a compliment and aid to our distinguished guests, a narrow – very narrow – board walk was laid upon the jellylike mass from the companion ladder to the door leading into the after cabin. Although a bit uncertain, it was altogether sufficient for its purpose. The look of consternation on the face of each one as he or she appeared up over the rail beggars description. Gingerly they crossed the Bridge of Sighs. There were no catastrophes; they all succeeded in reaching the doorway. They said little then, but later, I wonder!

That evening both ships were away together bound for Turnavik West, the summer fishing station of the Bartletts, some two hundred miles north.

Magazines and books – I wonder if any ship ever had as many. A kindly, thoughtful New York reporter, prompted by the wishes of one of the crew, had inserted a want ad in his paper stating that during the long Arctic night we had nothing to read. We never dared tell our Commander who this particular individual was, after seeing the expression on his face when he arrived at the pier one morning. A regular haystack confronted him. New York had done nobly and, I think, its best. Not a single American author was slighted; they were all there. And yet, in all this conglomerate collection, dealing with almost every conceivable subject under the sun, there was not a single Bible, a marked compliment to the reputations of the members of the expedition. For a moment Peary was too full of words for utterance, but finally he ejaculated in a pronounced staccato tone: 'Who in hell sent those books?' There was a deep silence. 'Throw them on the after deck. We'll chuck them overboard when we get to sea.' But we didn't. We peddled them out all along the Labrador Coast, real gifts to those poor people who are truly thankful for any kind of literature.

George Borup (left) and Donald B. MacMillan

We had the pleasure of doing this one day in a small fishing port. There was the customary hail from the oilskin-clad figure in a small fishing punt, 'Any books, sir?' I winked at Borup, who understood. 'Yes, come up alongside!' I yelled back. He did, and backed his boat under the quarter, with a broad smile of gratefulness. The books and magazines were conveniently tied up in bundles ready for instant and quick delivery. The first bundle was gladly and thankfully received and accepted. But when two, three, four, and five came tumbling over the rail in rapid succession, he dug his short crooked spruce oars into the water and rowed for his life, alarm for his safety written in every line of his face. When once away, he was the happy and proud possessor of the largest library in Labrador; and probably not able to read a word of it. I have boarded many a schooner with crews of ten men and not one of them able to read or write. What a pleasure it is to surprise a Newfoundlander by being generous! He has so little and prizes that little so highly that he really cannot understand why anyone should give something for nothing.

The weather was so fine and the sun so warm that Borup and I stripped on deck and threw buckets of sea water at each other, following a long period of several hours of packing and unpacking in the hot, stuffy lazarette. Thirty icebergs were in sight at the time, which was fairly good evidence that the water was not too hot for comfort, but certainly cold enough to stimulate. The waters of the Far North are about the same temperature winter and summer, 29.2° Fahrenheit.

Undoubtedly in the North there are more sudden changes in weather and varying conditions from day to day than farther south. I have known the barometer to fall from 29.73° to 28.35° in six hours; the thermometer to rise from twenty-one below zero to thirty-three above, a rise of fifty-four degrees, in twenty-four hours. July 22d was one of the most beautiful of days, yet that night it was raining and blowing from the northwest, and so rough the next day that work in the hold was impossible. Then, suddenly, a calm and one of the most beautiful of sunsets, accentuated in its beauty by being reflected from the surface of miles of scattered ice pans and the abrupt faces of many chalk-white icebergs.

On the morning of the twenty-fourth we anchored at Turnavik, to be met promptly by Captain Bob's father and his two brothers bringing us some fine Atlantic salmon (*Salmo salar*) and cod. Just out of the cold waters of this coast these fish are delicious. The taste is undoubtedly due to the character of their food – capelin and minute forms of animal life brought southward along the Labrador Coast by the Arctic Current.

Labrador is found on the Ribero map of 1529 as 'Tierra del Labrador,' with the note, 'This country was discovered by the people of Bristol, and because he who first sighted land was a labourer from the islands of the Azores is named after him.' This country has been known for its super-abundance of cod for the last three centuries and a half, ever since John Davis wrote, 'In this place at the Harbor mouth we found great store of cod.' In 1908 there were 1432 fishing schooners on the coast. Everyone went home loaded to the rails. The total catch of codfish alone was 289,000 quintals.

CHAPTER 6

✳

DAVIS STRAIT AND BAFFIN BAY

Our departure from Labrador on the morning of July 25th was the beginning of a new chapter in our work. Now we were really on our way to 'Greenland's icy mountains,' about which I had heard so much in my boyhood. Davis Strait and Baffin Bay! The very names conjured up all kinds of memories of stirring tales of explorers and whalers of old, those hardy mariners of Dundee and Peterhead, Scotland, who boldly pushed into the ice fields in early May, owners urging them on into the North, not alone because of the high value of oil, but because of the extraordinary price of thirty-five hundred dollars a ton paid for whalebone. Arctic whalers discovered lands and islands many years prior to their discovery by the explorers to whom credit is given. But it was the hope and purpose of each whaling captain to conceal from his contemporaries the fact that he had discovered new waters which were yielding his owners a profit of from fifty to a hundred thousand dollars a year. The purpose of the explorer, on the other hand, was to proclaim to the world that he had made an important discovery. A discovered land unrecorded might as well remain undiscovered.

The increase in the amount of daylight from day to day as one goes north should be explained, since the long Arctic day and equally long Arctic night are enigmas to the average reader. As twilight is in the east before sunrise and in the west following a sunset, so there is a continuous twilight in the North as the sun rolls along from west to north to east, a few degrees beneath the horizon, because of the inclination of the earth on its axis. With every degree of latitude that the ship proceeds northward, the sun is raised one degree nearer the northern horizon, or with every mile it is raised one minute of arc, until the day comes when it does not set, but skims along the edge of the sea and rises into the morning of the new day.

On July 27th we crossed the Arctic Circle, that imaginary line drawn 23° 28′ from the Pole, which equals approximately the declination of the sun at the time of the summer solstice. 'Within the Arctic Circle one sees the midnight sun.' This is not so; the truth of this statement depends upon where you are and the time of year. As a matter of fact, we did not see it until three days later beyond the Duck Islands.

Ocean currents, known as drift, stream, and submarine, are a wise provision of Nature for equalizing and tempering certain regions of the globe climatically. Think of the warm waters of the Gulf of Mexico flowing eastward through the Straits of Florida, thence northward like a mighty river, expanding to two hundred and fifty miles in width, lapping icebergs and ice fields into submission, bringing warmth to Iceland, where ice is a stranger, and so tempering the climate of the British Isles that, although situated from 50° to 58° North Latitude, 'no part at sea level has a temperature as low as 32° F.' Even during January, the coldest month of the year, the sea never freezes. Labrador, in the same latitude (50° to 60°), is locked in ice from November to July.

We were now steaming against an Arctic current flowing southward from the Polar Sea, bearing on its surface ten thousand square miles of ice to lower the temperature of the hot summer days in New England. Would a bottle with a letter enclosed reach home, and, if so, when? On Sunday, the twenty-sixth, I wrote a note requesting the finder please to return, stating when and where found. I threw the bottle, tightly corked and sealed with wax, into the sea on July 27th. Upon my return home in September of the following year, I found my letter on my desk with a letter from the captain of the Old Kinsale Life-Saving Station in Ireland stating that one of his men had found the bottle washing up in the surf. With considerable amusement I read Pat's letter to me on the back of my own, stating where he had found it, and ending with:

I would like to drink to the health of Captain Peary and his gallant crew. In joyful anticipation I thank you.

Five dollars forwarded by mail possibly enabled Pat to realize his ambition.

On July 29th we had reached 72° 55′ North Latitude, possibly the Farthest North of the Norsemen. Here was found in 1824 on the island of Kingiktorsuak, a runic inscription on a rock, which, translated, read: 'Erling Sighvaston and Bjarni Thordarson and Eindride Oddson raised these marks and cleared ground on Saturday before Ascension Week 1135.' One could hardly call this positive evidence. The date 1135 is uncertain, for the inscription might have been written many years later. But supporting this evidence, and as corroborative proof that the Norsemen did go far northward from their settlement along the western coast of Greenland, is an account in the Annals of Bjorn Jonsson of an expedition in 1266.

That summer [runs the narrative] came also people from Nordrseta, who had traveled farther north than we have formerly heard of. They saw no sign that Skraelings [Eskimos] had lived there except at Krog-fiordsheath, and it is thought that this must be the shortest way for them [the Skraelings] to go, from wherever they got there. Thereupon the priests sent a ship northward in order to explore the regions north of the farthest point which they had hitherto visited; but they sailed out from Krogfiordsheath, until they lost sight of the land. Then they had a south wind against them and darkness, and they had to let the ship go before the wind; but when the storm ceased and it cleared up again, they saw many islands and all kinds of game, both seals and whales and a great number of bears. They came right into the sea-bay [*allt i hafs-botninn*], and lost sight of all the land, both the southern coast and the glaciers, but south of them were also glaciers, as far as they could see. They saw signs that Skraelings had dwelt there in former times, but on account of the bears they could not land. Thereafter they sailed back in three days, and found some remains of Skraelings on some islands south of Snaefell. Then they sailed southward to Krogfiordsheath, one good day's rowing, Saint James's Day [July 25th]. It was frosty at night, but the sun shone both night and day, and was not higher in the south than that when a man placed himself athwartships in a six-oared boat [with his head] up against the railing [or gunwale] on one side of the boat, the shadow of that side [gunwale] which was nearest to the sun would strike his face; but at midnight the sun was as high as at home in the settlement when it is northwest. Thereafter they traveled home to Garoar.

If there is more truth than imagination in tradition, we may readily believe that these hardy mariners reached a much higher latitude, that they even crossed Melville Bay, and were seen by the most northern inhabitants of the world, who tell the following story:

Ships came in from the sea without masts and without sails, and the men were rowing. It was at the time of the going away of the little auks [September]. And now because of much ice one ship could not go on. Our people fastened strips of bearskin to the bottoms of their boots so they would not slip. For a long time they fought, but finally all the white men died.

This is the only recorded battle in the history of the Smith Sound tribe. We were now well among the icebergs. They were everywhere. Two hundred and eleven were in sight at once. Fulmars, glaucous gulls, murres, and little auks were in sight for every moment of the day as we passed Kasarsoak, Cape Shackleton, and the Horse's Head. In summer the North is far from being a dead world. Ahead lay the apparently peaceful waters of Melville Bay, for ninety years the battlefield of the Dundee whaling fleet, and the relentless ice field.

To the bay itself I gave the name of Melville's Bay, from respect to the present First Lord of the Admiralty. It is situated between lat. 75° 12′ and 76° 0′, and abounds with whales, many of which were taken by the ships which were persevering enough to follow us.

So wrote John Ross, K.S., Captain Royal Navy, in 1819.

Melville Bay! The very name brings up a kaleidoscopic picture of square-rigged ships, of shouting men, of 'tracking' to the accompaniment of fiddles, bagpipes, fifes and drums, of change of wind, of the pack in motion, of quick cutting of docks, of a squeeze, of cracking timbers, of abandoned ships a mass of flames, of ice littered with provisions, boats, equipment, and the long retreat to the Greenland shore. The year 1830 was a marked one, for twenty-one fine ships were crushed and torn to pieces. Four, however, was the average annual toll. Such dangers are not imminent in July and August, but in the early days of May, before the so-called fast ice leaves the land, there is an ever-present possibility of being beset and crushed.

In exceptional years Melville Bay may be completely blocked with ice, through which no ship could force her way. This condition is caused by a long continuation of southerly winds which drive the ice northward in the bay. The *Fox*, under the command of Captain F.L. McClintock in search of Sir John Franklin, was beset in Melville Bay on August 31, 1857. She was released the next year on April 26th, after drifting in the ice, first north, then west, then south, for a distance of 1385 statute miles.

The 'dreaded Melville Bay' of which I had read so much was so easily and quickly crossed that I could hardly believe it. Now we were in the real Northland off Meteorite Island, the most southern settlement of the Smith Sound Eskimo.

On August 10th, ninety years before our arrival, Captain John Ross dared to head northward through the ice pack of Melville Bay. There was every possibility that he would never return, but he persisted in going on. With an apparently endless ice field stretching northward ahead of his ship and hills in the distance, why should he take this chance? Who could imagine that life could exist at the so-called Top of the World. Yet he found there a happy race of people. As his experience is much like that of one who visits another planet and his report of meeting for the first time a people who are largely responsible for Peary's success and in whom all Arctic men are interested, I quote his narrative verbatim.

August 10, 1818. About ten o'clock this day, we were rejoiced to see eight sledges, driven by the natives, advancing by a circuitous route towards the place where we lay; they halted about a mile from us, and the people alighting, ascended a small iceberg, as if to reconnoitre. After remaining apparently in consultation for nearly half an hour, four of them descended, and came towards the flagstaff, which, however, they did not venture to approach. In the meantime a white flag was hoisted at the main in each ship, and John Sacheuse dispatched, bearing a small white flag, with some presents, that he might endeavor, if possible, to bring them to a parley. This was a service which he had most cheerfully volunteered, requesting leave to go unattended and unarmed, a request to which no objection could be made, as the place chosen for the meeting was within half a mile of the *Isabella*. It was equally advantageous to the natives, a canal, or some small chasm in the ice, not passable without a plank, separating the parties from each other, and preventing any possibility of an attack from these people, unless by darts.

In executing this service, Sacheuse displayed no less address than courage. Having placed his flag at some distance from the canal, he advanced to the edge, and, taking off his hat, made friendly signs for those opposite to approach, as he did. This they partly complied with, halting at a distance of three hundred yards, where they got out of their sledges, and set up a loud simultaneous halloo, which Sacheuse answered by imitating it. They ventured to approach a little nearer, having nothing in their hands but the whips with which they guide their dogs; and, after satisfying themselves that the canal was impassable, one of them in particular seemed to acquire confidence. Shouts, words, and gestures, were exchanged for some time to no purpose, though each party seemed, in some degree, to recognize each other's language. Sacheuse, after a time, thought he could discover that they spoke the Humooke dialect, drawling out their words, however, to an unusual length. He immediately adopted that dialect, and, holding up the presents, called out to them, '*Kahkeite*,' 'Come on,' to which they answered, '*Naakrie,*

Naakrieai—plaite,' 'No, no, —— go away'; and other words which he made out to mean that they hoped we were not come to destroy them. The boldest then approached to the edge of the canal, and drawing from his boot a knife, repeated, 'Go away; I can kill you.' Sacheuse, not intimidated, told them he was also a man and a friend, and, at the same time, threw across the canal some strings of beads and a chequed shirt; but these they beheld with great distrust and apprehension, still calling, 'Go away, don't kill us.' Sacheuse now threw them an English knife, saying, 'Take that.' On this they approached with caution, picked up the knife, then shouted and pulled their noses; these actions were imitated by Sacheuse, who, in return, called out, 'Heigh, yaw,' pulling his nose with the same gesture. They now pointed to the shirt, demanding what it was, and when told that it was an article of clothing, asked of what skin it was made. Sacheuse replied, it was made of the hair of an animal, which they had never seen; on which they picked it up with expressions of surprise. They now began to ask many questions; for by this time, they found the language spoken by themselves and Sacheuse had sufficient resemblance to enable them to hold some communication.

They first pointed to the ships, eagerly asking, 'What great creatures those were? Do they come from the sun or the moon? Do they give light by night or by day?' Sacheuse told them that he was a man, that he had a father and mother like themselves; and, pointing to the south, said that he came from a distant country in that direction. To this they answered, 'That cannot be, there is nothing but ice there.' They again asked, 'What creatures these are?' pointing to the ships; to which Sacheuse replied, that 'they were houses made of wood.' This they seemed still to discredit, answering, 'No, they are alive, we have seen them move their wings.' Sacheuse now inquired of them, what they themselves were; to which they replied, they were men, and lived in that direction, pointing to the north; that there was much water there; and that they had come here to fish for unicorns. It was then agreed, that Sacheuse should pass the chasm to them, and he accordingly returned to the ship to make his report, and to ask for a plank....

Captain Ross's first meeting with the natives of Prince Regent's Bay, August 10, 1818
Drawn by John Sacheuse, an Eskimo who had visited Scotland

Sacheuse was directed to entice them to the ship, and two men were now sent with a plank, which was accordingly placed across the chasm. They appeared still much alarmed, and requested that Sacheuse only should come over; he accordingly passed to the opposite side, on which they earnestly besought him not to touch them, as if he did they should certainly die. After he had used many arguments to persuade them that he was flesh and blood, the native who had shown most courage, ventured to touch his hand; then pulling himself by the nose, set up a shout, in which he was joined by Sacheuse and the other three. The presents were then distributed, consisting of two or three articles of clothing, and a few strings of beads; after which Sacheuse exchanged a knife for one of theirs.

The hope of getting some important information, as well as the interest naturally felt for these poor creatures, made me impatient to communicate with them myself; and I therefore desired Lieutenant Parry to accompany me to the place where the party were assembled, it appearing to me that Sacheuse had failed in persuading them to come nearer the ships. We accordingly provided ourselves with additional presents, consisting of looking-glasses and knives, together with some caps and shirts, and proceeded toward the spot, where the conference was held with increased energy. By the time we reached it the whole were assembled; those, who had originally been left at a distance with their sledges, having driven up to join their comrades. The party now, therefore, consisted of eight natives, with all their sledges, and about fifty dogs, two sailors, Sacheuse, Lieutenant Parry, and myself; forming a group of no small singularity; not a little also increased by the peculiarity of the situation, on a field of ice, far from the land. The noise and the clamour may easily be conceived, the whole talking and shouting together, and the dogs howling, while the natives were flogging them with their long whips, to preserve order.

Our arrival produced a visible alarm, causing them to retreat a few steps towards their sledges; on this Sacheuse called to us to pull our noses, as he had discovered this to be the mode of friendly salutation with them. This ceremony was accordingly performed by each of us, the natives, during their retreat, making use of the same gesture, the nature of which we had not before understood. In the same way we imitated their shouts as well as we could, using the same interjection, Heigh, Yaw, which we afterwards found to be an expression of surprise or pleasure. We then advanced towards them while they halted, and presented the foremost with a looking-glass and a knife, repeating the same presents to the whole, as they came in succession. On seeing their faces in the glasses, their astonishment appeared extreme, and they looked around in silence, for a moment, at each other and at us; immediately afterwards they set up a general shout, succeeded by a long laugh, expressive of extreme delight, as well as surprise, in which we joined, partly from inability to avoid it, and willing also to show that we were pleased with our new acquaintances.

Having now at length acquired confidence they advanced, offering in return for our knives, glasses and beads, their knives, sea unicorns, horns, and sea horse teeth, which were accepted. They were then instructed by Sacheuse to uncover their heads, as a mark of good will and respect to us; and with ceremonial, which they performed immediately, and of which they appeared to comprehend the meaning, our friendship became established.

One of them having inquired what was the use of a red cap, which I had given him, Sacheuse placed it on his head, to the great amusement of the rest, each of whom put it on in his turn. The color of our skins became next a subject of much mirth, as also the ornaments on the frames of the looking-glasses. The eldest of them, who was also the one who acted as the leader, addressing himself to me, now made a long speech, which being ended he appeared to wait for a reply. I made signs that I did not understand him, and called for Sacheuse to interpret. He thus perceived that we used different languages, at which his astonishment appeared extreme, and he expressed it by a loud Heigh, Yaw. As Sacheuse's attempt to procure the meaning of this oration seemed likely to fail, and as we were anxious to get them to the ship as soon as possible, I desired him to persuade them to accompany us; they accordingly consented, on which their dogs were unharnessed and fastened to the ice, and two of the sledges were drawn along the plank to the other side of the chasm; three of the natives being left in charge of the dogs, and the remaining sledges; the other five followed us laughing heartily at seeing Lieutenant Parry and myself drawn towards the ship, on sledges, by our seamen. One of them, by keeping close to me, got before his companions, and thus we proceeded together until we arrived within a hundred yards of the ship, where he stopped. I attempted to urge him on, but in vain; his evident terror preventing him from advancing another step till his companions came up. It was apparent that he still believed the ship to be a living creature, as he stopped to contemplate her, looking up at the masts, and examining every part with a mark of the greatest fear and astonishment; he then addressed her, crying out in words perfectly intelligible to Sacheuse, and in a loud tone – 'Who are you? Where do you come from? Is it from the sun or the moon?' pausing between every question, and pulling his nose with the utmost solemnity. The rest now came up in succession, each shewing similar surprise, and making use of the same expressions, accompanied by the same extraordinary ceremony. Sacheuse now laboured to assure them, that the ship was only a wooden house, and pointed out the boat, which had been hauled on the ice to repair; explaining to them that it was a smaller one of the same kind. This immediately arrested their attention, they advanced to the boat, examined her, as well as the carpenters' tools and the oars, very minutely; each object, in its turn, exciting the most ludicrous ejaculations of surprise; we then ordered the boat to be launched into the sea, with a man in it, and hauled up again, at the sight of which they set no bounds to their clamour. The ice anchor, a heavy piece of iron, shaped like the letter S, and the cable, excited much interest; the former they tried in vain to remove, and they eagerly inquired of what skins the latter was made.

By this time the officers of both ships had surrounded them, while the bow of the *Isabella,* which was close to the ice, was crowded with the crew; and, certainly, a more ludicrous, but interesting, scene was never beheld, than that which took place whilst they were viewing the ship; nor is it possible to convey to the imagination anything like a just representation of the wild amazement, joy, and fear which successively pervaded the countenances, and governed the gestures of these creatures, who gave full vent to their feelings; and, I am sure, it was a gratifying scene, which can never be forgotten by those who witnessed and enjoyed it.

Their shouts, halloos, and laughter were heartily joined in, and imitated by all hands, as well as the ceremony of nose-pulling, which could not fail to increase our mirth on the occasion. That which most of all excited their admiration, was the circumstance of a sailor going aloft, and they kept their eyes on him till he reached the summit of the mast; the sails, which hung loose, they naturally supposed were skins. Their attention being again called to the boat, where the carpenter's hammer and nails still remained, they were shewn the use of these articles; and no sooner were they aware of their purposes, than they shewed a desire to possess them, and were accordingly presented with some nails. They now accompanied us to that part of the bow from which a rope ladder was suspended, and the mode of mounting it was shown them, but it was a considerable time ere we could prevail on them to ascend it. At length the senior, who always led the way, went up, and was followed by the rest. The new wonders that now surrounded them on every side caused fresh astonishment, which, after a moment's suspense, always terminated in loud and hearty laughter...

They were now loaded with various presents, consisting of some articles of clothing, biscuit, and pieces of wood, in addition to which the plank that had been used in crossing the chasm was given to them. They then departed, promising to return as soon as they had eaten and slept, as we had no means of explaining to them what tomorrow meant. The parting was attended with the ceremony of pulling noses on both sides. After they had reached and crossed the chasm, they were observed by some men, who had been sent to accompany them, throwing away the biscuit, and splitting the plank, which was of teak, into small pieces, for the purpose of dividing it among the party. Soon after this they mounted their sledges, and drove off in a body hallooing, apparently in great glee.

But we were yet to make our first contact with the most northern people in the world. A solid field of ice barred our approach to the land where Commander Peary knew a certain number to be living, from whom he could learn the whereabouts of his favorite Eskimo dog-drivers, who, we afterward learned, had been watching the southern horizon for days, anticipating our arrival. Reluctantly we passed on and headed up the coast for Bushnan Island, so named by Captain Ross after his midshipman and clerk.

CHAPTER 7

✳

THE PEARY ESKIMOS

Naturally I remember every incident connected with my first meeting with a people living as man lived in the Stone Age. They have been designated as the Polar Eskimos, the Smith Sound Eskimos, and also as the Peary Eskimos. Anthropologists consider them one of the primitive peoples of the world.

Peary was the first to see a sealskin tent, or tupik, its color so blending with the gray rocks of the hillside that it was some minutes before the rest of us saw it, and then not until Captain Bartlett blew the whistle which brought the occupants out of bed and out of doors with a rush. Their yells evidenced their excitement. One ship a year would necessarily cause some sort of commotion. Beyond the point, at the bottom of the harbor, snuggling down between great massive hills, were two tupiks and a large number of dogs.

I cannot adequately describe my first impressions of these Polar Eskimos. What could be more primitive than a sealskin tent for a home during summer, a rock igd-loo, really a hole in the ground, for a dwelling during the winter, skins of the polar bear, seal, fox, and caribou for clothing, and meat from the sea and land for food, a large part of which is eaten raw and in a frozen state! No written language of any kind, no schools, no government, no village life, no king, queen, or chief, no money or even standard of value, no accumulation of property, no tenure of land or houses, no real knowledge or conception of the great busy world to the south!

Their interests in life are merely primary and essential – food, clothing, shelter, home. Free of the world, they live their life in their own way, untrammeled, unconventionalized, uncivilized, but they are very far from being savages. According to the best authorities, the transition from the upper status of savagery to the lower status of barbarism is marked by the invention of pottery. True, the Polar Eskimos know nothing of the manufacture of pottery, the material of which is wanting in the North, but they certainly exhibit as much skill in the carving of pots and lamps from stone as could be displayed in the baking of a piece of clay. When one studies further their remarkable adaptation to their environment and their resourcefulness in the utilization of all that this barren country affords, one is compelled to place them within the borders of civilization, their progress checked, not by mental incapacity, but by lack of material with which to work toward higher things.

The wildness and savagery of the whole thing affected me as nothing ever did, and, I am sure, as nothing ever will again. This was another world, as vastly different as I can conceive another planet to be. The dark sea spattered with level sections of the winter ice field, the talus slope, a chaotic mass of angular rocks, piled ever higher in endless confusion, seemingly alive with the ever-changing black and white bodies of the little ice bird – all was strange. Above the black cliff with its narrow green ledges and wheeling white dots, the large Nauya (glaucous gull) of the North sails majestically above his prey, confident, satisfied.

The plastic lip of the great ice sheet, an enigma to science, ever recedes above the cliff until lost in the blue of the horizon. On and on it stretches, filling valleys, leveling mountains, a rolling white world, five hundred thousand square miles in area! Living here as a part of it all, as puppet actors on a colossal black and white and green and blue stage, we find the Eskimo, the Innuit Race. How small they looked, and how much like animals, clothed as they were in fur, as they ran along the shore to meet us! Yellowish-white pants of polar bear skin, dark coats of ringed seal, buff boots of hairless skin, long flowing raven black hair, those who came to meet us were all men and boys. The women were standing at the doors of their sealskin tents, their dress quite different – sealskin coats, blue fox-skin trousers, and long ivory-white sealskin boots.

We watched our chance and ran in on the crest of a wave. A row of brown hands grasped the rail of our whaleboat, and then we noticed the smell! There is nothing like it anywhere. It pervades everything they have – their clothing, tents, sleeping-robes, kayaks, hunting equipment. It is the natural Eskimo smell, persistent, everlasting. There can be one source only – seals, the pure essence of blubber, with an admixture of walrus, narwhal, white whale, and polar bear. Incredible as it may seem, after living with this seal bouquet for several weeks, or four years, as I did later on, it becomes unnoticeable.

Here they were, smell and all, a malodorous throng, a laughing, black-eyed group of so-called savages, square-faced, heavy-jawed, slant-eyed, ruddy-cheeked men and boys, Peary's Eskimos of the Far North. All that I had read about Peary's unpopularity among these people was dissipated in a moment. First-hand information is as far apart from gossip and slander as the ends of the earth. I would not say that Peary was loved by these people of the North, or that there was even a deep feeling of friendship between him and a single member of the Smith Sound tribe, but he was certainly admired and deeply respected by every man, woman, and child, even to the point of fear. Had he been one of them, he would have lived and would have been known to younger generations as one of the Angakut, for no man could have done what he did unless he were in favor with the Good Spirits of the North who prevailed against the Evil Spirits. I well remember the awed silence which swept over the room when the Eskimos heard Peary's voice from the victrola long after he was dead. He never had a more respectful or a more attentive audience when he was alive.

And now Peary had arrived! The Eskimos rushed to the beach, laughing and jabbering, some bleeding at the nose, a common ailment of theirs when excited. The remedy is to plug both nostrils with grass. When one alone, the left, is plugged, it is evidence of a recent death in the family. An opened box of biscuits and a 'Help yourself' from Peary was his greeting. They did – a biscuit is a delicacy from the land of the white man especially prized by the children.

We strolled over to the tents, while Peary and Matt were finding out the whereabouts of their favorite Eskimo dog-drivers, who were scattered along the coast for more than a hundred miles. Our first impression of

their summer homes made of sealskin was their sensible shape, one which
cannot be described. It seems the best adapted to windstorms, of more fre-
quency here than rainstorms, of any tent I have ever seen. Without a single guy line of any sort, it is down on the ground as if it belonged there.
And it is surprising how comfortable their beds of flat stones covered with
grass – plenty of it there – can be. A shallow soapstone lamp, with ground
moss for a wick, seal, whale, or walrus blubber for oil, and soapstone
cooking-pot constitute their entire culinary department. Meats are merely boiled, never roasted, stewed, or fried, although I have known them to
use a thin flat stone as a grill when a pot was lacking. In the summer meat
is generally cooked; they prefer it that way. There are a few things, however, which they undoubtedly prefer in a raw state, such as the skin of the
narwhal and white whale, an extremely tough gristlelike substance reeking with oil, undoubtedly a source of vitamins.

The Eskimos eat little vegetable matter. I have known them to eat kelp
and rockweed when starving. The children eat the bark of the root of the
creeping willow in the spring, and the Eskimo hunter the contents of the
paunch of the caribou, but it may be safely asserted that as a people they
do not average a pound of vegetable diet in a year. That they are here and
have been for at least a thousand years is proof positive that a diet of flesh
foods is benign to a man living under the conditions of the North.

About half of all the meat that is eaten during the winter is raw and in a
frozen condition. Frozen raw meat is much to be preferred to warm, freshly killed raw meat. The harvest time for the bulk of their yearly supplies is
in May, June, July, August, and September. Placed in cache wherever killed,
it is frozen almost as hard as the proverbial flint when uncovered by the
owner some bright moonlight night during the winter. Thawing is an exceedingly slow process. In the meantime, all, family and friends, are helping themselves to a buffet lunch, the frozen hind flipper of a walrus, with a
knife or axe occupying the center of the floor. It is hack and eat, hack and
eat, sing and tell their stories, while the stars revolve in great and small circles and See-oog-ly (Arcturus) tells them it is long since they slept. They are
down to earth, their feet on the ground. Nature's children.

There is an old song which runs, 'The bear went over the mountain to see what he could see.' We did exactly that, and the trip was well worth while, for we witnessed one of the great wonders of the North. Marvin could talk a little Eskimo because of his previous year's experience, so he was delegated by Peary to cross the high ridge to the camp of an Eskimo, and to return with him and his dogs to the ship. Borup and I went along for the mere fun of climbing. We gained the top, and as we descended the southern slope we became lost in wonder at the abundance of bird life. I had read of famous rookeries, of the Bird Islands, of the Magdalens, of 'bird-covered cliffs,' of 'swarming ledges,' but this was beyond anything I had ever imagined. The air was filled with the sound of whirring wings and a medley of shrill musical notes. The birds resembled black and white balls, now like leaves of the silver poplar, now like snowflakes, as they dipped down, skimmed the tops of our heads, rose high in the air, turned to the left in a great circle, and swooped again to the talus slope.

They were the same birds that I had found washed up by the sea on the back shores of Provincetown during the bitterly cold days of January and February, as the wind came out of the northwest and the surf pounded and boomed upon the frozen shore. Why they came at that time only, and where they went soon after, we never knew, and the fishermen could not tell us. They were simply 'pine knots,' but we could never learn the reason for the name. In the North they were at home, and plainly glad to be so. Ornithologists know them as the Little Auk, the Dovekie, the Rotch; whalers, as the Ice Bird; Newfoundlanders, as the Bullbird. They are *the* bird of this world, and mean more to the Eskimo than all the others combined. They furnish him with clothing; they keep him from starvation; they fill his lockers for the long dark winter night.

At our feet lay a fifteen-inch dip net, made of sinew, with its twelve-foot pole neatly spliced and lashed. Crouching among the protecting rocks we waited. The birds shot over our heads like miniature express trains. Swish! Borup missed by a mile and laughed aloud at his failure. It was much like hitting a fast curve ball, but no pitcher ever developed such shoots in all directions. How those birds could dodge and duck! But we caught them,

exactly as primitive man caught them. We could have supported ourselves,
and with a few days of practice filled our winter caches to overflowing. I
have known of a woman who averaged one bird every minute. I have heard
of a man who netted eight with one sweep of the net. I have heard Langdon
Gibson, a former assistant to Peary, tell how he killed thirty with a single
shot. It is *the* bird of the North, and the first one in May is assured of a welcome after the long lean days of March and April.

Our object in calling at this settlement was to select the best Eskimo
drivers and the strongest Eskimo dogs for the work ahead. As far as I
could judge, it was pure selection, for all wanted to go, strange to relate,
with this 'tyrant,' 'martinet,' 'autocrat,' or whatever appellation was being
bandied about by his enemies at home. And why should they *want* to go,
leave home, be cooped up in a small dark cabin, work until their legs refused to obey and the sweat froze on their faces? There was the possibility that the ship would be crushed or that food would give out in the
reaches toward a dead world, far beyond their winter caches. I cannot
supply the answer of the why; certainly not for money or goods. They well
understood that each was to receive for the services of himself and wife
and dogs, for one year, a new .44 Winchester rifle. All dogs might die, per-
ish, be killed, or lost on the trail, but none was to be replaced.

It is true that they were to receive other things, such as snowshoes,
which they never use in their own country, a new sledge which would go
to pieces or be worn out before the battle was over, sheepskin coats – or
koole-tak, in their native language – not so warm as their own blue fox or
caribou-skin garment, sheepskin stockings, far more durable than their
own hareskin product, but not so warm. In other words, what was given
to them was to be used in the work – what they must have to make their
particular job a success. And when the work was done, they might return,
if they returned at all, late in the summer with but little time to fill their
meat caches for the winter.

Still they really got something. They joined a circus! They satisfied for
a time their desire to roam afield, ever persistent in an Eskimo, by nature
a nomad. They experienced adventure, excitement, social life, the very
things they crave. They saw new lands in which their fathers had lived,

new kinds of animal life, the great shaggy oo-mingmuk (musk ox), the old skulls of which could now be found moss-covered above their igd-loos on the hill. They saw the restless Polar Sea which pours an endless stream of heavy blue ice past their doors. They saw the white caribou, a new almost snow-white species named after Peary – *Rangifer pearyi*. They saw Arctic hare in droves: there was nothing like that at home. They leaned far out over the bow of the *Roosevelt* and saw great ice pans crack wide open. A strong ship! They heard the strange white men from the South laugh and talk and joke and play! They were permitted to enter their rooms and see everything from their wonderful rifles to their fountain pens. To them it was a new life, something different, out of the rut, a complete change. They had white biscuit, coffee, tea, milk, sugar, pemmican – white man's food. Yes, they would go, and there were many more than Peary could possibly use.

✳

ETAH AND WALRUS-HUNTING

When we steamed away from Cape York, a few days later, I counted the dogs on deck – one hundred and twelve in all, a fighting, snarling pack, all wondering why they were there, where they were going, and who was king. The tops of our cabin houses and forecastle head were littered with Eskimos and all their worldly possessions: litters of pups, tents, skins, soapstone lamps, pots, coils of line, harpoons, killing irons, paddles, bags of grass, and tin cans which are highly prized by every Eskimo woman as additions to her culinary department. Then there were large black seal-skin floats and long narrow skin kayaks. The circus was moving on to the next town.

I had often read of the Crimson Cliffs of Sir John Ross, first seen in 1818, and wondered why the name 'crimson.' It is true that there were patches of red snow, which might possibly lend their color to the name, to be seen as we steamed ever northward along the shore. After traveling this coast eight times and closely observing conditions, I am inclined to believe that the name might easily be derived from the red or orange-colored lichen which often grows squarely on the face of cliffs with a southern exposure. It is far more striking and more pronounced than red snow, which is really a tiny air plant living on the snow and known to botanists as *Protococcus nivalis*.

On the morning of August 3, we steamed into North Star Bay, so named because the British ship *North Star* wintered here in 1850, in search of Sir John Franklin. The Eskimo name is Oo-me-nak, derived from a heart-shaped mass of land seven hundred feet in height which projects from the mainland in the form of a peninsula. We found our consort, the *Erik,* awaiting our arrival. Captain Bob placed the *Roosevelt* alongside, preparatory to transferring whale meat and coal.

North Star Bay with its eight large sealskin tents deserved the name of city. Rarely are there more than five tents at one site. A population of twenty constitutes a large town. This is a wise precaution based on long years of experience, many of which were made memorable by trying conditions. In this year (1908) there were two hundred and eighteen people in the tribe, one hundred and twenty-two male and ninety-six female. In 1897 there were two hundred and thirty-four; in 1895 two hundred and fifty-three; in 1917, two hundred and fifty; in 1924, two hundred and seventy-six, and increasing rapidly. In 1855 Dr. Kane estimated the number to be about one hundred and fifty, and predicted that within a century the Smith Sound Eskimo would be extinct. The fact that there are many untenanted rock igd-loos in every settlement cannot be accepted as proof of a decrease in numbers. It merely attests to an increase in the number of individuals in that particular place that year; new igd-loos were built to accommodate the increase and later on abandoned. They have learned that in a country where life means struggle there is safety in small numbers. One Arctic hare would not do much to better conditions in a starving group of fifty people, but it might save the lives of one family. Furthermore, by locating up and down the coast in groups, more waters are covered and more game secured for the whole tribe. It is the total amount of meat in the tribe that saves all, not the catch of any one man.

The Eskimos fully realize the value of interdependence. When food is gone, pack up, roll a rock against the igd-loo door and visit Sip-soo. Prolong your visit until every scrap of food is eaten. Pack up, block the door, you and Sip-soo go and visit Arklio. You have heard that he still has three walrus in his cache. The bread-line increases in length, and is now leading to another village thirty miles distant, where there is still a bit of food left. When, finally, bones are picked, the procession moves on to Peteravik, where it makes its last stand against the enemy, for here walrus may be harpooned in the black pools at the edge of the ice. I lived here once for six weeks and watched the struggle. If those great cliffs which look down every spring upon a long white line of snow domes could only speak, what a huntsman's tale they might tell!

A knowledge of the Eskimo diet always arouses an interest in their health. Isolated as they must have been for hundreds and perhaps thousands of years prior to 1818, one can easily imagine an entire absence of all infectious diseases. What they have had in recent years may be traced to visiting ships. There was one striking case at North Star Bay. As I landed on the beach, I noticed a sledge and dogs. It was so unusual in the summer time with nearly all the snow gone from the land that we walked toward it at once. Well wrapped up and lashed to the sledge lay a man. His only movements were a slight turning of the head and a feeble lifting of the hand. We covered the outstretched palm with candy, which brought a smile to his pallid face, set in a frame of jet-black hair. 'Cursed by an Angakok many, many years ago,' was the explanation of the Eskimos; bony ankylosis, or arthritis deformans, would be the verdict of science. Helpless, yet helped by others for more than twenty years, he was down at the shore to meet us. Was this not an index of the character of some of the Eskimos at least? I have read that among the Eskimos of the North the old and weak and sick are left behind to die and are sometimes killed. Perhaps that is the case somewhere. Just where such things happen should be stated. Many are the tribes of the Eskimo and many are the lands they inhabit. It is estimated that *the* Innuit, as they call themselves, a word which means the People in the sense of the *only* people, number about thirty thousand in all, inhabiting the longest coast-line of any people in the world – from the Aleutian Islands in Behring Strait to the eastern shores of Greenland.

August 5th was a great day, for we had our first fight with the walrus. A man may hunt walrus for weeks and never have even a thrill, but the next morning he may have the thrill of his life. The animal is uncertain, and the Eskimos consider it the most dangerous of all. Today they are at you, an infuriated red-eyed mass of tough brownish skin, long white tusks, and raucous voice; tomorrow they are fleeing like sheep, looking back over their shoulders and fairly tearing the water apart in their fright and panic.

Hayes declared that it was simply a waste of time to try to shoot a walrus – 'Balls rebound from their hide like cork pellets.' Peary said, 'Look out.' Sverdrup: 'If an infuriated walrus gets his tusks over the rail of the boat, do not frighten him. Grasp the tusks gently in the hands and lift him back into the water!' There must be some mistake in that translation, for a walrus measures from twelve to fifteen feet in length and weighs from one to three thousand pounds.

Here they were before us, asleep on a pan of ice, five of them, excellent food for our dogs; in fact nothing is better for the purpose than walrus meat. A good team of ten dogs and plenty of walrus meat and the North is yours for the asking! At Bartlett's suggestion, I selected a crew to man the boat; Borup and I were to do the shooting; Bos'n Murphy to scull at the last moment, and five Eskimos to man the oars and harpoon whenever possible. Bob's parting words were, 'Don't shoot until they are harpooned.'

We rowed leisurely toward the pan, wondering what in the world to do and how to do it. Murphy had spent one year in the Arctic, but he was as confused in his plan of attack as we were. The Eskimos were unable to communicate with us or give us any instructions. It simply resolved itself into 'Go and get them.'

The five big brutes were sound asleep in the warm sun, a huddled mass of brown flesh. At a distance of fifty yards I motioned to Murphy, who was pulling the bow oar, to come aft and take my place at the steering oar and quietly scull up to the pan. I slipped one shell into the barrel of my .351 automatic, snapped in the clip holding five more, and crouched in the bow of the boat beside Borup, who was now whispering excitedly and wanted to let go everything he had in his German Sauer.

Two great heads broke water a short distance away, 'ooked' a couple of times, and disappeared. We were now within twenty feet of the sleeping five and slowly forging ahead, a bit too close for comfort. I motioned to the Eskimos to throw their harpoons. They shook their heads vigorously and whispered 'Naga' (No). It was clear that they wanted us to open the battle.

'Take the big one left, George; I'll take the one to the right,' I whispered. Before we could fire, their heads were up, and they were hunching toward the edge of the pan. Two dropped at the double report, but, to our amazement, managed to scramble into the water. It was bang! bang! as fast as we could pull the trigger, and after it was all over there was not a thing left on the pan but crimson spots.

Borup blinked at me and yelled, 'What do you know about that?' I had no time to answer, for they were back, mad clean through at having been disturbed, and apparently reinforced by all the walrus in the bay. There was a veritable pandemonium in the boat. The Eskimos were frightened, there was no doubt about that. They threw their harpoons at any walrus within distance, grabbed the lines, floats, drags, and tumbled them into the water – and yelled. Great Scott, how they yelled!

Borup and I kept busy snapping in clips and popping for all we were worth. Two big fellows hooked their tusks over the rail, one under the pointed barrel of Borup's rifle; he promptly pulled back and let him have it right in the face. It was more effective than the 'lift method,' for he instantly fell back and disappeared. Great bubbles rising to the surface told the story. He would never be back.

It was blood, foam, swirling water, great heads, white tusks, and 'ook, ooks,' for several minutes, when, so quickly that it was truly startling, they all disappeared. We were suspicious of some form of trickery or treachery, and could not believe our good fortune. We listened and looked and endeavored to peer down into the crimson-stained waters, but they were gone once and for all. Not so bad for our first experience! No one will ever know how many we killed, for when mortally wounded the walrus sinks to the bottom. Air bubbles, which continue to rise to the surface for some minutes, are an evidence that the walrus is either dead or dying.

The practice of the Fox Channel Eskimo is quite different from that of the Smith Sound native. He wounds the walrus in the body with his rifle, never in the head, which is more vital. The animal, weakening and with difficulty being able to keep afloat, pulls himself out on top of an ice pan and there becomes an easy mark for the harpoon.

Our five floats – inflated sealskin bags – were all upright in the water, denoting weight at the end of the line. One supported two walrus, giving us a total of six, which meant at least three tons of rich meat. This is why the Eskimo spends his time in the summer months in his kayak hunting walrus, white whale, and narwhal, and not on the land catching Arctic hare or catching brook trout. It would take some time to capture a thousand pounds of rabbits. The season is short; the winter is long; big game is needed to meet the demand for food.

When three more walrus were added to the number two hours later, and the Eskimos were working with long knives, almost knee-deep in entrails, meat, and blood, it was not a sight for the faint of heart or stomach. The dogs were full – that was the point. Without well-fed dogs Peary could do nothing.

Our interest was divided between looking for walrus and studying the map or chart. Every point now was notable for some historic interest. Picturesque Cape Alexander, just ahead, is almost exactly halfway between the Arctic Circle and the North Pole. Named after one of Sir John Ross's ships, it stands as one of the Pillars of Hercules, a noble headland guarding the entrance to Smith Sound, buffeted by wind, sea, tide, and ice.

But the center of the stage of the great drama enacted here for fifty-eight years is beyond. Cape Alexander is but the portal. Once passed one enters the real scene of action. At the right is Pandora Harbor called after the ship of that name, later to become De Long's *Jeannette*, in which Sir Allen Young brought the mail to the British North Pole Expedition of 1875–76. A few miles beyond is Port Foulke, the winter quarters of Dr. Hayes, where his ship, the *United States,* was frozen in during the winter of 1860–61. Then comes the Foulke Fiord, so named by Dr. Kane for William Barker Foulke of Philadelphia. The settlement here, known as Etah to the Smith Sound Eskimos, was our appointed place for meeting the *Erik,* which, under Peary's direction, left us at North Star Bay to gather additional Eskimos and dogs in Inglefield Gulf.

Our decks, now burdened with decayed whale meat, walrus meat, and dogs, were in such a shocking condition that Captain Bob resolved to clean up, and forthwith ordered the two hundred or more dogs transported to a small island in the middle of the harbor, henceforth known as Dog Island. We were well rewarded for our hard work in transport by the pleasure derived from seeing these poor animals jump and caper when they felt the soil beneath their feet.

Etah is not the thriving town which one might imagine from the frequent references to it in Arctic history. We found three tents which held possibly twelve or fifteen Eskimos at most. Every dwelling-place has its own particular reasons for its existence, selected by the inhabitants because of certain natural advantages. Etah has a beautifully protected harbor, a bountiful water-supply, southern exposure, millions of little auks, many Arctic hare, white whale, narwhal, walrus, eider ducks, and a good road along the edge of the Greenland Ice Cap leading to the caribou grounds in the North. While it is pleasant in summer, how the wind can blow in winter! Without a doubt it is the worst place on the coast from September to May. It lies in a veritable funnel through which the cold heavy air of the Ice Cap pours down from a height of nine thousand feet, and on out to the open water which is always present throughout the year between Littleton Island and Cape Sabine.

On our arrival it was truly beautiful in its ruggedness, its dark blue waters reflecting the thousand foot cliffs, its glittering glacier touching the calm waters of Alida Lake, and, especially, in its marvelous pattern of colors on the north shore when reflecting the bright sunlight of a summer day. The natural slaty gray of its rocks blends marvelously with the grass-covered green slopes, the uniformity of which is broken by huge boulders ablaze with orange-colored lichens. I can think of nothing with which to compare it save a beautiful Turkish rug. Northern lands and waters have a certain charm in their variety and in their blending of colors, quite unlike that of more southern climes.

Just south of the entrance to Foulke Fiord and partly protected from the sea by three islands is the small indentation in the land known as Port Foulke. The sites of the headquarters of past expeditions are always of

The *Roosevelt* at anchor at Etah

interest, especially to one who has read their narratives so many times that he feels almost personally acquainted with every member of the crew. Next afternoon we rowed across the harbor to visit that historic place. All points were easily recognized from their descriptions by Dr. Hayes in 'The Open Polar Sea' – the high gravelly bank, the bold water, the brook, the miniature lake, the almost flat plain, and the grave of Sonntag, the astronomer, marked by a headstone on which was cut:

In Memory of
August Sonntag
Died, Dec. 1860
Aged 29 Yrs.

Five of the *Roosevelt*'s crew
Left to right: Thomas Gushue, first mate;
John Connors, seaman; Charles Percy, cook; George A. Wardwell,
chief engineer; Banks Scott, second engineer

Note that the exact date of his death is omitted, for it was never known. He sledged south with an Eskimo and was found dead in a snow house weeks later. The Eskimos declared that the white man had fallen into the water and had perished of cold, a story which for certain reasons was not accepted at the time. Sixty-four years later an old woman told me that the man was designedly drowned by the Eskimo driver, who wanted every-thing on the sledge for himself. Such stories are so common among the Eskimos who boast of their courage in killing a white man that we pay lit-tle attention to them.

We found the bones of Sonntag in one pile of rocks and the stone in another, so we rebuilt the grave and set up the stone at its head. When I saw it last, seventeen years later, the headstone was still erect and the grave undisturbed.

Saturday, August 8th, was 'Littleton Island Day,' an excursion to a place famous in Arctic history, to determine the character of the ice northward and secure, if possible, eider ducks for food. We were hardly out of sight of the ship before we began shooting and continued intermittently throughout the trip.

It was with mixed emotions that we stepped on the island where Dr. Kane, America's second Arctic explorer, had landed fifty-five years before. He described his visit as follows:

> Our stores deposited, it was our next office to erect a beacon and intrust to it our tidings. We chose for this purpose the western cape of Littleton Island as more conspicuous than Cape Hatherton; built our cairn; wedged our staff into the crevices of the rocks; and, spreading the American flag, hailed its folds with three cheers as they expanded in the cold midnight breeze. These important duties performed – the more lightly, let me say, for this little flicker of enthusiasm – we rejoined the brig early in the morning of the 7th and forced on again toward the north, beating against wind and tide.

We found the beacon, or cairn, still there; we could see it plainly as we approached the island. The same cairn was used as a depository for the mail in 1876. Here Greely left a supply of coal in 1881, and here Beebe cached stores for the Greely party in 1882.

Littleton Island, with its two companions, Eider Duck Island and McGary's Rock, is known to the Eskimos as the best breeding place for eider ducks. As we walked over the island, we could well believe it. There were nests everywhere, many still lined with soft gray eider down. Although it was late in the year we found a few nests which contained eggs still warm and others with young. The mother birds had undoubtedly been robbed earlier in the season and were now endeavoring to hatch their second and perhaps their third clutch. Beneath piles of rocks were hundreds of eggs which the Eskimos had gathered during the last week in June and placed in cache for the winter months. When lying on frozen ground and protected from the rays of the sun, the eggs soon become chilled. By the middle of September they are frozen hard enough to be eaten 'as is,' the lollypop of the Eskimo.

Many of the eggs when fresh are poured and blown into the cleaned intestine of the walrus, an Eskimo sausage often eaten when traveling from village to village. We found dead eiders in several of the caches. They are captured in three ways: either killed with stones, trapped by rawhide snares, or caught with the hands on the nest. I did not believe this possible, but six years later I saw it done by a small boy who crept forward on his stomach, face to the ground, up to within grabbing distance of the tail feathers of a mother duck.

Tired with rowing, running over the island, and shooting – we had killed one hundred ducks – we lay down on the bare rocks of the north side of the island and tried to sleep. Bob and Borup crawled under the sail of the whaleboat and succeeded in dozing off in a few minutes.

For some time I watched the low midnight sun rolling along the northern horizon and studied the contour of the great white hills across the sound and the black bold-looking headlands leading northward to the Polar Sea until lost in a narrow dark ribbon on the horizon. I wondered which was Cape Sabine, the scene of the Greely tragedy. As the ice field before me shifted back and forth, now blue water, now white ice, I could easily understand why these men dared not take the chance of crossing. They were familiar with the details of the drift of the *Polaris* party which at this very spot became separated from the ship and drifted some fourteen hundred miles before being rescued off Gready Harbor, Labrador. It was late in the autumn; it was the twilight of the long winter night. They were not ice navigators; not even water men. They were enlisted men of the United States Army, many from Western forts.

Before I realized it the night was gone, and Bob was 'boiling the kettle' and Borup was knocking down the eiders as they came winging along the shore. As they saw our little pond, they set their wings for a landing. George was a good wing shot and thoroughly enjoyed the sport.

Chilled through by the cold north wind we were glad to feel the handle of an oar again, and sense the boat jump ahead as we straightened our backs and stiffened our legs against the edge of the thwart in front of us. We were off for home. As we passed Cape Ohlsen we could see what looked to be a flock of ducks at the head of a small bight to our left. We left George on the end of the point to bag them as they flew out and headed in. Not ducks – brant geese, a real dish! Twelve out of fifteen was our score. The remaining three flew over our heads and sat down right in front of George. He got them all.

Off Sunrise Point a strange bird swung in toward our boat. Bang! George got him, a northern puffin, a rare bird so far north as Etah. It is the *Fratercula arctica naumanni,* the large-billed puffin, not the common one of the Labrador Coast, which is slightly smaller.

For the next three hours we were shooting, yelling, pulling our hearts out, and towing dead walrus against a strong tide. When it was over we were back at Littleton Island with not a cartridge left for anyone of the four rifles. It was time to go home. We reached the ship at one the next morning with one large and two small walrus.

There is so much to see and to do in the North that every day is fully occupied. On August 12th we planned a visit to Wreck Beach of the *Polaris* Expedition. Near here she was beached and stripped of everything of value that could be utilized in building some sort of winter shelter. In the spring she was carried away by the ice, ever drifting toward the south, and sank a short distance from the northern end of Littleton Island. Panikpak, whose mother sewed for the white men in their improvised home, well remembers and describes even the personal appearance of some of the men and has often pointed out the exact spot where the *Polaris* now lies.

Although this had happened thirty-five years before, the beach was littered with evidences of the occupancy by white men. We found first three pairs of leg irons – white men are sometimes troublesome in the Arctic. There were numerous pieces of copper and bronze work marked U.S.N.Y.W. 1871 (United States Navy Yard Washington). There were checkers, nails, broken bottles, coal, iron bands, boom fittings, and one long piece of manilla rope, the life of which, however, was gone, for with our united strength we easily broke it.

The *Erik* with a load of Eskimos, dogs, and walrus had arrived while we were away. On the thirteenth we were busy transferring everything to the *Roosevelt* – tons and tons of coal, food supplies, skins for clothing, narwhal tusks, kayaks, harpoons, killing-irons, sealskin tents, soapstone lamps, moss, grass, drying-racks, birdskins, ducks' eggs, dog harnesses and dog sledges – everything belonging to the fifty Eskimos who were to be a part of our family for the next year. If anything should happen to the *Roosevelt*, these natives were prepared to abandon ship, walk over the ice to the shore, pitch their tents, and begin housekeeping at once. This is their land; they are at home anywhere.

The already too deeply laden *Roosevelt* seemed well on her way to the bottom; her scuppers were almost awash. Although she was built with sharp bilges so that she would rise when squeezed, her low freeboard now negatived all plans and purpose of her designer. Pressure applied above the water-line is deadly, for it eliminates the only possible avenue of escape – up and out. But to load to the limit and beyond was necessary, for her way to the North and the way home the next year was a long, long one. She must take everything that would ensure a continuance of this passage, and especially fuel.

The *Roosevelt's* engines, capable of developing a thousand horse-power, of the inverted compound type, driving a single eleven-foot propeller, two water tubes and one Scotch boiler, could certainly eat up coal. So far as I know, her excessive coal consumption was her one great failing. She was strong, she could buck the ice, she could steam, she could sail, she was livable; but she could not leave any port in the United States, steam into the Far North, and reach home again with coal in her bunkers.

The last days at Etah were busy days. We were going into dangerous waters. In attempting them, the *United States* retreated well-battered, the *Advance* never returned, the *Polaris* was on the bottom, the *Proteus* was crushed, the *Alert* and *Discovery* were both at times in serious danger, and the *Roosevelt* herself had had many a narrow squeak in 1905–06. Careful preparations must be made to guard against all contingencies.

Provisions for a retreat southward over the ice were hoisted to the deck and placed upon the rail, ready at hand to be seized and thrown into the boats. All the boats were provisioned with pemmican and equipped with shotguns, rifles, and ammunition; all oars were numbered; every man was assigned to his place. Snowshoes were lashed in the rigging. Provisions and coal were placed in cache at Etah against a possible retreat southward over the ice field by sledge or in open boats down Kennedy Channel, Robeson Channel, and Kane Basin.

We could not be sure that they would not be disturbed by the Eskimos. Commander Peary took no chances. He left in charge of this station Bos'n Murphy and William Pritchard of the *Roosevelt,* and also Harry Whitney, one of the sportsmen on the *Erik,* who requested permission from the Commander to remain here a year and await our return in 1909.

✳

NORTH TO THE POLAR SEA

Saturday, August 15th, it snowed – the first herald of the approaching winter. The Commander was getting impatient. The seventeenth was a dirty disagreeable day – it snowed again. We worked through it all, chasing our now two hundred and forty-six dogs over the island, rushing into the ice water, thigh deep, to grab them by the nape of the neck as in fright they plunged in to swim toward the mainland, then dragging them over the rough ground to the boats, tumbling them in and then lifting them up over the rail of the ship – hard, cold work. We were wet through and dead tired, so tired, in fact, that we never knew of the commotion caused an hour or so later by many of them falling between the two ships where they were in danger of being crushed. Commander did not call us; he did the work himself and rescued them all.

From the top of the highest hill the three-hundred-mile road to the North looked good. In the Arctic one must take advantage of the open door, for it may close within a few minutes and remain closed for even a year. So it was rush, rush, rush. The dogs were on board, the last ton of coal had been taken aboard from the *Erik* and stowed away in the already bulging bunkers. The Eskimos, our native dog-drivers, their wives and children were coming out in boatloads – forty-nine in all, twenty-two men, seventeen women, and ten children.

If it were ever justified to call a ship a madhouse, the *Roosevelt* was the ship. The quarter-deck was filled to the rail with tons of whale meat; the waist of the ship between the for'ard and after house was a solid, fuzzy mass of dogs, at times a rolling ball of snarling, snapping fur – a general free-for-all fight. All the twenty-two kings were ambitious to remain king. Twenty-one were dethroned within the next ten days. And yet we and even the small children could walk fearlessly through the mass of dogs. I have never heard of a single case of man, woman, or child ever having been attacked by a Smith Sound dog. I have known of many along the Labrador Coast – children torn to pieces, eaten, and parts of the bodies even buried.

At 4.45 P.M., August 18th, it was time to go. With colors flying, and dangerously deep in the water, we steamed out of Etah Harbor, waving good-bye to the men of the *Erik* and answering the three long blasts of her whistle. We now felt that we were really away. We had severed the last link which bound us to civilization, our supply ship. We were beyond the home of the most northern people and were as completely cut off from the world as if we had reached another planet.

Our route was through the waters of Kane Basin, Kennedy and Robeson Channels. Only four ships had preceded the *Roosevelt*: the *Polaris* under Captain Hall in 1871; the *Alert* and *Discovery,* of the British North Pole Expedition of 1875–76; and the *Proteus,* of the Lady Franklin Bay Expedition of 1881. The *Polaris* reached latitude 82° 11' N., but, as we know, sank the next year just north of Etah. Encouraged by the high latitude which the *Polaris* had attained, the British, under Sir George S. Nares, attacked the Pole by the 'American Route,' but they had to fight their way northward inch by inch. One sentence is an epitome of it all: 'The next thirty hours were spent in constant struggles with the pack, the ships being moved from the shelter of one iceberg to another as circumstances rendered necessary; and, owing to the unsteady wind and the variable tidal currents, we were never quiet for more than an hour at any one time.'

The *Discovery* wintered at Lady Franklin Bay, latitude 81° 40' N. The *Alert* pushed on to Cape Sheridan on the northern shores of Grant Land, 82° 25' N. The struggle to reach such northern points was one continuous fight, and the return the next year was just as hard.

In 1881 the *Proteus* had a comparatively easy time in reaching Lady Franklin Bay – it was an open season. But when she returned in 1883 with the same place as her objective, she encountered the impenetrable pack a few miles north of Cape Sabine.

Here is the story of her end:

The *Proteus* was a staunch vessel, and nothing showed it more than the way in which she stood the terrible trial of that July afternoon in Kane Sea. Had she not been of extraordinary strength and endurance, the ice, which was from five to seven feet thick, would have made short work of her. As it was, there was ample time for preparation, supposing that the ordinary precautions of ice-navigation had been taken. The nip was about three o'clock. At half-past four the starboard rail was crushed in. At this time, Lieutenant Garlington and a part of his men were in the hold getting out stores, and another party under the Sergeant was at the same work in the forepeak, where the prepared depots had been stowed. Presently the ship's side opened with a crash, the ice forced its way into the coal bunkers, the water rushed into the hold, and the deck planks began to rise. The pressure of the floes kept the ship up, and the stores which had been got on deck were thrown upon the ice. In the hurry, a third of what was thrown overboard was lost by falling too near the ship. The whale boats, one of which had become jammed and was saved with difficulty, and the dingy, were got out by Lieutenant Colwell, who was the last man to leave the ship. At a quarter past seven, as the tide turned and the pressure slackened, she began to sink, and soon passed out of sight.

The conditions which render this passage so dangerous are clearly revealed by a study of the map. There is a long narrow channel leading from the Polar Sea through which the heavy floes are driven by tide and current into a basin or reservoir, roughly eighty miles in diameter, always a congested area, with an outlet which is only twenty-five miles wide. The pressure upon the converging points, Cape Sabine and Cairn Point, can hardly be imagined. It is simply appalling! I have watched and listened to it for hours, amazed and even dumbfounded at the stupendous power exhibited by Nature, as the ice driven on by wind, tide, and current seemed bent on destroying everything in its path. Solid white today, but the glitter of an open lead tomorrow. Could we get through?

It looked like a clean run to Victoria Headland, but at eight-thirty we met scattered pans, the outer guards of the solid pack. By ten o'clock we were across Smith Sound and passing Payer Harbor, named after Julius Payer, the distinguished Arctic explorer, which had been the headquarters of Commander Peary for sixteen months in 1901–02. Through the glass I could see the cairn built by the Nares Expedition on the summit of Brevoort Island in July, 1875.

Within fifteen minutes we could see the site of Camp Clay of the Greely starvation party of 1884, with Cocked Hat Island beyond. Within an hour we were blocked by the ice off Victoria Head, and we continued to be all night. Captain Bob took advantage of the delay to load fresh water from a pan of ice. All salt-water ice eventually becomes fresh. One of our distinguished representatives in Washington once inquired of Commander Peary as to the number of *barrels* of fresh water he carried on his sledges to the North Pole!

Commander Peary realized the possibility of a 'squeeze' and a hurried abandonment of the ship, and instructed me to equip all boats as follows: one set of five oars, two boathooks, one pair of row locks, one bailer, one liquid compass, one oil stove, four one-gallon tins of oil, one gallon tin of oil with patent nozzle, one Springfield rifle, one hundred cartridges, one shotgun, fifty shells loaded with No.2 shot, one miner's tent seven feet by seven, one box of matches in tightly corked bottle, two tins of biscuit, twelve tins of 'blue' pemmican, ten tins of milk, two tins of sugar, two pounds of tea, two pounds of coffee, one harpoon, line and float. With all this equipment, and our emergency bag of clothes which we were ordered always to keep in readiness, we could live for a long time even in an open boat.

All through the nineteenth we were locked in tightly ten miles from land, with not a living thing to be seen but the bosun-bird, or jaeger, both the parasitic and the long-tailed. A field of ice under such conditions ceases

A difficult corner

The *Roosevelt* nipped by the ice in Robeson Channel

to be attractive. It is a prison wall. One wonders whether it will ever open again. It is not the one year's ice which retards progress and completely blocks the way. Although the ice freezes from six to eight feet thick during one winter, after it has been acted upon by a warm spring and summer sun, it is easily split by a good strong ship. The ice which blocks and is ready to crush any ship which floats is that which breaks away from the so-called glacial fringe of Grant Land, a great wide white collar which has been thickening for years and is released only under certain conditions.

On the twentieth we had thick weather and a fine drizzle – an ice-eater, the sailors called it. That afternoon the weather and ice conditions were

so favorable that Captain Bob worked the ship through the field as far as
Cape Prescott and Cape Durville. There the rudder chains gave out and
had to be replaced with rope of walrus hide, which is of sufficient strength
for such work, but almost too elastic.

On the twenty-first, we drifted slowly south. At four o'clock the wind
began to blow from the west, a favorable direction, for it would tend to
set the ice off shore and thus open the way northward. During the night
we heard the churn of the screw and the deep breathing of the pistons and
knew we were going somewhere, and it proved to be in the right direction.
By three o'clock we had covered half our distance to Cape Sheridan and
by five o'clock the next morning we had passed Lady Franklin Bay with
clear blue water ahead. To avoid finding a few pans later, Captain Bob
headed east to Thank God Harbor, where Charles Francis Hall had
berthed the *Polaris*.

Hall's men really believed that in his zeal and ardor for polar work he
would lead them to their death. Undoubtedly they were not in sympathy
with his ambition to reach the Pole, but it seems hardly probable that to
thwart his purpose they would resort to murder as has been alleged.
Knowing that he had bitter enemies aboard the ship, his friends and sym-
pathizers declared for years that he had been poisoned.

The Government edition of his work gives the story as follows:

Upon Captain Hall's arrival at the *Polaris,* he went on board, and was
assisted by Mr. Morton in getting off his fur clothing. He spoke very
encouragingly of the prospects of the expedition, and added that he
expected in a couple of days to start upon another sledge journey
which would complete the fall work. He had not been in the cabin
more than a half-hour when John Herron, the steward, brought him a
cup of coffee. He drank it, and was immediately taken very sick. He
vomited a good deal, retching violently. He went at once to bed. Dr.
Bessels, who was at the observatory, was summoned, and after examination expressed grave fears that the sickness might be fatal. At 8 P.M.,
he announced that Captain Hall's left side was paralyzed, and that he
had had an apoplectic attack.

On the 25th, Captain Hall felt much better, although he had suffered very much during the night. He was able to eat some chicken and arrowroot. In the evening he again became very sick and was in great pain from his constant efforts to vomit. After having passed another very uncomfortable night, the morning of the 26th found him much better. The fever which accompanied the attack had left him, and with the exception of being very weak, he seemed quite well. During the day, Dr. Bessels administered quinine to him and applied cold compresses. On the 27th, Captain Hall was worse, and his condition was critical. Dr. Bessels said that if, in his present state, he had another attack, the result would be fatal.

In the evening the doctor proposed to bleed him, but Hall resolutely objected. On the 28th, he was very much worse, and symptoms of mental aberration began to appear. He no longer recognized those about him. He refused to take medicine.

On the 29th, his condition was generally the same, except that he showed marked evidences of insanity. Every effort was made to keep him quiet and free from excitement. Divine service was held in the forecastle.

On the 30th, Hall remained in the same condition as on the two preceding days. He refused all medical aid and all nourishment, under the impression that an attempt might be made to poison him.

On the 31st, having enjoyed a good night's sleep, he felt much better. He talked rationally, except that he still entertained his former apprehension, to which he steadily adhered. The refusal of all medicine seemed to be beneficial, and he improved rapidly, and on the 1st and 2nd, appeared to be well, though weak. He took a little nourishment, but the same suspicions still haunted him when he seemed otherwise to be perfectly sane. He would take no food from anyone but Hannah, whom he worried with many anxious inquiries regarding it. On the 3rd, Captain Hall talked as if in the full possession of his faculties.

On the 4th, after much persuasion, he submitted to the doctor's treatment, who prescribed a mustard bath on this and the next day. He ate a large quantity of cooked seal meat contrary to the doctor's directions.

On the 6th, he looked and felt well, and strong hopes were entertained for his recovery. Notwithstanding the injunction of Dr. Bessels, he got up and dressed, remaining up nearly all day. He was to all appearances perfectly sane, and employed his time in getting in order the records of his sledge journey. He dictated for hours to Mauch, and began to interest himself in the ordinary duties of the ship. That night, however, he had another attack and became alarmingly ill. Early on the morning of the 7th, he sank into a comatose state, breathing heavily, during which his body was rubbed with mustard. In this condition he remained until 3.25 A.M. of the 8th, when he expired.

With glasses we could see two small houses, one an observatory for Dr. Emil Bessels, scientist, and the other a storehouse built by Captain George E. Tyson, the assistant navigator. Commander Peary pointed out to me where in 1905 he had found the two boats abandoned by Tyson and Myers thirty years before.

Captain Bob now turned back toward the shores of Grant Land for safety, for the ice which was swinging south from the Polar Sea was the heaviest we had seen – hard, blue, deep. We were soon blocked off Lincoln Bay, and in a bad place, because of a rapidly running tide. Commander Peary and Captain Bob realized the danger; they had been through it three years before, and they knew that safety lay in hugging the land and grounded bergs. We thought that they were hugging a bit too close when the sharp edge of our porthole cut a biscuit out of a small floe berg which reached from the sea up to the bottom of the boat hanging on the davits.

This brush with tides and swirling ice cakes in Lincoln Bay was the most exciting part of our trip so far. It had been the same on the previous expedition at the selfsame place, when the *Roosevelt* lost a part of her stem, had her rudder damaged, and was forced aground, in fact so high up on the shelving beach that Captain Bob and Peary almost despaired of getting her off again.

All through the night of the twenty-fourth it seemed to be one continuous bang and bump. As the 'growlers' and heavy pans swept around

Cape Union on their way south in the Arctic Current, they seemed to say, 'Ah, there she is!' and down they would come to take a crack at her. I now realized for the first time that no ship, however strong, can be built to cope with a shifting ice field, driven on by strong wind and tide. Her only hope for safety is in her *small* size. Right here where we were a fifteen-foot dory would be a thousand times better than the largest ship ever built. Pull the dory up on top of an ice pan, get in, sit down, and light your pipe – you are absolutely safe – your little ship cannot be crushed. The turns are sharp, leads are narrow, waters are shoal where safety lies. The small ship wriggles through or lurks in safety behind a protecting ledge.

Captain Bob worked the *Roosevelt* northward to Cape Union on the twenty-fourth, hugging the land for safety. Now we could look out into the Great Polar Sea, white to the horizon, with old bluish pans with rolling surfaces, twenty to forty feet in thickness and some of them a quarter of a mile square, very different from the one year's level ice field of Melville Bay. It must have weighed the astounding amount of a million tons, or roughly one thousand times the size of the *Roosevelt*. She looked small and felt smaller as she dodged back under the lee of the Cape to await a more favorable opportunity.

After being on board ship so long, loaded as we were with fifty Eskimos, men, women, children, babies, two hundred and forty-six dogs, tons and tons of whale and walrus meat, it is easy to imagine how good the land looked and how we wanted to feel good clean dirt under our feet.

The previous expedition had killed Arctic hare and even musk-oxen right here in Lincoln Bay. Commander Peary granted us permission, and George, Dr. Goodsell, and I, accompanied by two Eskimos, were away at once with instructions to listen for a recall signal at any minute.

Every small boy likes to 'cop' ice cakes, and in the North men become boys again. We had a bully time for the next half-hour jumping, jumping, jumping. Just as we reached the shore there was a long blast from the steam whistle, Captain Bob's peremptory summons to return at once. Our eagerness to obey resulted in a wetting for Borup, the doctor, and one of the Eskimos. It was now ebb tide and the ice was on the move. I found my

boathook most useful in vaulting from pan to pan, and in helping the doctor and Borup out of the water.

Captain Bob, high up in the ice barrel, could see every move we made
and knew that he would soon be needed. He gave the *Roosevelt* full speed
ahead and forged up to the pan on which we were standing and wondering what to do next. Amid laughter and good-natured raillery the boys
warped us in over the rail – the 'tenderfeet' on their first expedition.

Naturally I noted every living thing so far north and in so different a
world from our own. I did expect to see the ivory gull (*Pagophila alba*), for
it is a Far North bird, but not the fulmar (*Fulmarus glacialis*) in this latitude. We saw them both. The sea-pigeon (*Mandt's guillemot*) was evidently breeding here, for it could be seen going in and out of cracks of the rocks
just above the water's edge. The young, nearly white, were seen daily
swimming in pools along the shore.

On the twenty-fifth, seven narwhal were reported by Captain Bob
from the crow's-nest. These waters seem to be a favorite resort for these
creatures, which pass by means of the channel from Melville Bay, where
they are very common, to the Polar Sea.

On the twenty-sixth, I found two young old-squaws (*Clangula hye-
malis*) swimming in a pool of a partially frozen pond. Probably they had
been abandoned by their mother, who realized that winter was at hand
and that her little ones, born late in the season, would never grow sufficiently to start their long flight southward. This is the common practice of
the mother eider in the Far North. On the same day we secured a second
specimen of the long-tailed jaeger (*Stercorarius longicaudus*), not merely
a transient. We found its eggs the following spring.

Little ringed seals (*Phoca foetida*) were very common and frequently
seen lifting their heads above the surface of the water, puzzled by the high
black sides of the *Roosevelt*.

For eleven days the battle waged between the *Roosevelt* and the drift
ice issuing from the Polar Sea. One day we advanced a few miles northward along the shore, only to be driven back the next. We were ever on
duty, slept in our clothes, and expected to be called at any minute. With
change of wind or tide, it was out of bed with the cry, 'Let go all lines!
Haul in! Pay out!' The rope would hardly be made fast to a grounded

berg, a huge anchor to keep us from drifting southward, when the yell of Commander Peary or Bartlett would come, 'Let go!'

We lost part of our rail from the port quarter. A small berg paid us a visit. As it grated along the side, hoping to get a grip on our greenheart sheathing, we endeavored with picks and ice lances to hew away the more dangerous projecting points. Our puny efforts were almost ridiculous. The berg did what it wanted to do – lift off a section of our rail. With a 'Take that for coming up here so far north,' it gave us a final kick and sailed off down the shore.

On the night of the thirty-first I simply had to go somewhere. I jumped over the rail, ran across the drift ice to the land, up the cliffs to the north, and ran on and on until I was thoroughly tired and reeking with sweat. With no hat, coat, or mittens and the temperature seventeen below freezing, it was now necessary to keep on to keep warm. A snow bunting was all the life I saw.

Standing on the heights above the sea at the most northern point of Cape Union, I looked down at a narrow lead of open water which extended around the Cape and on into the north. Possibly the *Roosevelt* could make it, so I turned back at once to inform Commander Peary and Captain Bartlett. There far below me the ship, the most northerly in the world, looked like a toy boat in a small glassy pool. She was biding her time for the final dash. The long dark winter night was near. It had to be done within a few days, or not at all.

I reached the ship at midnight and notified Captain Bartlett at once. Commander Peary suggested to the captain that he climb to the top of Cape Union and observe through a good glass the action of the ice on the ebb tide. The captain wanted company, so both Borup and I went back with him. This second trip was well worth the time and effort, for we selected for the ascent the most inaccessible part of the cliff simply to try ourselves. Cliff-climbing can furnish thrills!

When we reached the summit, we found the lead had closed. There were patches of blue here and there, but the floes were too large, the corners too sharp, to attempt a passage. We were boys again while watching the changing ice field as the tide ebbed. Every teetering or balanced boulder was a temptation. It must go over and down. We tugged and pushed and rolled to our hearts' content, and loud were the exclamations of delight as tons and tons leaped into space, bounded as they impinged against the talus slope, and disappeared with a mighty splash into the sea. From the sea thousands of years ago, now back into the sea for thousands of years to come!

We arrived on board ship in time for breakfast. My all night out, running, perspiration, with no hat, coat, or mittens, may have been the cause of it – I never knew and the doctor could not tell me. The next day I had a temperature of 102. For the next three weeks I was out of the game. I remember little about it. I heard the chug of the engines and felt the impact of hard, heavy ice.

On September 5th, George stuck his head in the door and yelled, 'We're there, Mac!' Where, I didn't know, but I supposed it was where the Commander wanted to be. The *Roosevelt* was on time. Later on I learned that she had arrived at the very place on the very day three years before, and that we had steamed farther north than any ship had ever steamed – the *Fram* drifted – and had returned to the mouth of Shelter River, Cape Sheridan, a position some two miles north of the winter quarters of the *Alert* in 1875.

The next six days are almost blanks. Commander, always considerate and ever kind, never failed nightly to open his door and play for me my favorite pianola record 'The Wedding of the Winds.' The twelfth was memorable – the birthday of the Commander's daughter Marie, who was born in 1893 at Redcliff House in Murchinson Sound, Inglefield Gulf, some eight hundred miles from the North Pole. Bear steak and frosted cake! A northern dinner, a southern dessert! Throughout the day the flags snapped in the wind from bow to stern, from rail to truck.

✳

ARCTIC TRAVEL

Twice now the *Roosevelt* had done the thing for which she was designed and built and had placed Peary at the edge of the Polar Sea, within striking distance of the Pole. For the time being her work was done and she could rest. The dogs were tossed over the rail and away they scampered over the ice for the shore. The men rejoiced with the dirty devils. They were followed by the whale meat. Again the men rejoiced. Next went the food for the expedition, the field equipment and boats.

Now if the *Roosevelt* were destroyed, crushed by the Polar pack, burned or carried away by running ice, the work could go on just the same. Any or all of these disasters might easily happen as she was placed in winter quarters, if they could be complimented as such. On the port side was the straight shore of Grant Land without harbor, bay, bight, or even slight indentation; on the starboard side was the heavy pack ice of the Polar Sea, which is never at rest winter or summer.

Commander Peary had carefully considered the possibility of losing the ship. It was true that she was more than a pawn, but not so valuable but that the game could be played without her and even won. With this possibility in mind all equipment needed for field work was landed at once. A large house was constructed out of boxes, and one of our large sails provided a roof. Here was a shelter if we were compelled to abandon ship during the winter. Our whaleboats or dog teams could take us south during the spring.

The attack on the North Pole was really launched on September 16th, for on that day sixteen heavily loaded sledges started northwest along the ice foot to establish depots at Porter Bay, Cape Hecla, and, eventually, Cape Columbia, ninety miles distant. Cape Columbia is the most northern point of North America and lies in 83° 7′ North Latitude, four hundred and thirteen miles from the Pole. For this reason Peary planned to have his base there. The ice of the Polar Sea works from west to east along the northern shores of Grant Land and Greenland, so it is best to advance the base well to the west to counteract the effects of this current. On each of his efforts to the Pole, the Commander increased his distance westward on leaving the land. In 1902 he left Cape Hecla, thirty-six miles west of our ship; in 1906 Point Moss, forty-nine miles west; now he planned to leave Cape Columbia, ninety miles to the west and north.

Those were busy days, but I could do nothing but listen to the shouts of the men, the loading of the sledges, and the pistol-like reports of their rawhide whips. Sixteen more sledges left the ship on the twenty-first. Through the porthole I could see the long black line winding in and out along the ice foot, with a yearning beyond description for the Great Out-of-Doors, for sunlight, for air, for action. My temperature was now 101. With the boys all gone the ship was a grave. But only for a few hours – they were back at night. The twenty-four miles to Cape Belknap and return made only a joy ride along the level ice foot, which, with its interminable winding in and out of bays and inlets, demanded constant attention to dogs and sledge. Still that added zest and enjoyment to the whole thing. How different the work of Commander Peary, accompanied and assisted by his faithful Eskimos, experienced dog-drivers all, from that of those gritty Englishmen who toiled and labored at this very place in 1875! The following excerpt from 'Voyage to the Polar Sea,' by Captain George Nares, reveals marked changes in methods of travel, so marked that people can hardly credit the results:

On the 14th [October] Dr. Moss walked out to Dumb-bell Bay on snow shoes, and there met Commander Markham and his three sledge crews, struggling homeward through deep snow.

I did not expect Markham on board until the following day; but so great was the discomfort of passing another sleepless night in the stiff and shrunken tents and hard-frozen blanket-bags and clothing, that he made a forced march to get on board, sending Lieutenant Parr in advance to report his intention. I ordered a hot meal to be prepared, and all hands from the ship walked out to meet the travellers. They fell in with them at Point Sheridan, as they were struggling through the last of the deep snow before reaching the mile and a half of hard level ice leading to the ship; this was the first level ice they had met throughout their journey.

The men were in wonderful spirits, but although all were able to walk, several were severely frost-bitten. The journey had been most severe; but Markham had nevertheless succeeded in establishing his depot at Cape Joseph Henry. All made light of numerous unavoidable hardships they had undergone, remarking laughingly but truly, 'We could never have learnt our work except by actual experience we have gone through.'

Sledge travelling during the autumn is necessarily accompanied by greater hardships and discomforts than during the spring, to say nothing of its usually being undertaken by inexperienced men. During the spring the weather, and consequently the travelling, is constantly improving, and the equipment, moistened during the earlier days, can usually be dried before it becomes very bad. During the autumn the temperature, too warm at first, steadily falls, and each day adds its modicum of dampness to the tent, blanket-bags and clothing, until at last they contain so much moisture and become so frozen and contracted in size as to be almost unserviceable. The sodden blanket-robes frozen as hard as boards can scarcely be unrolled, and the stockings and foot-wrappers, put on damp in the morning, are by night frozen so hard into the canvas boots as to refuse to separate unless cut apart or melted inside the blanket-bag by the heat of the body.

Markham's journey of nineteen days was accompanied with the usual hardships and sufferings. The deep soft snow, reaching sometimes above the knee, was nearly impassable; being a totally new experience the travellers were unprepared for it. In the daily endeavor to advance, the three officers in front of the party treaded down a road through the snow, and as the most severe labour devolved on the sledge in front, its crew was augmented. The order of march was changed daily as well as the leading men on the drag ropes; when the snow was very deep, the whole party of twenty-one men had to drag the sledges forward one at a time. The newly formed ice was so weak that it became necessary to cross it with half-loads, and the unfrozen water-spaces near the shore were so frequent that land travelling along every bend of the coast line had to be resorted to. A large water-pool in the neighborhood of Cape Richardson obliged the travellers to cross a hill two hundred and fifty feet high.

Out of the party of twenty-one men and three officers, no less than seven men and one officer returned to the ship badly frostbitten, three of these so severely as to render amputation necessary, the patients being confined to their beds for the greater part of the winter.

The sledges with their cargoes on four occasions broke through the ice, and individual men frequently. These being made to change their clothing escaped any bad consequences. The frost-bites were attributable entirely to the wet sludgy state of some of the ice that had to be crossed.

The water that had oozed through the ice remained unfrozen, although the temperature was upwards of forty degrees below freezing point; consequently whenever the travellers, inexperienced as they were at the time, were forced to drag their sledges over a road of this nature, their feet became wet and frost-bitten a considerable time before they discovered it when changing their foot-gear in the evening; by which time the mischief had attained such an advanced stage as to defy all restoration of the circulation.

The experience of these men was very different from ours throughout every stage of the work, naturally and necessarily so. We have here a group of men laboring along hauling their own sledges, often by standing pulls, inexperienced, poorly clothed, with crude equipment, endeavoring to learn through mistakes the technic of Arctic sledging, mistakes which entailed untold suffering and the loss of their lives. The Peary methods were the result of his own experience over many years combined with the experience of the most efficient men in the world in Arctic work – the Eskimos. Without their help the North Pole would never have been attained by dog team.

On the twenty-second, some of our hunters arrived with fourteen caribou, thus assuring us of fresh meat for weeks to come and eliminating all danger of scurvy. If an expedition is so fortunate as to secure an ample supply of fresh meat, the dread disease is the last thing to be feared. It is true that we were well supplied with lime-juice tablets – we were compelled to be, I believe, by the laws of our country. For a century at least lime juice has received credit for eliminating the ravages of scurvy. Recent investigation has disclosed the fact that the cure should be attributed to lemon juice and not to lime juice at all. But even lemon juice suffers a marked loss in potency when it is stored for even so short a period as two weeks in a cold place, which invariably happens on a Polar trip. With a knowledge of these facts we hold the key to the secret of the hitherto unaccountable breaking-down of the health of several Arctic expeditions, which lacked sufficient fresh meat in their dietary, but had an ample supply of lime juice.

In the absence of lemon and orange juice and fresh vegetables of many kinds, which are undoubtedly a preventive and a cure of scurvy when given in sufficient quantities, plenty of fresh meat, and much of it eaten raw and in a frozen state, is an excellent and efficacious substitute. We are compelled to recognize the truth of this, for we have never known of a case of scurvy among the Smith Sound tribe, who are practically entirely meateaters. That this is due in no way to racial immunity is proved by the fact that I lived for four years among them, without fresh vegetables or fresh fruits of any description, and enjoyed good health every moment of the time.

With no scientific basis for it, Commander Peary was always a firm believer in the potency of fresh yeast bread and canned tomatoes as antiscorbutics. He simply judged from his own experience and general good health. It is now proved that tomatoes, even when subjected to the heat of canning, are rich in vitamins.

We were facing the winter with confidence one mile and a quarter north of the Nares Expedition which consisted of sixty-one men. According to the official report, before a year had ended nearly everyone on board the *Alert* showed signs of scurvy, even the cat!

Commander Peary was a good physical director. After five days of rest from the first twenty-four-mile run, he dispatched the sixteen loaded sledges again on the twenty-first with their objective Cape Richardson, eight miles beyond Cape Belknap. The new men under his command were learning field work with all that the term implies – harnessing dogs, lashing sledges, setting up tents, building snow houses, chipping holes for hitching-strap, feeding eight frantic jumping dogs, cooking in low temperatures, and keeping comfortable at night without a sleeping-bag. Borup and the doctor had much to tell on their return, experiences both laughable and tragic, such as their dogs disappearing in the distance. Nothing can bring more disgrace than to have one's team arrive home without him. It is a long walk, with humiliation at the end of the trail.

Another seven-hour run on the twenty-sixth fitted them for what seemed then the big trip of the twenty-eighth to Cape Columbia, a distance of ninety miles. The British expedition required *twenty-nine days* to cover this distance; Peary's men would do it in three, and return laughing and yelling like a crowd of schoolboys. The answer – dogs. It is no wonder that men who travel afoot, men who pull their own sledges, men who do not know the true value of the Eskimo dog in sledging, who do not differentiate between the value of dogs really driven and those merely used as draught animals, question the rapidity of some of Peary's travel. But these bundles of bone and sinew are a great part of my story.

I drove up the road with Borup for a mile or so, for I was now able to be out. Every tail curled, every trace as straight as a solid bar, the sledge going like a well-oiled machine, the pure joy of a dog team! It is not alone in watching the play and swing of muscled legs, the smooth gliding of space beneath the runners of polished steel, the pure air, sunlight, wind, drift, but also in the companionship of ten good friends, no two alike, each with his individual traits. Life on the trail would be far less enjoyable if it were not for the personality of each dog. They are willing to go where you go and as far as you want to go. With all his experience and the best of men, Peary could never have succeeded without his dogs and the North Greenland dogs are by far the best in the world for work over the ice.

With the sun gradually going south the days were becoming shorter and shorter, colder and colder. On October 4th the thermometer registered zero. On this northern shore of Grant Land the British Expedition experienced 73° below zero, or one hundred and five degrees below the freezing point of fresh water, and this at a time, March 4th, when we would be sledging with our dogs towards the Pole. How could men endure such extreme cold? Before the year was over we knew.

We watched the approaching darkness, the 'dreaded Arctic night,' as it has been called in many a narrative. I had read much of this phenomenon, but I had not realized that only one expedition has ever had real darkness for twenty-four hours during the winter. That was the Nansen Expedition of 1893-96, when the *Fram* was locked in the ice north of Siberia and slowly drifted within two hundred and forty-three miles of the Pole. Many have claimed to have experienced darkness throughout the twenty-four hours, but a few slight calculations will disprove the claim. Darkness occurs when the reflected light of the sun disappears from the heavens. This is not possible until the sun is eighteen degrees below the horizon. Roughly, we were at 82° 28′ North Latitude, or 7° 32′ from the Pole. On December 22d, the middle of the long night, the sun would be at its farthest south, 23° 27′ south of the Equator, or 15° 48′ below our horizon. On our shortest day, therefore, there should be a glimmer of twilight in the south, and this proved to be the case.

Even at the Pole itself there are not six months of darkness. The sun sets on September 21st and returns on March 21st, but during this non-sun period there are nearly two months (fifty-three days) of twilight in the autumn and an equal amount in the spring, leaving only two months of real darkness during the winter.

It is true that on stormy days in December, midday was as dark as midnight. As far as I could judge, the physical and mental effect of such an experience is nil. There were no 'increasing gray hairs,' no 'faltering steps,' or 'premature ageing,' or 'insanity,' all of which have been attributed to the effects of an Arctic night. One thing alone was noticeable and we all commented on it when the sun returned to the ship – lack of color in the faces of the men. But in a few weeks they were as brown as berries, and in a few months almost black, tanned by the reflected rays of the sun when sledging over ice and snow fields.

Commander Peary and Captain Bartlett were taking chances in wintering the *Roosevelt* as they were. It did not seem possible that a ship could winter in safety on this straight shore, and sound reasoning was against it. But it had been done by the *Alert* and by the *Roosevelt* in 1905–06, and they hoped it could be done again. We were up against a shelving bank of mud and sand exactly three hundred and forty-eight feet two inches from high-water mark. Outside of us was a floe berg seventeen feet high; beyond that was open water, a lead, five hundred and ten feet distant. Its presence was a bit ominous, since it permitted motion of the great Polar pack which, under certain conditions, would make mince meat of the ship. Before spring the pressure of the pack had heeled the *Roosevelt* so far to port that, in order to keep the dishes on the table and soup in our plates, we were compelled to level up the dining-table by placing blocks of wood under the legs. Aside from this nothing happened, although, at times, pressure portended trouble.

Commander Peary was always energetic and loved the open. He could stand ship life no longer, and on October 2d he was away with six of his favorite Eskimos, two of whom had accompanied him on his long journey in 1906 along the northern shores of Grant Land far west to the northern end of Axel Heiberg Land.

'Piblockto' was now common among the women. What this disease is no one knows. I believe, however, that it is a form of hysteria, not caused by fright or joy or sorrow, but possibly by jealousy, abuse by the husband, or a craving for affection. After crooning for a time, accompanied by a swaying back and forth of the body and a beating of the hands, with an 'I don't care' yell they were off for the hills or for the Polar Sea, ripping off their clothes with teeth and hands, spitting, biting, clawing, if restrained in any way. Heavens, what a time!

The show was always well attended. Everybody was up to see what would happen next, and something always did happen with startling rapidity. We found fat old In-a-loo flat on her back far out on the packed drift ice, blowing like a porpoise and cramming pieces of ice under her sealskin coat on her bare breast. We handled her with gloves. Although she was well along in years, she could certainly scratch and kick. With a sling around her waist the boys 'heave ho'ed' her over the rail. Her husband promptly sat down on her feet, a son on each arm and a lady friend on her head, and there they remained until the tumult subsided. Weak, dazed, and with eyes bloodshot, she was finally put to bed. When in the unladylike condition of 'piblockto' her special forte was an insane desire, followed by the attempt, to walk across the ceilings of our cabins. She never quite reached the top. Commander Peary informed me that when 'possessed by the Devil,' as the Eskimos think they are, this particular woman was an adept at imitating the noises of birds and the cries of all the animals of the North.

Ahl-nay-ah, nicknamed Buster by the men, was the star actress. Her performance was 'impeccable,' as the dramatic critics say. She was the most accomplished singer on board. Without the singing a woman about to have piblockto really could not do her best, for the curtain rings up with music to attract attention.

Our chief engineer, dear old George Wardwell, dead now, weighed two hundred and forty pounds and wore union suits. Buster weighed a scant one hundred and had no union suit. The chief would have given away his heart. Buster was well clothed; by wrapping the garment around her twice she had two union suits! It is a well-established and accepted fact that women like good clothes and want us to know that they have good clothes. In the silence of one mid-afternoon out popped Buster from Eskimo headquarters and, with a Comanche yell, cleared the rail. She had it on! the pleats were out. She looked like an animated misshaped balloon. Pursued by a highly interested conclave of sailors, she struggled valiantly to gain the first rampart beyond the box house. She fought hard, but she was finally captured and subdued and led back to the ship, hair streaming, lips protruding, and blowing like a bandmaster every note in the scale and some beyond it. No one knew exactly what to do with her, since she had no husband, the only woman in the tribe who hadn't, and consequently there was no one to take charge of the runaway. Someone suggested, 'Lash her up!' She was wrapped in a blanket, arms pinioned to her sides, flat on her back on a two-inch plank, and hoisted up to the fore boom where she remained, swinging to and fro in the wind, not all faculties subdued, for she could still sing and spit, which she did high into the air! Life was not monotonous on the *Roosevelt* at the edge of the Polar Sea.

✳

CHAPTER 11

THE ARCTIC NIGHT

The Scotch word 'cairn' is almost synonymous with explorer. Wherever he goes we find his cairn, or at least should find one; *for it and the enclosed record is the explorer's only proof that he has actually visited that spot.* Man may come and go, but what proof have we that he reached that particular point unless man follows and finds evidence of the visit? Observations as proof to others mean nothing as I shall demonstrate later. Unfortunate is he who reaches a point not on land, where no record can be left. Happily the South Pole is on land, and irrefutable proof can be found there of man's attainment. When Scott reached the South Pole, he found Amundsen's tent pitched, a record inside, and the Norwegian flag flying.

These cairns and their contents have always had a peculiar fascination for me. I take more real pleasure in hunting for records than in the pursuit of the polar bear, or walrus, or musk-oxen. They mean much more than meat, unless one is in dire need. In the past I have had the pleasure of finding four of Peary's records, six of the Nares Expedition, three of the Kane Expedition, and one of the Sverdrup Expedition of 1898–1902. In discovering evidences of a former expedition there is a thrill which persists, but there was a special thrill when I held in my hands the cap-lining of the immortal Kane, with the mark of 'O K.', scratched by the head of a bullet. Later I learned, through relatives of Dr. Kane, the mystery of the 'O K.' It appears that the family name at that time was not 'Kane,' but O'Kane.

Upon reaching the pinnacle of fame as he did upon his return in 1855, it seemed wise to Dr. Elisha Kent O'Kane to omit and forget the 'O' and the apostrophe!

The large cairn erected by the British was plainly visible from the deck of the *Roosevelt*, as it stood outlined against the sky on the brow of a distant hill south and east. Although I knew that Peary had removed the record two years before, it still held attraction for me, for it was built by plucky Englishmen who did a noble piece of work, although they failed to reach the Pole. Think of them plodding along these northern shores, harnessed to their sledges, each man hauling two hundred pounds and often more, one sledge carrying the astounding weight of twenty-two hundred pounds! Poorly equipped, poorly fed, down with the scurvy, up to their knees and thighs in snow, no snowshoes, resorting to standing pulls, 'One, two, three, pull! – at times advancing only ten yards in one hour, they were heroes. They showed the way with the loss of four good men.

As I walked south for a mile or so, I found the grave of one of these men, Niels Christian Petersen, a Dane, Eskimo interpreter of the expedition, once honored by his king with the silver cross of Dannebrog. Interpreter with Penny of the Franklin Relief Squadron, with Dr. Kane in 1853, with Captain F. L. McClintock in 1857, and then with the Nares Expedition, he died in the North which he loved, looking out over the ice fields of the Polar Sea from the most northern grave in the world. The headstone was of hard wood, covered with sheet copper, the lettering beautifully done. A solid stone slab covered the top of the grave:

> May 19th, 1876, Niels Christian Petersen was buried today on the brow of a hill a quarter of a mile from the ship where the snow never collects; the grave will therefore always remain conspicuous. No documents are buried near it, so it need never be disturbed. Nares.

On the evening of October 7th, I stepped backward a thousand years and possibly many more. How often, when reading of primitive peoples and their simple modes of living, thinking, and reasoning, we wish that we might have talked with them for at least one day. The day was here for me, and many happy more were to follow. In addition to our box house ashore, ready for occupancy in case of emergency, there were two Eskimo igd-loos, where a few of the Eskimos lived and where many gathered nightly to get away from the crowded conditions of the ship. Late one evening, as I happened to step out on deck, I heard singing in the distance. I walked across the ice, crawled through the narrow passageway and looked into the darkened interior. The singing ceased at once. I entered, sat down on the bed platform and waited patiently. The only occupants were an old woman and two girls aged about fourteen or fifteen. The woman was perspiring freely; the two girls were highly wrought up. Slowly and faintly the humming began, a mystic chant, attended by the swaying of the body and rhythmic beating of the hands in lieu of a drum, the old, old song of primitive man, swelling gradually in volume, the hoarse guttural note of age blending harmoniously with the clear treble of youth, the old teaching the young. As the singing continued, the two girls became actually frenzied and were simply beyond control. Physical exhaustion alone quieted them to a knowledge of their surroundings.

This, my first experience, I can never forget. The dim half-light of the primitive dwelling beneath winter snows, the faces faintly discernible through a mass of tangled raven-black hair, the swaying, sweat-covered, glistening bodies, the violent gestures, the fervid notes, all made a lasting impression. I was no longer living in the world of the present; I was back in ages long ago. I was a contemporary of the cave man.

Since then I have attended many such sessions, have listened to other chants, to stories of the days when men were strong, to stories of the creation of the world, and the one man and the one woman, when all was darkness and there was no light and no death and men lived on, but nothing was ever so impressive as that night beneath Cape Sheridan!

When one sees the rolling barren hills of the northern shores of Grant Land, its snow-filled valleys, its black ragged cliffs, a land unfinished or long since dead, one of the most forbidding in the world, it comes almost as a shock to learn that even here there is something alive, with red blood, meat, heat. The transformation of dry frozen grass and wind-blown snow into something which moves and breathes and sees and hears – a great strong vigorous animal – may be simple to the chemist or to the physiologist, but it is a mystery to me. My first impression was that there could be nothing eatable in this barren northern land. Everything gives that indication – the short season, frozen ground, extreme cold, and lack of sunlight. One would think that here must be the end of all animate things. So our eyes popped a bit when Commander Peary and his hand-picked Eskimos dashed up alongside the ship on October 9th. The gallery was full, admiring the sledges stacked up with black skins and ferocious-looking heads of the musk-oxen – that Far Northern animal which looks like a cross between a mountain goat and a buffalo, with extremely dangerous-looking horns, whose function is not to strike or pierce, but to rip and toss. Peary and his men had killed fifteen in as many minutes, more meat than many an Arctic expedition had had in a year. But the center of attraction was a sledge carrying on its very front the light straw-colored skin and head of a polar bear, the real King of the North.

When the last sun sinks slowly below the ice horizon and twilight deepens, and the Eskimos, tired with ever striving, gather in their primitive homes under rock, grass, skins, and snow, stirring tales are told of life, real life, where man lives more in a moment than the ordinary man lives in a week, and there is no story quite so thrilling as that of *Nannook*, no picture so impressive. He is emblematic of the North, an integral part of our conception of it. This hardy animal seems absolutely ignorant of the severity of the elements. Unlike his southern cousin, the black bear, hibernation, a winter's sleep, is unknown to his restless nature. He is up and at it in all kinds of weather, asking no quarter, plodding through darkness, blinding drift, extreme temperatures, always comfortable, a type perfected through the ages by the environment. The Eskimos respect him for what he is – a real one!

That night I walked up the trail leading to the north, now well marked with the parallel lines of sledge runners and footprints of many dogs, the beginning of that long white road leading to the end, the objective of three hundred years of effort. With prayers, cheers, and banners flying, Markham and his men, thirty-two years before, had stepped out lightly, hopefully, visualizing success. They had returned weary, dejected, beaten, faces blackened with frost, almost bewildered by the savagery of wind, cold, rough ice, open water, pressure ridges, everything antagonistic, inhospitable.

It was not so tonight. The North was in her friendliest mood, alluring, enticing. Nothing can be more beautiful than a moonlight night in the Arctic. It is beauty plus something indefinite, indescribable, mystic, creating within a great indefinable yearning for something unattainable. At home the moon is a great silver disk, resplendent with reflected light, but here it is a deep crimson oval distorted by refraction as it appears over the rim of the Polar Sea. The colder it is the greater the distortion, a shortening of the vertical axis, a flattening of the true circle into an ellipse, a weird spectacle.

As the moon mounted into the sky, it assumed its true proportions, its familiar color, and turned the surroundings into a fairyland. The long shadows of the floe bergs, the shorter ones of the crushed ice adjoining the ice foot, the high lights on the hills, the dark valleys, the glistening snow fields stretching back into the interior, with silence whispering to silence, immeasurable – it was another world. Surely it could not be the same one in which men and nations were striving, pushing, jostling, crowding to acquire.

Nothing could have been a greater contrast between the North and the South, a contrast further accentuated by the long-drawn note of a wolf or of one of our dogs searching for his own kin among the hills, calling back through the centuries. A single low reply came from the ship, then two, then three, and now from a hundred throats, deep, far-reaching, musical, the acme of loneliness, one of the wildest calls in Nature.

As I approached the ship, the silence was broken by the laughter of children at play on the wide level ice foot. There they were playing in the moonlight at the top of the world, real children of Nature who play as southern children play, unmindful of a mere six below zero or the long night to come.

On October 11th the large party came in from Cape Columbia, all looking brown, healthy, physically fit. They had landed the large dépôt of supplies at this northern point, ninety miles from the ship, in readiness for the great task to be undertaken in the early twilight of the long summer day. This preliminary work was an important part of the whole plan of attack. It served to break in new dogs and accustom them to their strange team mates. It also tested the strength of the sledges, the mettle, the endurance, the resourcefulness of the men, the warmth of the clothing, the reliability of our cooking equipment. It acquainted the men with the trail, the character of the ice foot, the sea ice, and the short cuts across necks from bay to bay. Finally, it was excellent training for Borup, Goodsell, and the younger Eskimo drivers.

Most Arctic expeditions considered fall sledging and winter work so dangerous and barren of results that, to while away the time and to kill the tedium of the so-called Arctic night, schools were established, plays were acted, papers were published, anything and everything to keep the men interested and happy until the real work began in the spring. Peary's work was already begun and it continued throughout the winter. The North Pole was not reached in a day.

CHAPTER 12

✳

SURVEYING IN GRANT LAND

A survey of Clements Markham Inlet was the first task allotted to me by the Commander. It did seem good to be getting ready to go somewhere; not that life on board was in the least monotonous, but taking and developing photographs day after day for the Commander and taking meteorological observations for the Government were rather prosaic occupations with the other men in the field driving dogs and being initiated into Arctic work. Every minute counted for efficiency in the great work to come; thoroughly to be acquainted with that demanded not months but years.

As always, the Commander was kindness itself in helping me in every way to prepare for my trip. Because of my recent illness, he even supplied me with a polar bearskin sleeping-bag, the only one on board, I think, for it was not part of the Peary system to use bags. This one accomplished its purpose, but it was far too heavy and too warm for that time of year. Since that time I have used sheepskin, bear, musk-ox, seal, caribou, eider-down, and blanket bags. At sixty below zero there is nothing quite so satisfactory, warmth, weight, and feel considered, as a good close-fitting late fall caribou-skin bag. The new eider-down robe is an excellent substitute, and in some ways much to be preferred.

The blue foxskin 'kooletah' – hooded coat – lent me by the Commander is without doubt and argument the warmest, softest, lightest, and most comfortable Arctic garment worn. Perhaps it ought to be, considering that it is made of ten blue foxes and one white, and would sell, if marketed, for at least a thousand dollars. Such a coat has only one drawback – that under the stress and strain of lifting, pushing, and working with a heavy sledge, the stitches pull.

On October 14th, fourteen sledges and one hundred and forty dogs were lined out along the ice foot. It was an animated sight. The dogs were yelping, jumping, tugging at their traces, eager to get away. The men were shouting to each other as they loaded their sledges, and at intervals, to restrain their impatient dogs, snapping their whips with a loud report. Two of the sledges and two of the best men, Eging-wa and Oobloo-ya, were to accompany me in my work; twelve sledges were to go to Cape Columbia with full loads of five hundred pounds each.

As I sat on the leading sledge and looked back over that long line of fast-stepping dogs, sledge beyond sledge following the coast, I realized as never before the magnitude of the whole thing and what Commander Peary had been through during the past years in trying to do the seemingly impossible. He who does not know the zest and keen pleasure of putting his wits and his strength against the elements has not really lived. Now I could easily understand why Peary pressed on and knew how tremendous was the personal satisfaction to him with one more obstacle overcome, one more barrier passed, one more fact recorded. People at home do not seem to understand. Fame, money, love of adventure, leave of absence on full pay, were the least of all motives urging him on and out over treacherous ice fields from which he might never return. His own record was written on the northern skyline – 87° 6'. It must be passed!

That night we slept at Porter Bay, a run of thirty miles for the dogs. Here George Porter of the Nares Expedition died and was buried in the sea ice. And here his fifteen shipmates struggling homeward from the Polar Sea were so exhausted that eleven were carried to the ship on relief sledges. After such a disaster, one is not surprised to read in Commander Markham's report:

I feel it impossible for my pen to depict with accuracy, and yet be not accused of exaggeration, the numerous drawbacks that impeded our progress. One point, however, in my opinion is most definitely settled, and that is the utter impracticability of reaching the North Pole over the floe in this locality; and in this opinion my able colleague, Lieutenant Parr, entirely concurs.

The 'utter impracticability' did not cause Peary to swerve one iota from his purpose.

The next morning the thermometer read twelve below zero. A deep red in the east portended wind – 'Red in the morning, sailors take warning. Red at night, sailors' delight.' A strong cold wind is the worst enemy of the Arctic man. It blinds with its stinging drift; it freezes face and hands; it not only stops dogs and men dead in their tracks, but actually blows them away. I have seen an Eskimo and his dogs being helplessly driven to leeward across a field of smooth ice.

If it were not for the wind – and how a man curses it! – one feels confident that he could go anywhere and do anything. And yet, as with so many evils, it has its good qualities, and we bless it. We are bounding along today over a hard rolling snow field. 'Wonderful going!' we exclaim. But the wind makes it so; all the loose freshly fallen snow has been driven away, and all the snow under our feet is so compact that we can hardly dent it with the heels of our boots. The wind really makes long daily journeys possible. Fortunately, extreme temperatures such as sixty and seventy below zero are never associated with wind. If they were, man would soon go into a hole, the first one he could find, and stay there.

In spite of our warning we were away at nine-fifteen in the morning for the crossing of the Fielden Peninsula. We anticipated trouble, for a land crossing in the Far North generally means grit and gravel, which ruins the carefully polished steel runners. We always stick to the sea ice whenever possible. Within fifteen minutes it began to blow, dead ahead; within fifteen minutes more we knew we were through for the day. The drift blinded the dogs and froze the cheeks of the leading men. Someone must lead, and to pick the route must face the wind, and that someone suffers. We in the rear buried our faces in the skins which covered the loads for protection and to breathe against a wind which fairly whistled through the narrow pass. Our faces numb with pain, we were glad to reach the shore of James Ross Bay and take refuge in the lee of a provision cache. Enough for one day! Tents were pitched, but they are miserable contraptions for cold, windy weather as they slat and bang all night.

The wind subsided in the early morning and tempted us to try it again. Old Torngak, the Evil Spirit of the North, must have chuckled in his sleeve as he saw us packing and lashing our sledges. By ten o'clock it was blowing again, as hard as ever, which discouraged our Eskimos who declared that it was impossible and wanted to camp.

Captain Bartlett and I plodded ahead on snowshoes, tramping down the drifting snow, going over the trail four and even five times. Even then some of the Eskimos were compelled to throw off half their loads. My two men were not loaded so heavily, and they were the only two to reach the shores of Sail Harbor with full loads. Some of the men failed to arrive at all and had encamped for the night back in the hollow of the hills.

The next morning I left the Columbia Division, which was under the command of Captain Bob. He started back on snowshoes to round up his men, while I headed, with my two sledges and two Eskimos, up the coast for Hamilton Bluff at the entrance of Hamilton Inlet where I was to begin my survey. I shall never forget that survey, for in the next few days I walked in and out eighty miles, and counted every step! The Lord deliver me from a repetition of any such work! – not the walk so much, but the count, which refused to discontinue itself for days after I reached the ship. Walking necessitated counting, so closely were they associated in my mind. I counted as I walked to the breakfast table; I counted as I walked to the instrument shelter; I counted every time I walked, thirty inches to the step, twenty-four hundred steps to the mile; eighty miles, 192,000 steps!

The counting was loud, determined, and decisive at times, especially so on one day when I rounded a point of land and heard the rapid firing of two Winchester rifles. Wolves, bears, caribou, or musk-oxen? Any one made a strong appeal to stop the everlasting counting, plant the transit in the snow, pocket my notebook and pencil and run. I finished my five hundred, made a rapid note of it, and ran.

By this time the whips were snapping, and I knew that something was down; that the two men were endeavoring to keep the dogs from tearing it to pieces. I rounded another point and was astounded to see a mass of flying black hair pursued by twenty dogs galloping down the hill and out onto the bay ice. There he fell, jumped to his feet, and with the dogs clinging to him like leeches headed straight for me, as if for protection, a pitiful sight. Here was being played the oft-repeated tragedy of the North – a pack of wolves dragging down their quarry. There is no law in Nature but the law of the strong. I spread my arms. He swerved a bit to the right and fell, exhausted, mouth open, almost at my feet, covered with the growling, yelping throng, completely overwhelmed with numbers – a year-old musk-ox.

Eging-wa was now calling from the hill – 'Tu-a vi' – for me to hurry, as there was one still alive. I found the dead bodies of three cows, and a yearling standing in the midst of them, head down and trembling. It seems a shame to shoot them, and it would be if fresh meat were not a necessity. In all my experience seeing musk-oxen means getting them. What they would do if one approached on foot, I do not know. Sverdrup states that one of his men did so and would have been killed except for the arrival of a dog who diverted the attack. I can easily conceive its happening in the spring of the year when the bulls protect the mothers from the attacks of the wolves.

We have found this animal as far north as land goes, at the most northern point of land in the world, Cape Morris Jesup, the tip end of Greenland, three hundred and eighty miles from the Pole. Feeding as it does on frozen grass on wind-swept stretches, fat and in good condition, the musk-ox is so far north that it is safe to say that it will never be exterminated by man as was once feared. Explorers are not numerous enough for that. Its only enemy is the wolf, and possibly the polar bear, although as yet there is no real evidence of this.

My only reason for including the bear is based upon an experience in 1916 when traveling along the southern shores of Ellef and Amund Ringnes Islands where bears are plentiful and musk-ox tracks were seen. There were four sledges and thirty-nine dogs. As we approached a small frozen-in berg, a bear popped out from behind one corner and ran directly at us – Noo-ka-ping-wa and I were leading by some three hundred yards. This was a new experience for us both, for all the bears we had seen up to this time had turned tail and run. The 'evidence' was but a few yards away. He stopped, turned and ran. Was his direction merely accidental, or did he deliberately plan the attack and realize his mistake too late? Wolves had done that very thing a short time before, mistaking our four teams traveling slowly in close formation for a herd of musk-oxen. As the twelve white bodies bounded down the hill, it was a beautiful sight, and, for a few seconds, a bit exciting. The thrill of such a moment justifies somewhat the long hours of plodding, plodding through deep snow, pushing heavy sledges, facing biting winds.

But to revert to the musk-ox. It is one of the oldest animals on earth. Its contemporaries, the woolly mammoth and woolly rhinoceros, are long since dead. Typically Arctic, with its long undercoating of wool it withstands the coldest temperatures, feeding on high windswept areas of which there are many, and even in valleys, nuzzling the snow away where the ground is but lightly covered. Upon sighting the dogs, the oxen scurry to a vantage-point of land, at times far up the talus slope, with their backs to the cliffs. If in the open and attacked suddenly, they huddle, all facing out, forming roughly a circle. There is nothing of the trained soldier in the attack. The musk-ox charges at a dog with head well down to catch him, if possible, on his outward and upward curving horns to toss and rip. There is no order in the charging as to number or time; both depend upon the number and nearness of the dogs.

Following the charge, which rarely exceeds fifty feet, the musk-oxen return almost immediately to the herd, a precaution against being cut out and surrounded by the pack. The circle formation with all facing out is their defense against the wolves and their only safety. Their meat is as delicious as good beef. Because of the extreme length and coarseness of the hair, the skin is of little value. The Eskimos sometimes use it as a cover for the grass on the bed, and I have seen outer garments made of it, when caribou and fox skins were not available.

At the bottom of this same inlet, some fifty feet above high-water mark, I found a log of wood a foot in diameter and about twelve feet in length. Its presence could be accounted for in only one way – it drifted there. I regretted that I was unable to determine the species, for this information would have been of value, but it was clearly a coniferous wood, probably pine, larch, or fir from Siberia. Later, we found similar trees at high-water mark. This was the first evidence I had noticed of an uplifting of this part of the North. When the snow had left the land, there was evidence all along the shore and even to the height of a thousand feet, where we found mud beds, rippled rocks, and various kinds of broken and some whole shells. Limestone with embedded fossils could be found within a ten minutes' walk of the ship. George Wardwell succeeded in getting a fine collection.

The ice sheet in this inlet deserves more than a passing notice, as it was not the ordinary one-year formation of six and, according to our measurements, never more than seven feet in thickness which is found in lower latitudes. Under the warm rays of a long summer sun, the latter melts or breaks up into large flat sheets, which are driven out by winds and tides into Kane Basin and Baffin Bay, and then on along Baffin Land and the Labrador Coast in the so-called Labrador Current. The ice in this inlet was entirely different, and resembled rather the hard blue rolling surface of a glacier which, judging from all appearances, had been there for at least a century. Later I discovered that ice of this same character was to be found all along the shore, as far west as Ward Hunt Island, really glacial ice afloat. At no place was it connected with the true glaciers, as there are none on this coast which reach the sea. This must be the 'paleocrystic ice' of Nares and Greely and the 'glacial fringe' of Peary.

Are such inlets in the Far North the source of the huge low blocks of ice so prevalent in lower latitudes in certain years? Obviously they are liberated into the ice streams flowing south under the three following conditions: A very early spring, extremely high spring tides, and strong offshore prevailing winds. In 1912, the year the *Titanic* met with disaster, there were many such bergs, or low ice sheets, in the North Atlantic. They are very difficult to see at night from a ship's bridge seventy-five feet above the water, since they are not outlined against the lighter color of the sky.

Now it was plug, plug, count, count, and sight, sight every day, yet putting new land on the map has its thrill. As we swung along back on the western side of the inlet, we discovered a cairn, which proved to be one of Peary's filled with polar bear meat.

The discovery of this bear meat led to a laughable incident that night. Naturally I wondered how it would taste, so bear was on the menu. The boys chipped the ice and passed the pot in through the tent door for me to place on the oil stove. After a long day we were ravenous, but we boiled the meat long and hard in the hopes of making it tender. Once Eging-wa removed the cover and jabbed his long hunting knife through the cloud of steam to test the meat. 'Not done yet,' he said.

Our patience finally yielded to the pangs of hunger; we whetted our knives, removed the pot, and sat up close to our table, fairly drooling with expectation. When the cloud of steam rolled away, we peered into the water long and earnestly. Not a thing there! We had forgotten to put in the meat!

Oobloo-ya and Eging-wa fell back and roared with laughter. This was my first insight into one of the characteristics of the Eskimo. The average white man would have cursed his head off. It is needless to say that the meat was not boiled so long the second time. Polar bear is stringy and tough and decidedly not a delicacy. It is much better eaten raw than cooked, but only in a frozen state. Then it is really good, for freezing removes the peculiar rancid taste.

By Sunday, the twenty-fifth, we had completed the eighty miles, so we sledged out for the tip end of Cape Colan, beyond which we could see evidence of drift and heavy wind. I hoped to pick up Captain Bob's trail and follow it to the east. There is a tremendous difference in the speed and spirit of a team of dogs when breaking a trail and following one. At the Cape we found a split stick upright in the snow – the Arctic man's post-office – holding a note which read:

Surveying Clements Markham Inlet

MY DEAR MAC:
Have part of the load to Good Pt. and will have the other load and a half tomorrow. The wind and snow have played hell with things and the God damned dogs I don't know what is wrong with them. Hope you are well.
Sincerely
BOB

A pressure ridge at the edge of the Polar Sea

I left here a sketch of the Inlet, which showed the caches of musk-ox and bear meat; he was to get them and bring them out to the ship if he had time to do so. I also left a leg of musk-ox and a leg of bear meat, which I knew he and his men would enjoy.

The wind had now increased and was driving the snow down the coast a hissing, seething mass, fortunately at our backs. Away we went with it, laying a course by compass of south 21° west. Within an hour we were animated balls of snow; our fur clothes were driven full of it. We couldn't see fifty yards. Finally, we camped on the sea ice, for we knew that unless our course was true, we should have miles of unnecessary work the next day.

There was another new dish for supper – pemmican. This is an Indian word from the Cree dialect and means a 'fatty food.' The chief ingredients are dried beef – the Indians used dried buffalo meat – and suet. It is pleasant to the taste and most satisfactory in cold weather, for the suet content is about thirty-eight per cent. The white man has added raisins and sugar, with the result that pemmican is a highly concentrated and nutritious food, undoubtedly the best ever adopted for Arctic work.

On the trip to the Pole we had eight ounces of pemmican in the morning and eight ounces at night, with no other meal during the day. Commander Peary considered that only two other things were necessary to the diet – hot tea and hardtack. How simple this bill of fare was when compared with those of other expeditions! For breakfast, eight ounces of hardtack, eight ounces of pemmican, a tin cup of tea. For supper, eight, ten, twelve hours later, eight ounces of hardtack, eight ounces of pemmican, a tin cup of tea. Day in and day out it was the same, and, strange to say, we never tired of it. For cold hard work man wants tea, not coffee or chocolate. Tea is light to carry, easily and quickly prepared, and is stimulating and refreshing. It puts a man on his feet, ready to start again. Tea is a more powerful stimulant than coffee, with few, if any, after effects.

The weather was clear the next morning, and we could see across Clements Markham Inlet, but even before we were through breakfast, it was hissing again. One generally defies the weather when on the homeward trail, so we started. We held fast to our compass course of south 21° west, the wind aiding us against error, but, since winds are subject to change in direction, we checked the course at intervals of fifteen minutes with the railroad transit. We hit Sail Harbor square in the eye. To make the land through the loose deep snow, which generally prevails when coming down upon a weather shore, we had to lighten our loads and 'double-bank' – to go over the trail twice with half loads. How the dogs wagged their tails and rubbed their faces in the snow when they reached shore after their exertions! We pitched camp for the night, fed our dogs, and sat down to a good supper of tea and musk-ox meat.

The next day was almost a repetition of the last few hours of the day before. It was yell, push, snap the whips, and tramp down the trail on snowshoes – heart-breaking work with poor results. The days were now short, for the sun had been gone for fourteen days, and we were unable to keep the trail in the gathering dusk. However, we succeeded in reaching the eastern shores of James Ross Bay, passing on the way a large number of boxes of biscuit and pemmican, evidence that Captain Bob was having his troubles. Bob would push through with full loads if anyone could.

October 28th was worse – there was water under the snow. Every snowshoer knows what this means – snowshoes a mass of slush and ice and as heavy as lead. But we plodded across the neck to Porter Bay, where we were startled to see two black objects rushing to the top of a hill. At first we thought they were musk-oxen, but within a few seconds the sharp eyes of Oobloo-ya recognized them as Innuit. They proved to be the brothers of my two men, In-yu-gee-to and Ootah, who were taking loads of whale meat for Bartlett's division in order that he might conserve on pemmican; they were also to hunt caribou. How their tongues wagged as they gave and received the latest news! The inland hunting party under Marvin had bagged nineteen caribou; Henson's party came in with eight.

The three days which these men had taken in coming from the ship portended trouble for us, for the dogs often covered the distance of thirty miles in one day. The portents were right. The next day was a hard one with only eight miles to our credit on account of the darkness. How Ootah kept the trail, now covered with soft snow, was a mystery to me. It was by feeling with his feet! With not the faintest sign of a dog's foot or sledge runner, I wondered, and then watched him plodding along ahead of the dogs, unconcernedly on snowshoes, chewing on a caribou bone. Finally, I noticed that he hesitated, stepped a bit to one side and went on. The old trail there was under a new layer of snow and a little harder to the feet than the area just outside it.

The next day In-yu-gee-to and Ootah branched off for the hills to hunt caribou, while we went on for Cape Richardson. There we met two more men, their thin beards, eyebrows, and long black hair so covered with condensed moisture from their breaths that I failed to recognize them. One proved to be another brother of Eging-wa, and a fine young fellow by the name of Sig-loo. They urged us to go on to their camp at Cape Belknap which we reached at eleven-thirty, after a long hard day.

After seventeen days of hard walking and good substantial food, such as tea, biscuit, pemmican, polar bear meat, and musk-oxen, one feels like stepping out to the end of the world. Just to swing the arms and legs is pure joy. The next morning I strapped on my snowshoes and raced the dogs to the ship. They were wallowing through snow and were, consequently, handicapped. I reached the ship at 1 P.M., reeking with perspiration, a half-hour ahead of the dogs. To my surprise I learned that it was twenty-six below zero, a temperature far too warm for the clothes we were wearing, walking rapidly as I had been. A bath, a shave, a good meal, a good bed, was too good to be true, and I could not sleep. I probably missed the slat and flap of the canvas tent, the noise of wind and drift.

CHAPTER 13

✴

CAPE COLUMBIA

Sledges were coming and going constantly; everyone was busy. Some were sledging supplies; others were a hundred miles in the interior keeping the expedition well supplied with meat. The morning after my return to the ship, Commander Peary called me to his room and informed me that previous to our departure he had received orders from the United States Government to take a series of tidal observations along the northern shores of Grant Land and Greenland. He wanted me to go to Cape Columbia for that purpose. This would be a real night trip of about two hundred miles up and back. The Eskimo women at once began work on my clothes – a close-fitting blanket shirt and bearskin pants. A trip to the summit of Cape Rawson and back, a few days later, tested their warmth and fitness for such work.

On November 6th I received the following orders:

PEARY ARCTIC CLUB
North Polar Expedition 1908
S.S. Roosevelt, Nov. 6, 1908

Instructions
Dear Sir:
Proceed to Cape Columbia with your party comprising your sailor, Jack Barnes, and the two Eskimos, Eging-wa and In-u-gee-tok and

their wives, for the purpose of obtaining a month's series of hourly tidal observations.

Your personal interviews and instructions from Dr. Harris render it superfluous for me to give you detailed instructions. I will, however, note one point. In addition to your hourly observations, you will take additional readings at closer intervals during a period of one hour immediately before and one hour immediately after the culmination of high and low water to more clearly trace the tidal curve at those times.

The peculiar condition of the wide permanent glacial fringe at Cape Columbia will make the problem of a satisfactory location of your tide gauge somewhat difficult, but I have confidence in your ability to solve it.

I feel confident, also, that your personal ability, general training and experience, together with Dr. Harris's instructions, and my suggestions, will enable you to do work that will be of distinct credit to you and the expedition, and secure results that will be essential for reference in every future discussion of the tides of the Arctic Ocean.

As you are aware, Prof. Marvin will take simultaneous observations at the *Roosevelt*. The question of time, therefore, as also the establishment of a reliable bench mark for future reference, are two vital points which must claim your constant and best attention.

You will keep the two Eskimo men in the field hunting every practicable opportunity. You will start on your return to the ship on the completion of a lunar month of observation and not later than the 14th of Dec. in any event.

Very truly

R.E. PEARY

PROF. D.B. MacMILLAN:
Supplemental Instructions
Dear Sir:

While the tidal observations are your main object at Cape Columbia, the opportunities in other directions afforded by a month's stay at the most northerly limit of all North American Lands are not to be thrown away.

In connection with your tidal observations you will make hourly observations of temperature and atmospheric pressure, with full notes in regard to weather (direction and force of wind, clouds, fog, snow, etc.) movements of the ice when practicable, presence of open water, aurora, etc.

Very truly yours

R.E. PEARY

As my party numbered six, with two heavily loaded sledges, Commander Peary planned to send with us for a part of the distance five dog teams, driven by Oobloo-ya, Sig-loo, Poo-ad-loo-na, Koo-la-tinah, and We-shark-ab-see. The explorer terms these 'supporting parties.' A flashlight of our departure hastened it; it was a new experience for the dogs.

Since the wives of the two Eskimos accompanied us on the trip, Jack and I knew that we must walk the two hundred miles. The snowshoeing was ideal, but it was a bit soft for sledges. We easily kept ahead of them. In eight hours and a half we were at Cape Richardson where we found a tent, stove, and nine musk-ox skins, which made an excellent bed in spite of the familiar smell of a cow barn.

Koo-la-tinah and We-shark-ab-see left us here to return to the ship. Sunday, November 8th, was so dark that the two girls picked the trail by the light of a lantern. The ice foot was overflowed in many places by the recent high tides. As it was covered with a thin layer of snow, its real character was not revealed until we stepped and drove into it, with the result that our snowshoes were covered with slush and our sledges were stuck fast. To extricate them meant hard work on the part of the drivers.

With an increasingly cold wind and drift, the two women, although far superior to any white man in detecting the faintest sign of a trail, began to wander, unable to see by the feeble light of the snow-covered lantern. Eging-wa now went on ahead and I was left to drive the team. When the dogs heard him call from the Porter Bay cache, I happened to be just ahead of them, a bad place to be in when dogs are in a hurry. They scooped me up, snowshoes in the air and flat on my back on the ten traces. I grasped the prongs of the sledge to prevent it from going over me, and rode into town a ludicrous figurehead, with the men and women screaming for the dogs to stop.

The cache village had one resident who sleepily lifted his head out of a snowbank – a stray dog. Why should he go home to the ship when there was plenty of whale meat here? We found a sheltered spot on the sea ice in the lee of a small berg and pitched our tent. In the fall of the year it is difficult to find snow of the proper degree of hardness out of which to build snow houses. The two girls, both young wives, were soon in their reindeer sleeping-bags, plainly tired by their fifteen-mile tramp through loose snow and cold from facing a zero wind.

Upon stepping out of the tent the next morning, I found the stray dog dead in front of the door, a bullet hole through his head. I was puzzled to know why anyone would shoot a poor, harmless, and even friendly animal. My limited vocabulary of Eskimo words struggled for some time before the full explanation dawned upon me. The night before I had given each man an eight-pound tin of pemmican for his dogs. Sure of this, I had sleepily refused to donate a second one to the cause when Oobloo-ya came to my tent soliciting food for his dogs. I did not know at the time, or rather did not understand, that the stray dog in an unguarded moment had bolted, so Oobloo-ya declared, the whole eight pounds. The dogs had worked hard during the day; they would have to work hard tomorrow; they deserved their food. There was only one way to get it. Shoot the dog, open him up, and there it was! This Oobloo-ya did. His dogs were fed.

Our third day, November 9th, was a hard one. The sky was completely overcast and the trail badly drifted so that we were compelled to go into camp at 7 P.M. in James Ross Bay. We looked out of the tent an hour or so later, and what a change there was! The clouds had disappeared and the moon was up. The high hills of Cape Joseph Henry and Hecla stood as great white silhouettes against a star-besprinkled sky. The Arctic was back again in all its beauty.

The tenth was a beautiful day without wind or drift. We did not mind the deep snow on the pass to Sail Harbor, not even the patches of bare ground. The moon was out and we could see Cape Colan; though ten miles distant it seemed but a mile away. New bending ice turned us south a bit from a direct line; but by holding close to the edge of it we found excellent sledging and made fast time to the Cape. I knew that Commander Peary had left a cache here three years before, so Jack and I hunted up and down the shore until we found it – nineteen tins of pemmican, one tin of biscuit, one ice pick, one ice lance, and a flag.

By four o'clock the next day we could see on the horizon the high bluff of Cape Aldrich, capped by the Cooper Key Mountains of Cape Columbia. Anxious to make our objective in such fine weather, I promised all sorts of good things to my Eskimos if they would make it. But thirty miles with heavily loaded sledges in soft snow was almost too much to expect of our dogs.

We slept that night for the first time in a snow house, regal apartments in comparison with a canvas tent in low temperatures. How unfortunate that previous explorers had no knowledge of the building and use of such quarters. Three of us in an hour could build a good house, eight feet in diameter and eight feet high; and enjoy doing it, for it is a work of art.

It is well worth going North just to see a good Eskimo work in snow. Not row on row, layer on layer, as described in many books, but spirally from right to left, or counterclockwise, since the block of snow is held by the left hand and fashioned or fitted with the right. The blocks for such a house number between fifty and sixty and are roughly 24 × 18 × 6 inches in size. Naturally the size varies with the quality of the snow. When the dogs have been fed and the entrance sealed tightly with a close-fitting block, there is a feeling of security and coziness which one never gets in a tent in cold wintry weather.

A snow house, it is true, is never really warmed, at least not for any length of time, if one respects his house and wants to live in it. Clothed as we are for the trail, it is too warm when cooking is in progress. The house begins to drip; water runs down the sides wetting our sleeping-bags, sealskin undercover, clothes-bag, and equipment in general, unless we are careful to enlarge the hole in the top of the igd-loo. The temperature in the room is regulated by the size of this hole which varies from two to four inches in diameter. If it is too cold, stick in a mitten; if too warm for the safety of the house, pull it out. Without the Eskimo stove lamp or our own Primus, which we generally use, the temperature within varies according to the number of the occupants, the sole heat being that radiated from the bodies.

Several years later I found, after a number of experiments, that we radiated about ten degrees of heat with four persons in an igd-loo. If it were fifty below outside, by sleeping inside we raised the temperature to forty below.

The greatest recommendation of the snow house on the trail, where fuel must be conserved and where the ration is twelve ounces a day, is not warmth, but protection from wind and drift, peace and quietness inside and the elimination of the weight of a tent when traveling. To unbend a frozen tent, pound it with the fists, kick it with the feet, set it up against wind and drift, with fingers white and stiff with cold, is not a comfortable job. By the end of a trip a tent has doubled and trebled its weight, with ice, as the result of the condensation of the steam when cooking and the moisture of the breath. It can be called anything but a tent.

The weights furnished by Sir George Nares are of the greatest value in comparing the work of the early expeditions with those of Peary. Upon leaving the ship the tent of the British Expedition weighed thirty-one pounds fourteen ounces. Upon their return it weighed five hundred and fifty-one pounds! Their floor cloth weighed eleven pounds four ounces; when the trip was over, its weight was seventeen pounds. A coverlet weighed twenty-one pounds and one ounce. At the return it weighed forty-eight pounds! *These weights ever increasing were carried throughout the trip.* Under the Peary system there was no tent, no floor cloth, no coverlet. Stay-at-home critics who have never seen an ice floor or a snow house, however, have made themselves ridiculous by denying that Peary had a system. It would seem in the face of these facts that he eliminated at least a quarter of a ton of weight and the men were more comfortable than had a tent been carried.

In the morning we kick the door out of the house and leave it as a home for the next party traveling our way. They will be glad to see it, since they will save one hour in getting their supper and getting to bed!

A beautiful morning, and Cape Columbia was calling. A long low spit reaching seaward from the black bluff of Cape Aldrich must be what we are looking for. It answered the Commander's description of the place where we should find a large provision cache, which was sledged there by Bartlett's and Borup's division a few weeks before.

By this time it was blowing and drifting, with the thermometer registering thirty-eight below zero. As we groped through the smother, we found the boxes barely discernible in the dark. We knew that our future month's location depended upon the site of our tidal gauge, which, after repeated trials to find the right depth of water, might have to be miles away, so we thought it best to pitch the tent for the night and establish permanent quarters later. When this was done, we began at once our attack on the sea ice with the help of a lighted lantern.

Between the wind and drift it was cold work digging down through four and a half feet of ice, only to be rewarded with gravel – no water at all. We were still on land. All along this coast it is the same; the angle of slope is so gradual from the foothills to the sea that it is impossible to determine from the appearance of the ice whether one is on sea or land.

We went out a quarter of a mile beyond this hole, and again tried digging down through five feet. We achieved the same result, the ground. We gave it up for the night, and what a night it was at this Cape Horn of the North! By morning we were partially buried under the weight of snow which was actually pressing the canvas down on our bodies. The Eskimos dug out, drove their snowshoes into the snow, ran lines to the sides of the tent, and pulled it back into shape. There was a gale of wind and a temperature of thirty-six below zero.

On the fourteenth it was a little warmer, only twenty-five below, so Oobloo-ya, Poo-ad-loo-na, and Sig-loo were encouraged to start for home.

On the fifteenth we struck water nine feet in depth under the high bluff of Cape Aldrich, an excellent place for our tidal observations. After this strenuous work, we had our supper, and enjoyed it – a stew of tomatoes, canned hash, and crackers, all mixed in with tea – by mistake!

The sixteenth was a busy day. Our plan was to sink to the bottom a butter box loaded with rocks, which would hold upright a staff graduated to a tenth of an inch. This was sufficiently long to project well above the surface of the sea ice, and thus record the rise and fall of the tide. By actual calculation Jack and I cut and removed three and a quarter tons of ice. Our two Eskimos were busy building our snow house. When it was completed, it measured eleven feet seven inches by twelve feet, with a height of eight feet two inches. This was the igd-loo itself; the bed platform was seven feet five inches long and a foot and a half above the level of the floor.

As a protection against dampness and cold we placed on the snow bed, box boards, snowshoes, and sheepskins. The women then lighted our oil stoves and closed all openings. Within an hour or so the thermometer registered forty-two above zero, or ten degrees above the freezing point. The snow melted; the sides ran water. Then they extinguished the lamps and opened the door. The sudden lowering of the temperature stopped all melting and resulted in a hard glazed surface, which strengthened the whole structure against violent winds and abrading drift. As we were to live in this house for at least a month, we lined it with our canvas tent as a further protection. All in all we had most livable quarters.

We should need the pemmican for the Polar Sea, so the Commander had rationed us from the ship's stores – tomatoes, corn, brown bread, beans, salmon, hash, condensed milk, biscuit, and tea. With two meals a day, this would give each one of us for each meal one-third of a can of tomatoes, brown bread or beans, or one-half of a can of corn, salmon, or hash. To supplement these stores, we hoped to secure a number of musk-oxen, and we were encouraged in this by finding fresh and numerous tracks in a small bight east of the camp.

Jack and I began our work, six hours on, six hours off, continuously for one lunar month. To be doubly sure of our comfort, Commander Peary had insisted upon supplying us with a small iron wood stove, since the pemmican boxes which would not be carried on the Polar Sea were available for fuel. Upon his return from a cold series of observations, Jack rubbed his hands together and declared he was going to have a 'damn good fire.' To prove his statement he crammed the newly set-up stove full of wood and applied a match. I think it began to smoke when he reached for the match, and to show what it could really do, it soon put every stove to shame that I have ever seen.

Through the gathering cloud I heard Jack wheeze, 'Every new one smokes,' and that is the last I heard clearly, that is, the last complete sentence considered in good form. The ejaculations, exclamations, words of extreme disgust, and oaths were most pronounced. I crawled under the bedclothes; the women retreated to the limits of the igd-loo and buried their faces in the musk-ox skins. Eging-wa was more practical: he dove out through the hole in the floor and knocked a hole in the roof. For a couple of days Jack eyed that stove with suspicion.

In trying to put in a bench mark on the eighteenth with the temperature at thirty-two below zero, I began to appreciate why explorers have the tangent screws of their transits covered with chamois or flannel. The metal burned like hot iron. And to read the vernier by the light of a flickering frozen lantern in a strong wind – it simply can't be done!

We had broken two of the three globes for our lantern. If the other one went, how were we to get home with the moon in its last quarter? It looked like trouble ahead. On the nineteenth it was thirty-eight below zero and we had no wood. We had to go back to our small oil stove and wear more clothes in the igd-loo. Eging-wa and In-yu-gee-to had tried hard, but they had failed to find fresh meat. Undoubtedly the musk-oxen heard our dogs and retreated to the hills. We had to feed our dogs with the Commander's precious pemmican, but we hated to do it, for we knew how much it would be needed later on when the real work began.

We kept religiously at our observations, lying on our breasts on the sea ice for hours, chipping, chipping ice from the freezing gauge at thirty and forty below zero. As we took observations every fifteen minutes for six hours and later on every five minutes, we sincerely hoped that they proved or disproved something. After we returned home, we received a letter of commendation from Dr. R.A. Harris, the tidal expert of the Coast and Geodetic Survey. Our observations, taken in the middle of the Arctic night, at four hundred and thirteen miles from the Pole, were evidently of value to someone.

Finally, it became so uncomfortable, exposed as we were to wind, drift, and low temperatures, that I had my Eskimos build a small snow house over the tidal hole. This served to protect the light as well as ourselves. We resorted to the use of a candle to save oil. A candle burns in a peculiar way at low temperatures. The heat from the flame is sufficient to melt only that part of the candle in immediate contact with the wick. Thus the flame works down *inside* the candle, leaving the outer walls standing, but perforated like lacework.

The thermometer now dropped to forty-two below. In trying to save fuel during my watch, I frosted both heels. At the time I failed to realize the seriousness of the incident, but it proved to be the beginning of more serious trouble on the real trip, and one which finally turned me back toward home.

Thanksgiving Day was one I shall always remember. I started the day by having a good wash – some of us wash once a week, and some not at all. The night before I had told the Eskimos about the day. That on Thanksgiving fathers, mothers, brothers, sisters, friends, all assembled around a great table heaped high with food, and that tomorrow we should have something extra on our usual bill of fare. Corn seemed to be the popular meal, so when we gathered around the Thanksgiving board each sat down to his one-half can of corn, eight small crackers, and a cup of tea. But the *pièce de résistance* was cooling.

I had wondered what to have as a surprise for the Eskimos. Reared on Cape Cod as I was, I had visions of a real Cape Cod Cranberry Pie. I had the cranberries, a jar of them given me by Charlie the cook, but no flour. Perhaps crackers would do. I pounded them up into a meal, put them in a pan, poured in water and stirred. It looked like chicken feed. As I stirred, it occurred to me that our mothers used shortening for some reason or other. What should I use instead? I had a tin box of musk-ox tallow for frostbites, why not use that? I heated it and poured it in. My intended crust now looked a bit slippery, but I spread it on the plate and dumped on my thawed cranberries. With a spoon I dribbled the straps across one way, then the other, to make the little red squares which were a delight in our childhood. Really, it was a most palatable-looking pie.

I fashioned an oven for our oil stove from a five-gallon oil tin. Shortly we heard a sizzling and a sputtering which was most unusual in pie-baking. The shortening was boil-over into the stove! My red squares had lost their color. It didn't look like a pie. I couldn't cook it. It was forty below. I would freeze it. We left it in a snow bank for an hour or more, and then served. My Eskimo friends were kind enough to express their appreciation of the new dish. Jack and I enjoyed it thoroughly.

Upon my return to the ship, I learned that my recipe was somewhat unique. When I told the boys about my pie, they inquired what I had used for shortening. 'A tin tube of musk-ox tallow which I found in my kit,' I answered. Dr. Goodsell, to make sure that he had heard aright, inquired again. With a rather amused expression, he exclaimed: 'That wasn't tallow. Thinking that possibly you might have frozen feet, I included it with other supplies. That was a tin of boric acid salve!'

But it was really a good pie! Cigars and a flashlight of the group completed our most northern Thanksgiving Day.

CHAPTER 14

✳

ESKIMO COMPANIONS

There was a certain incongruity, in such an inhospitable region at a temperature of forty-five below zero, in studying with my transit telescope the 'Sea of Tranquillity,' the 'Sea of Serenity,' and the 'Lake of Dreams,' yet there they were on the face of the moon. The Eskimos have a strange way of knowing when the moon will appear, and they never fail by a day – by the dimming of the stars and the disappearance of those of the fifth and sixth magnitude.

To the Eskimos the moon is a man with a torch that merely glows in pursuit of a woman, his sister, who has a flaming torch. Their house above is one, but it is divided into two parts into which they go when they are gone from sight. All through the winter the sun remains indoors; all through the summer she is out. Many of the glittering stars in the heavens are the spirits of their people. This is a common belief among primitive people the world over; it is even entertained by the southernmost people in the world, the Patagonians.

Ursa Major, the 'Big Dipper,' to the Eskimos is seven reindeer feeding on the hills of heaven. The Pleiades, the 'Seven Sisters,' is a team of dogs in pursuit of a bear. The three stars in Orion's Belt are three steps cut in the face of a glacier. Arcturus, ever revolving about the horizon, is their clock or guiding star, by which they know how long they have been traveling and how long they have slept. There is a land beyond to which we go when through with this life, and there we shall live much as we are living here.

That is why, when one dies, a man's hunting outfit is carried to the grave; that is why some of his dogs are strangled, for he will need them in the world beyond. A woman's needle, thimble, thread, and knife are placed with her, or in a small grave at her feet, as are also her cooking-pots – but the last are broken to release the spirits, which go on into the next world to be with their mistress and to be used in the world above.

They tried to tell me much more, and much that I could not understand, of their customs and ways and the life beyond as we sat in the igdloo at the edge of the Polar Sea and listened nightly for Tornarsuit, the evil spirits of the North. Torngak, the greatest of them all, was heard repeatedly. He was in the moaning of the winds, in the rush of drift, in the cracking of the sea ice. He stood at our door for hours, and even in the snow passage, listening, always listening. We could hear him as he crept softly up over the dome of our snow house so that he might peer through the small four-inch hole in the top. Twice Eging-wa, with loaded rifle, dropped through the hole in the floor, stole quietly to the end of the snow passage and fired into the darkness. Yes, he was there! he is always in such places when one is far from home, and it is dark, and the wind blows, and it is cold.

There are other spirits moaning in the tidal cracks, the souls of those who perished in kayaks, who were lost at sea, who paddled away to the hunting grounds, but have never returned. All sounds, signs, fatalities, deaths are attributed to supernatural agencies. We should expect to find such superstitions and beliefs among a people living in such a hostile environment, where the cause and meaning of dreams, echoes, the laws of sound, reflection, refraction, physical forces, physical processes, and a multitude of other things are entirely unknown. Naturally intelligent they have wondered. But lacking even the rudiments of learning, they are lost in a maze of speculation and superstition. Their only resource is the propitiation of the spirits or an appeal to their Angekok, their medicine man, who, inspired by the Gods, uses his powers for good and sometimes for evil. Through long periods of fasting, which leads to mental disturbance, he has acquired a power which is the envy of all. As among many primitive peoples in other parts of the world, illness is looked upon as the presence of an evil spirit within the body which must be expelled. This is done by beating a small drum, shouting, gesticulating, and making frightful faces. Since the Angekok has the power to expel evil spirits he has the power to summon them, and is, therefore, greatly feared. With the years, this power is being lost. Men are not as they were.

Here, in constant communion with four Eskimos, I had a favorable opportunity for a study of the Eskimo language which philologists assert to be one of the most difficult in the world. After twenty-three years of association with five different Eskimo tribes, I can readily believe that this is the case. Any knowledge of the Eskimo language possessed by any man who has not spent at least ten years with the Innuit is almost wholly pretentious. Moravian missionaries who have spent thirty and even forty years with the Eskimos have told me that they are still learning the language. I can testify to this – Latin, Greek, French, and German are comparatively simple.

When I started North on my first trip, someone casually remarked to me that there were but a few words in the Eskimo tongue, as their possessions were so few – a logical conclusion, perhaps. It was possible that there might be five hundred words, certainly not a thousand. I have now arranged alphabetically and spelled phonetically three thousand and thirty-seven words, and I know that there are many to be added.

'Kanok atinga?' is the key to the language for the beginner, for the use of this phrase enables him to learn the Eskimo word for anything which may be seen and which can be designated with the pointed finger. 'Kanok' is the interrogative 'what?' 'Atinga' its name. So 'Kanok atinga?' was in daily use.

But we soon learned this: each word is exact, decisive, fully expressive. Where we are indefinite and must resort to several words fully to cover our meaning, one word of Eskimo expresses all. The incorrect use of new words led to many a laughable and, at times, embarrassing situation.

As I lay back in bed one day in the snow house, to my surprise I could see stars through a hole in the roof. The heat rising from our stove had melted through one of the snow blocks. I suggested to Eging-wa that he repair the damage by putting in a new block. After he had disappeared through the hole in the floor – all doors are in the floor – I turned to Too-cum-ma, his wife, and pointing to the hole asked, 'what do you call that?' Her answer sounded like 'Oop-sha-sul-nee-eye.' Here was one more word for my new Eskimo dictionary, the word for hole.

A few days later, as I was entering the house by way of the lone snow entrance, which is also used as a storehouse, I caught a leg of my bearskin pants on the iron strapping of a box, tearing a hole some six inches in length. Here was my first opportunity to make use of my recently acquired word. I asked the girl to get her needle and thread and sew up the hole in my bearskin pants. She fell back on the bed and began to laugh. She whispered to In-you-wah-o, and they both laughed and continued to do so for some time. When the laughter had subsided, I ventured to inquire what it was all about.

It was the usual reply: 'You used the wrong word. You asked me to get my needle and thread and sew up the snow hole in the roof of your bearskin pants!'

A hole in a pair of bearskin pants was quite different from a hole in the roof of the house. The word for a hole in skin, in wood, in iron, in ivory, in the ground, in snow – all were utterly different.

'Now, listen,' I said. 'I do not want any of these; I simply want to learn the word for hole.'

After thinking for a moment, she replied:

'We have no word for hole in the language. If it is a hole, it must be in something, or it would not be a hole.'

In other words, there is a definite word for every kind of hole under the sun. I started a new Eskimo dictionary that night.

On Wednesday, December 9th, one of the women, in the midst of laughter, song, and story, heard the faint snapping of a whip. As we had every reason to believe that there were no dog teams within ninety miles of us, we thought the sound was merely her imagination. But she said again, 'Nar-la!' (Listen!) Sure enough, we could hear it now, far out on the sea ice, heading for the provision cache at the end of the Point. Poo-ad-loo-na and Ah-wa-ting-wa had been sent by Commander Peary to see us home. We learned by letter that Borup and his Eskimos were at Sail

Harbor, transporting supplies; that all the other divisions were in the field hunting, Henson in Clements Markham Inlet, Goodsell at Black Cliffs Bay, and Bartlett at Lake Hazen – all this in spite of darkness, wind, and cold.

Next day the four men made a final determined hunt for musk-oxen. My men had tried repeatedly during the past month, but had failed to see a living thing. The hunters were back in eight hours, eyes badly inflamed by wind and stinging drift, reporting that land work was impossible on account of the lack of snow, 'rocks and sand everywhere.'

The statement that in the Far North there is not so much snow on the level as in the New England States seems almost incredible, yet it is a fact. When it snows, there is usually a strong wind which sweeps the snow over the hills and flat plains and on into valleys and sheltered places. Because of the small amount of open water, the source of moisture in the air, there is a proportionately small amount of snowfall. We always dreaded a crossing, a route which leads from sea or bay or inlet ice over a neck of land to the sea ice beyond. Then we strip for action, prepared to push heavy sledges over bare ground, unless we can find a sheltered valley which often serves as a catchbasin for wind-driven snows. Then all is well!

In order to obtain better results, if possible, on December 12th we took a tidal observation every five minutes for fifteen hours. With watch in the palm of the hand to keep it from freezing, and the hand inside of a polar bearskin mitten, we lay on our breasts in front of the water hole, chipping, chipping with the knife, and snapping our feet together at forty and the next day at forty-five below zero. To cheer us up, we hummed the old familiar songs and rambled in our thoughts to our homes and friends two thousand miles south.

It was cold work; and yet, strange to say, I hated to leave our snow igdloo snuggling up under the big black cliff on the northern shores of Grant Land. It had been a unique experience to live so long in darkness and desolation, and with a primitive people in a primitive way. We had thoroughly enjoyed associating with these people, now our friends, and had learned much to compare with the so-called progress of man. I had gained a new perspective.

Finally, the day came when the last observation had been taken and recorded in our tidal book. The lights in the igd-loo were extinguished. One by one, we dropped through the hole in the floor, crawled through the long passageway leading to the open air, and looked east toward home.

The sledges were packed, and off the dogs went with a rush over the rolling glacial fringe to the more level sea ice beyond. I was curious to know how the Eskimos would keep their course for Cape Colan, thirty miles away. On our right hand, as we traveled east, we could see the faint outlines of the great white hills which roughly paralleled our course. I noted that they preferred to take a direct course instead of following the irregularities of the coastline, so I asked Eging-wa what he was heading for. He pointed to a star on the horizon.

I recalled the story of the sailor who steered by a star and fell asleep to find, on wakening, the star over the stern of the ship. He concluded that he had passed it! If my Eskimos followed that star which was revolving about the horizon one degree every four minutes, as all stars do, we would run ashore, and eventually be back on our course and then out toward the North Pole. Eging-wa knew this, and kept it ever on his right, *increasingly as we traveled*. Not a bad method of keeping a course by dead reckoning!

That night we had our first experience with a piblockto dog. What this disease really is we do not know, but it would appear to be some form of rabies, of which there are two in the Far North, and this particular form is fatal. The first noticeable symptom is restlessness, which is followed by whining, by a peculiar muffled bark (most unusual for an Eskimo dog), bloodshot eyes, dropping of the lower jaw, drooling at the lips, and trembling. The affected dog runs amuck through the village, attacking any and all dogs in sight, until it is set upon by the pack and almost eaten alive.

One can safely handle his own dog, even when it is in this condition. I have frequently taken an afflicted dog in my arms and carried him to a safe or more comfortable place; have stroked his head until he was apparently asleep. I have never known of a man, woman, or child in North Greenland to be bitten by a 'mad' dog. One of my dogs was attacked and severely bitten on a certain day and hour, which I recorded in a notebook. The incubation period in this particular case was fifty-one days. The dog died in thirty hours.

The Eskimos say that the same malady is also common among the wolves, white and blue foxes, and even Arctic hare. I have had a blue fox deliberately jump into the middle of my ten dogs. It may have been suicide, but he must have had something serious the matter, if not piblockto. A white fox entered the igd-loo of one of my native dog-drivers and grabbed him by the back of the leg. A clear case of piblockto.

As we traveled along that night, I heard a commotion in one of the teams and, later, saw a dog go by me in the darkness with dragging trace. I knew instantly that his driver had cut him loose. Within a few minutes the poor demented thing was back, charging into team after team, and being terribly mauled and bitten, until pulled out of the fray by the hind leg and driven again into the darkness with the rawhide whips.

I suggested to Eging-wa that he shoot the dog to put him out of his misery. Pointing to a star and moving his hand to the right, he replied, 'When the star is there, the dog will die.' I learned later that for some reason or other there is a decided aversion to shooting a dog or even drawing blood. It is something more than economy of ammunition. When necessity calls for it, and this is so even with small polar bears, they strangle by tying a tight cord about the neck.

Our piblockto dog finally disappeared, but Jack, my sailor, was not quite sure that this particular dog would not be back. With hands gripping the upstanders of the sledge he stepped along gingerly, peering into the darkness in all directions. Eging-wa, a practical joker, did not fail to notice this. Gradually, he dropped back on the trail, stole quietly up behind our unsuspecting nervous wreck and, with a terrifying growl, grabbed him by the seat of the pants! Jack did not look or think; he went, with a 'My God!' scrambling over the upstanders to the top of the load, while the two women burst into roars of laughter.

A long delightful tramp of twelve hours and a quarter through the starlight brought us to the snow house at Cape Colan. The next march took us to Porter Bay, which we reached at half-past one in the morning.

A piece of sweet chocolate lying in the middle of the snow bed in one of the igd-loos was like manna in the desert to me. Interpreted in the language of the trail, I knew this to be a 'Hello, Mac,' from George Borup.

A combination of rough ice and darkness on December 16th, almost the middle of the long night, made rather a hard day of it. When I went up to the Arctic I had never visualized myself as sledging by the light of a lantern! We camped at Cape Richardson in a good snow house.

Thursday, the seventeenth, our forty-first day from the ship, was overcast and snowing. We had to keep close to our light or be lost in the dark. After six hours and a half of plugging on, stumbling, and now and then falling into an unseen hole, we suddenly saw a light, and then a great black object – the *Roosevelt*. As usual her rail was lined with faces anxious to welcome the new-comers and learn the news.

CHAPTER 15

✳

ARCTIC TECHNIQUE

After such a period in the field, ship's food invariably causes indigestion. The quality is not responsible – it is the quantity consumed, and the variety – everything goes. And how a man gains in weight! A pound a day for several days is not uncommon, even two pounds a day have been recorded.

It seemed good to be back. All the boys were at home – Bartlett, Marvin, Borup, Goodsell, Henson – and all had something of interest to tell. Among the two hundred and more dogs, I found my pets, who were accustomed to walk with me over the hills daily. They wagged their tails vigorously, bending their bodies in semicircles to manifest their pleasure.

December 21st, or the 22d, is known as the winter solstice, the day when the sun is at its farthest south. Consequently, it was our darkest day. It was our coldest up to date, fifty-three degrees below zero, and it happened to be clear, as we hoped it would be. There was twilight in the south, as there should be. This is by far the most important day in the North, for it marks the turning-point of the sun. Commander Peary ordered the men to fire a salute, and issued orders to the cook to give the Eskimos a banquet of musk-ox, biscuit, and coffee. Hearing that the sun was returning, one of the Eskimos, who had imbibed too freely of gin and water, started south over the hills to meet it. They brought him back with a frozen hand.

Christmas Day was not forgotten and was observed happily. At the Commander's request, I arranged a program of sports to be held on the flat stretch of ice between the ship and the shore. Fortunately it was comparatively warm – twenty-one below zero. Probably it was the coldest track meet ever held, and without a doubt the most northern. Here is the program:

2.00 P.M.

50 Yard Dash

First Heat	Eskimo Children
Second Heat	Eskimo Women
Third Heat	Eskimo Men
Fourth Heat	White Men

2.30 P.M.

Tug of War

Men Aft

vs.

Men Forward

3.00 P.M.

Distribution of food and presents to Eskimos

4.00 P.M.

Dinner

5.00 P.M.

Throwing Dice

for Prizes

8.00 P.M.

Finger Pulling

Back Pulling

Head Pulling

Boxing

9.00 P.M.

Grand Concert on Graphophone by

Chief Steward Percy

10.00 P.M.
Flashlight Picture of Group
by
George Borup

10.30 P.M.
Pipes – Cigars

GOOD NIGHT

During the morning I was busy in the tidal igd-loo with observations, Captain Bartlett and George Borup helped me in every way. When I came out of the igd-loo at two o'clock the race-course looked like Broadway – there were fifteen lanterns. Everyone was enthusiastic and ready to go.

The races were hotly contested, and the race between the women who carried their babies on their backs was distinctly amusing. Those little black-eyed tots, peering from the sealskin hoods over their mother's shoulders, must have thought their parents had gone plumb crazy as they swept down the lighted line to the finish. If a mother had stumbled, her baby would have won the race!

The dash for the Eskimo men was won by Sig-loo, who later accompanied Peary to the Pole. Since then he has lost both feet, in sliding over the face of a glacier down into a mass of rough rock. Ross Marvin easily finished first in the white man's race.

We in the after cabin were sure of the tug-of-war with George Wardwell, our big engineer, two hundred and forty pounds, as anchor. Dr. Goodsell weighed two hundred and was a bull in strength. Captain Bob could pull off the side of the ship. Henson and Borup were light but good. We had the surprise of the day; we lost by six inches. In spite of their forced inactivity, the sailors were in fine physical condition, and, incidentally, a fine group of men. We had an exceptional crew. No happier body of men ever wintered in the Arctic.

A wonderful dinner of roast musk-ox, plum pudding, candy-decorated cake, and other good things followed. Our dining-room was decorated with the now historic American flag which waved at the North Pole and the flags of previous expeditions. Commander was at his best, always a most congenial table companion, always solicitous about our comfort and happiness. If ever a man was a father to his men, he was on his last expedition. All that I had ever heard to the contrary was entirely dispelled from my mind after living with him for fifteen months. Considering the cares, the worries, the strain, the responsibility, there must have been much more in the man than he ever let us know.

On Christmas night, I wrote in my journal:

Our first Christmas in the Arctic has been a most enjoyable one, plenty of everything, even good feeling and good cheer, which are of far more importance than an abundance of good food. We are happy. With us the 'dreaded Arctic night' does not exist. The days are all too short for what we would like to do. The sun has not even been missed. It will be welcome when it comes, but it is not essential to our happiness, or, thus far, to our good health. I think we are all, with one exception, in better physical condition than we were when we left New York – heavier, healthier, and as happy as can be, all eagerly looking forward to the more serious work on the Polar Sea.

With Christmas over, our out-of-door work continued. Captain Bob, Borup, and Goodsell received their instructions the next day. The captain was to cross Robeson Channel and hunt musk-oxen in Greenland. George was to go inland to hunt caribou in the Lake Hazen region. Goodsell was to go to Clements Markham Inlet to hunt anything and everything. Winter and darkness meant nothing to Commander Peary or his work.

On the twenty-ninth Marvin and Captain Bob got away for Greenland, the former to take a series of tidal observations at Cape Bryant to supplement those I had taken at Cape Columbia. Judging by the sound of the ice, as it crunched and ground just outside of us, such a trip was the height of folly, but we knew that they would make it, and have a good time doing it.

Borup and the doctor left on the last day of the year. That New Year's Eve was to be remembered. It was forty-eight below zero, but who minds in bright moonlight? They would have a wonderful time! And they did.

Their camp was located on a plateau at an altitude of two thousand feet. With four oil stoves going full speed ahead, the thermometer registered seventeen below on the bed platform inside of the igd-loo. George declared that the machine broke when he stuck it outside.

They herded Arctic hares in the moonlight almost as if they were sheep. George claimed that Panikpa got six with one shot, by lying on his breast in the snow and firing through the huddled mass with a heavy .40-82 rifle. The hunters were lost in a blizzard only eight hundred yards from their igd-loo. To build a shelter to keep from freezing, they were compelled to stamp out blocks of snow with their feet, for they had left their snow knives in their snow house.

Meanwhile all were busy on the *Roosevelt* in preparing for the great work. Commander Peary knew that every detail of his equipment must receive the most careful attention if he were to win out after so many failures through so many years.

The sturdy *Roosevelt* had done her part of the work. That much could be crossed off the list. Personnel was the next great consideration. Without good help Commander Peary could do nothing. Fortunately, on this last expedition, he had many of his Old Guard with him. He had studied their whims, their weaknesses, their strong points. Unless something unforeseen happened, or some undue influences were brought to bear, he knew that he could depend on them to the limit.

The next consideration was the food-supply. Man can do nothing without good food, which means energy, which means go. Commander Peary had read, he had studied, he had tested in his long experience practically everything recommended by fellow-explorers. Jellies, jams, cheese, fish powder, erbswurst, acidic fruits, chocolate, malted milk, beef cubes, and concentrated patent foods – all had been consigned to the ash barrel. He was down to earth, to three things only as necessary for life and strength for at least four months.

If Peary were not back in that time, he would not need food; he would never come back. No man returns from the Polar Sea after June 1st. Explorers who talked glibly of flying over the Pole in aeroplanes and of walking back to Cape Columbia or Morris Jesup, if they were forced to land on the Polar Sea, have learned. Little did they know the real character of this mass of drift ice. Amundsen learned later after he was forced to live on it for a month and spend the time in building a runway for his plane. And he was lucky.

The daily ration, as I have indicated, was to consist of sixteen ounces of biscuits, sixteen ounces of pemmican, four ounces of condensed milk, and one-half an ounce of compressed tea per man. Here were the proteins, fats, and carbohydrates of a balanced ration as determined by science.

The biscuits, each weighing one ounce to facilitate rationing, were packed in hermetically sealed rectangular tins of twenty-five pounds weight. To ensure compact packing, the length of the box corresponded to the width of the sledge. The pemmican, about thirty thousand pounds in all, was packed in exceptionally strong eight-pound tins, which were so scored that when the tin was cut from the contents there remained an eight-pound block of frozen food, each pound plainly indicated and so easily rationed.

There were to be eight dogs on each sledge, so there was one can of pemmican per team per day. One glance at a sledge told us the possible number of days of travel. Whereas the men required thirty-two ounces of protein, fat, and carbohydrates for such strenuous work, the dogs needed but sixteen, an amount proportionate to the respective weights. A strong Eskimo dog weighs about eighty-five pounds. Our heaviest dog weighed one hundred and twenty-five pounds. He was too heavy for good work and was ordered back early in the game.

The next item in the equipment was the clothing. Expeditions have differed as widely in dress as they have in food. The most pathetic picture to me in all Arctic or Antarctic work is that of Scott and his men standing at the South Pole – pathetic for two reasons. First, although they had won the Great Prize, they had lost it; second, they were so poorly clothed, a natural result of their inexperience.

For cold work, with the temperatures between forty and eighty degrees below zero, there is absolutely no choice between woolens, windproofs, or fabric of any kind, and fur, Nature's gift to animals for their protection against extreme temperatures. The Eskimo has used it for centuries, and continues to use it now, fully appreciating its superiority over any manufacture of civilized man. With use there must be knowledge of how to wear it, and this knowledge must be gained from the Eskimo. Ignorance of this has cost many, many men dearly, in toll of suffering and failure. Woolens permit an excessive loss of heat and energy through radiation; windproofs frost up and freeze stiff. They are both out of the question for effective and successful work on journeys of a thousand or more miles in February and March. During the past twenty years I have tried a variety of store clothes and have offered them to my men as possibly superior to Eskimo clothing. They were always discarded early in the game.

Commander Peary provided each man with the following clothes:

1. One blanket shirt with hood for head protection, this to be worn without covering in excessively hard labor such as hewing ice for the improvement of a sledge road; when handling a heavy sledge through a broken ice field and over pressure ridges, and in ascending glaciers.

2. One sheepskin coat similar in construction for ordinary sledge work.

3. One caribou-skin coat to be exchanged for the sheepskin at the end of the day's march, a much warmer garment when sleeping in the snow house at night.

4. One pair of polar bearskin pants, strong, durable, warm.

5. One pair of bearskin boots, made from the skin of the forelegs, with heavy square flipper soles, for extremely cold weather.

6. One pair of caribou-skin boots.

7. One pair of sealskin boots.

8. Three pairs of sheepskin or hareskin stockings, all to be worn with a thick padding of grass in the bottom of the boot – the real secret of warm feet.

9. Underneath all a light woolen union suit to absorb the moisture of the body.

With a pair of dark sun glasses to prevent snow blindness, the above constituted our wearing apparel. In effectiveness and economy of space, no expedition has ever been so well equipped to withstand the rigors of the North. Read the accounts of previous expeditions and read of their struggles with frozen boots, clothing, sleeping-bags – they seem like a labor of Hercules.

The type and construction of the sledge cannot receive too much thought and attention. Peary had now been going North for over twenty years and had made a careful study of each and every type of sledge. To suggest, as a recent writer has, that he should have used the Hudson Bay type of sledge because it is only half so heavy, is to exhibit a complete lack of knowledge of sledging or of Polar ice. It is true that Amundsen started toward the South Pole with sledges as heavy as those Peary used, and at once halved their weight when *he saw the conditions of the southern ice.* Sledging over sea ice and land ice are not comparable. Some Alaskan dog-drivers criticized the Peary sledge, but they exhibited as great a lack of knowledge of the ice of the Polar Sea as the stay-at-home critics. Peary knew all sledges, and he also knew from actual experience the exact conditions they would have to meet. It is absurd to suggest criticism of Peary on this point when he had been learning and experimenting for more years than his critics had been reading about the subject. The facts about the Polar ice are roughly as follows:

The Polar Sea is not a pond or a big lake. It is a great crushing, grinding, moving field of drift ice, at rest neither winter nor summer. As the ice forms, it slowly moves from the northern shores of Siberia across the top of the world to the waters of the North Atlantic, an endless stream of ice pouring southward between Spitzbergen and Greenland. As a result of this motion we have pressure incalculable, which causes the enormous pressure ridges which rise to a height of fifty and sixty feet, a chaotic mass of ice blocks varying in size from mush to a small house. This motion is also the cause of the so-called leads, stretches of open water, which are even more effective as barriers than pressure ridges, which can be surmounted by dint of hard work.

If the sea ice were smooth, as it is in Labrador, or as level as the Great Ice Cap of Greenland, a toboggan could be used successfully. In fact, in traveling inland on his first trip across Greenland in 1892, Commander Peary made a sledge out of two skis which weighed twelve pounds and carried two hundred pounds. Later, he built one of fifty pounds, which, by actual test, carried *one thousand pounds.* But such a sledge would not last an hour when drawn by a team of eight strong dogs through, on, and over the rough sea ice between Cape Columbia and the Pole.

Nor is the openwork sledge, as used in Alaska, or by Shackleton and Scott, adapted for Polar Sea work. The struts, oftentimes inclined at a sharp angle, when going through rough ice not only interfere seriously with the progress of the sledge, but even bring it to a sudden stop, which is a severe strain on harnesses, traces, dogs, and men. At low temperatures a projecting spur of ice can completely wreck a rapidly traveling sledge; and it does travel rapidly when, freed from dogs, it is permitted to bound and leap full loaded from the summit of a high pressure ridge. The solid-sided sledge is to be preferred when traveling through and over rough ice. To economize on weight, naturally one would select the strut sledge for level going.

The latest model of the Peary sledge was twelve feet long, two feet wide, and seven inches high, with a strong blunt nose to resist shock, with a knockabout bow for rough work. Bound with rawhide to give elasticity and flexibility, the whole structure was rendered immune to shock and less liable to breakage. Many northern men declare that these qualities, so much desired in every wooden sledge, can only be attained by the use of rawhide lashing. After experimenting for several years, I am inclined to believe that an all-steel sledge is superior in many ways to one made of wood. It certainly can be built much lighter in weight and still possess the same desirable qualities.

✳

Theorists have shown as great lack of appreciation of the difficulties and conditions of the Polar Sea as the Peary critics. One actually asked Commander Peary why it had not occurred to him to use skates! Another engineer (?) suggested that he set up a portable sawmill on the shore of the Arctic Ocean; saw out the necessary building material and construct a protecting shed for his men and dogs to the Pole. The correspondent stated that in this way trains at certain places in the Far West are protected from terrific snowstorms. It would not be necessary to consider food as a part of the equipment, no, not even dogs and sledges, since it would be a simple matter to pipe hot soup to the men three times a day!

I received a beautifully drawn set of blue-print plans for an attack on the Pole, with the request that I do my best to interest Commander Peary in this new method. A specially constructed 'knock-down' house was to be taken into the North and placed on the ice. This house, about ten by twelve feet in measurement, contained a set of tanks filled with hydrogen gas. In the center of the room was a small oil engine which caused a heavy chain loop to revolve out through the front window, to travel along the surface of the ice – really a tractor – and in through the rear window. When the moment came for the departure of this promising expedition, the valves of the tanks were to be opened; the gas was to escape by tubes leading through a hole into a balloon deflated and neatly folded upon the roof, which, when sufficiently buoyant, would gently lift the whole structure from the surface of the ice, but only a few feet. The engine would then do its work; the result would be progress, and progress eventually would mean grasping the three-hundred-year-old prize! Two thousand dollars was an unbelievably low price to pay for success in such an important undertaking, but the man with the idea was not mercenary; he was inspired by patriotic motives only, and would sell at this low figure.

To my objection that this animate house might experience some difficulty in crossing the numerous leads of open water, he promptly replied that he had considered that point, and had succeeded in overcoming that difficulty by installing extra gas tanks. The additional contents of one, possibly of two, would cause this house of refuge to jump the lead! To my objection that if we encountered a real gale, the whole outfit might go

The Peary type of sledge
Designed for the rough ice of the Polar Sea

skipping and jumping like a jack-rabbit down into Canada, he called my attention to the 'compressor' which I had failed to notice tucked away in one corner of our 'very comfortable quarters.' It was a simple matter to deflate the bag, fold it up, anchor ship, go to bed, and await more favorable weather – a combination flying-tractor-house de luxe!

As far as I can determine, the Peary expeditions were the first to attempt Arctic work without the use of sleeping-bags, a radical departure from the universal custom. A good sleeping-bag weighs from twelve to twenty pounds, and, in the hands of an inexperienced man, will easily double its weight. The novice inevitably persists in getting into his bag with coat, pants, boots, and even his cap on! Every ounce of moisture carried into the bag is condensed into ice, and, during cold weather, remains there unless the bag is repeatedly turned inside out, beaten with a stick, and placed in the sun.

Sledging on the Polar Sea

Clothed as we were with Peary, we were really walking in our sleeping-bag, which was always ready for use. Around the bottom of our caribou-skin 'kool-e-tah,' or hooded coat, there was a series of rawhide loops through which ran a rawhide drawstring. At night we drew this up tightly around our hips and down between our thighs, pulled our arms out of the sleeves and in on our warm bodies, threw one empty sleeve over the face to prevent it from freezing, and there we were in a sleeping-bag. We were very comfortable, too, if we managed to keep dry during the day.

For the weight of the sleeping-bag on the sledge, Commander Peary substituted sixteen pounds of pemmican, or two days more of travel for the dogs. Conditions and rate of travel might be such that these two additional days might place him at the Pole. The elimination of weight is the great problem on every hard Polar trip; for every pound saved in weight of equipment results in so many more pounds of food and so many more miles toward one's objective.

A stove for Arctic work should be so designed that one obtains the maximum amount of heat for the minimum expenditure of fuel. Commander Peary had experimented with standard oil stoves, and with various new-fangled camp cookers, all of which seem to work well at home, but rarely well in the North. With one of the latter he was almost painfully patient. It had every chance to make good. He was hungry – one always was on the trail – and his fingers in contact with cold metal were white with cold. He jerked his neck out of his collar; his face twitched a bit. Finally, he grabbed the stove by one of its legs, and, whirling it around his head, threw it with all his might far off in the rough ice.

Arctic men generally consider that the so-called Primus stove is the most satisfactory for their work. It is small, compact, light in weight, fast, and economical in its consumption of fuel. With about eight ounces of fuel and an improved ice pot, it will convert ice into a gallon of boiling water in about twenty minutes when the temperature is even as low as fifty below zero. Yet Peary improved even on this. He designed a stove which, with six ounces of fuel, would convert ice into boiling water in nine minutes. We were asleep and resting for the arduous work of the morrow when men of other expeditions were sitting, cold, tired, hungry, around a sputtering, smoking contraption.

We had one unreasonable and selfish objection to this invention – the Peary stove went out in nine minutes. After a long hard cold day and the igd-loo was built, our dogs fed, and the door sealed, we yearned for just a little crumb of comfort, for something warm. It seemed a bit of Heaven to place the stiff, cold, frostbitten hands and horny fingers on the warm cylinder of the only nine-minute stove. But it was the perfection of efficiency, and we had not come on the trip to keep warm.

In 1906 Peary failed mainly because a six-day gale separated him from his men and from his supplies which had been left on the surface of the sea ice. It had been planned that these supplies should be sledged forward by the supporting parties and used upon his return trip. This disastrous and

almost fatal experience convinced Peary that his former plan was impracticable, and that he must keep his supporting parties together with him.

A supporting party is a division of men, dogs, and sledges, feeding the
leader, his own men, and dogs, in order that he may conserve his own supplies for the last stages of his journey. The number of Peary's parties must
depend upon the distance to be covered, the amount of food to be consumed, and the *probable* rate of travel per day over the ice of the Polar
Sea. The last is a most uncertain factor, since conditions vary from day to
day, from week to week, and from year to year. The real purpose and value
of a supporting party is to advance the base of supplies nearer one's objective, and thus lessen the danger of starvation, if held up by open water, or
by a rate of travel, which, owing to unusual conditions, might be below
the average.

As a result of his experience, Peary had decided upon five supporting
parties under the command of Borup, Goodsell, Marvin, Bartlett, and
myself. Each party was to feed the main party for five days and, when no
longer needed, to return to the ship. When the Commander reached the
Pole, if he succeeded in getting that far, he would have ample food on his
own sledges for the return trip.

Each division was to be under the command of a white man and was to
be outfitted completely as a self-supporting and independent unit. That is,
each was to carry its .44 Winchester rifle, to ensure getting game along the
shore in the event of separation from the main party. Each had its own
cooking outfit, its snowshoes, its snow knives for building igd-loos, and
each its 'ah-wa-tak,' or sealskin float, to be inflated and placed beneath
the sledges in the event of open water cutting off the retreat later in the
season. Every possible emergency seemed to have been considered and
every precaution taken against disaster.

CHAPTER 16

✳

PLANNING FOR THE DASH

Although the sun was not to return to the ship until March 1st, Commander decided to begin his attack on February 15th. The twilight days were short, but a fair average mileage could be made to Cape Columbia, which was now really the base of the expedition. The men had been traveling all winter; they were as hard as nails, ready to go, in marked contrast to the condition of men who had been housed in a ship for months.

Captain Bartlett left the *Roosevelt* with his division on the fifteenth; Henson and I with five Eskimos followed on the eighteenth. My team, made up of dogs from everywhere and anywhere, even from Eagle Island, Maine, gave me no end of trouble. They were afraid of each other, of the Eskimos, and of the other dogs. Henson, an expert dog-driver, and his fast-traveling Eskimos, soon left me far behind struggling with a heavy load and a green team.

It has never been fully brought out that the Peary Expedition which reached the Pole differed from the expeditions of other explorers in that the dogs were *driven*, and by experts at that who with a turn of the wrist would avoid obstacles which would put a novice out of business for hours. There was no leading dogs here; no inexpert driving by men who had taken up the whip for the first time on the trip. Dog-driving is an art which requires long practice and years of experience. And it can be cruelly hard work when the sledge is heavily loaded and rough ice bars the way.

Once the technique of the long thirty-foot whip is mastered, one's troubles are largely diminished. It is not the pain of the lash that is the incentive for speed or work; it is the dog's knowledge of the fact that pain can and may be inflicted at any moment. There is far more snap and crack of whip and jargon of Eskimo words with no meaning whatever than real pain.

When your dogs realize that you are a novice, a tenderfoot – and it is almost ludicrous how quickly they sense it – wagging of tails and fun begins! I have seen a white man vigorously wave a tent pole to create a swishing and – hoped for – terrifying sound. I have seen him throw a snowshoe, which, on account of its crazy motion and attendant peculiar sound, really scared his dogs into action. The snow beater, a club of wood, is a favorite throwing stick. Borup nearly wore his out.

Snapping a long rawhide sealskin whip is much like casting a fly, but with the speed increased a hundred times. The motion is not so much from the shoulder as it is from the elbow, with a quick snap of the wrist. Realizing the importance of the whip, following my return from Cape Columbia I collected the bodies of eight dead dogs and harnessed them to a biscuit box near our tidal igd-loo where I was at work. Between observations I drove my dead team, all frozen stiff and propped up in the snow. It was good practice flicking the back of each dog. A perfect shot was signalized by a white puff, for I had sprinkled their bodies with snow.

The night of that eighteenth of February Koo-la-tinah and I slept in a snow house at Cape Richardson. We were forced to buck through drift the next day to overtake Henson and his men at Porter Bay. In the morning, according to Commander Peary's orders, we each added ten gallons of alcohol to our loads from the cache and sledged across the Fielden Peninsula and James Ross Bay and down into Sail Harbor, where we slept. At Cape Colan we added pemmican, oil, and biscuit enough to make up the maximum load of five hundred pounds, the weight the Commander planned for the Polar Sea.

This weight was not planned with a knowledge of the combined pulling strength of eight dogs, but with a knowledge of the *lifting and pushing power of a man*. With good going the dogs would run off with a thousand pounds and even more. It is known to a driver of a Smith Sound team that the dogs rarely or never start a loaded sledge. If the sledge is deep in the snow or in slush, or frozen down, or on the slope of a hill, one dog cannot do it, nor can five. All must pull together and keep pulling. If a dog sets into his collar and does not get results, he quits; and it would be a miracle if they all did their best simultaneously. If, on the other hand, the driver pushes on the upstanders and in this way starts the sledge, and keeps it going for only two or three seconds, the dogs all straighten out their traces and walk off with the load. I have gone into this in detail, because critics of Peary's work and particularly of his speeds have not understood this point – and it is an important one. The limit of weight of a loaded sledge upon the Polar Sea depends, not upon the number of dogs, but upon the strength, skill, and experience of the driver, for he is called upon to start the weight a dozen or more times a day, to wrestle with it to prevent it from being overturned, to struggle with it to prevent it from side-slipping into a deep hole, and to lift it bodily out of that hole if it does, while the dogs sit on the bank and wag their tails. This is no task for an amateur; an experienced skillful driver adds miles per hour to the speed of progress.

When a man claims that he had a thousand, fifteen hundred, or eighteen hundred pounds on his sledge, depend upon it that he was not working on the Polar Sea. He was traveling over a relatively smooth surface or downhill somewhere, if he was traveling at all. Twenty dogs on a sledge would not have increased distance or lessened labor in rough ice, but would have resulted in a waste of twelve pounds of food a day.

On the twenty-first we could see dog teams ahead of us on the trail and concluded that we must be overtaking the Goodsell division which had left the ship two days ahead of us. We slowed up in sight of Camp Crane at Cape Aldrich, in order that the men of the advance parties might occupy my big igd-loo built in November. On the twenty-second Bartlett's, Borup's, Goodsell's, Henson's, and my own divisions were all there in camp. It was a busy scene with men drying clothes, feeding dogs, repairing sledges, dog harnesses and equipment.

We now had orders to bring up everything on the trail to the base camp. Heavy wind and drift kept us in camp on the twenty-fourth, but

Borup and I doubled our teams and got away early on the twenty-fifth. Within a few hours we met Marvin and his men, then the doctor and his men, and, within another hour, the Commander himself. The great white hills must have wondered what it was all about to see twenty-six men and one hundred and fifty dogs passing and repassing.

We shook hands with the Commander and were surprised to hear him say, 'Borup, your face is frozen,' and, turning to me, 'MacMillan, your nose is gone.' It was there, but as hard as wood. We had no idea it was cold enough for that. In reply to our question, 'How cold is it?' he answered, in a matter-of-fact way, 'About fifty-seven below.'

The books tell us that when the finger, foot, nose, or ear is frozen, the Eskimo rubs it with snow. As a matter of fact this is never done. Snow at fifty-seven below zero would simply freeze the nose harder, if possible. The heat of the warm hand is the only remedy. If an Eskimo's feet are freezing, he puts them on his wife's stomach – a natural and comfortable warming-pan – not in a snow bank!

On February 26th the thermometer stood at fifty-eight below zero; on the twenty-seventh we never knew how cold it was. We were quite certain that it was the coldest of the year, since we could lie down on a snow bed and be comfortable at fifty-eight below, but that night no one slept. *The Eskimos declared that it was the coldest night they had ever experienced.* Whiskey and gin were frozen solid. Kerosene oil, water white, froze into white mush. Our condensed milk was as brittle as rock candy. Every exhalation was a surprisingly long stream of heavy vapor. Our hemp-woven traces were nearly as stiff as sticks. Our steel sledge runners had a peculiar singing sound as they traveled over the snow. Each dog team had its own smoke screen, the result of the exhalations of the eight dogs. And most striking of all, and something which I have never known to happen before or since, a few of the dogs lifted one foot and then another from the snow when at rest. It was cold, the absolute zero for us.

A certain scientist has written, 'Little bugs were cooled to minus three hundred and eighty degrees below zero, and, when warmed up slowly, they scampered merrily away!' Well they might! Think of it – a bug!! The comparison is rather humiliating to a would-be explorer. We were some time warming up, and we didn't scamper merrily away. We were glad to see the first streaks of dawn, for now we could get out and begin work, which meant warmth. Fortunately for the Arctic traveler, low temperatures only occur under a clear sky and when the air is perfectly still. As we journeyed on toward Cape Columbia clouds were gathering on the horizon, and, within a few hours, there was a noticeable change.

Years before I had read of how fatal it was for a man in such low temperatures to breathe through his mouth, and how 'Lung tissue was rapidly destroyed'; that one must carefully inhale through the nostrils. Theoretically this may be correct, but actual experience proves such statements to be based purely on the imagination. Throughout the trip I noticed that every man, white and native, breathed through his mouth when working on the trail. In fact it was absolutely necessary to do so for two reasons: first, a more rapid and needed supply of air is drawn through the mouth; second, no man preferred to suffer the excruciating pain of drawing a stream of frozen air through the small passages of the nose.

We were disillusioned on many things. One in particular was the generally accepted belief that to eat snow was injurious to the health and even at times fatal. This theory is not even theoretically sound. Snow is refreshing, but exasperatingly lacking in thirst-quenching qualities on account of the small content of water. At times I have thought that it even intensified the desire for more. Naturally, one would not put a handful of snow at sixty degrees below zero into a mouth which has a temperature of ninety-eight and four-tenths plus. That is, he would not do it twice. When working and perspiring freely, I have eaten snow all day long, but only after raising it to the melting point by holding it in the hollow of my hand inside of a bearskin mitten.

On the twenty-seventh, we were back at Camp Crane, where the most casual observer would have realized that something important was about to happen. Every man was on his toes; the very air was tense with expectancy. Loads were scattered, sledges were bottom up. Files were going, runners were being polished, harnesses mended, traces knotted, dogs exchanged, crossbars repaired, holes drilled, cracks lashed, whip stocks strengthened, new tips replaced. Commander was everywhere directing the work. The first division, the advance party, was to leave in the morning, a pioneer party under Captain Bartlett to select the trail and lay out the course toward the North Pole, four hundred and thirteen geographical miles away.

With the end of the day, with the work done, we gathered in Commander's snow igd-loo for advice, suggestions, and final instructions. It was the night before the Big Game, but a game almost ghostlike in comparison to that attended and spurred on by bands, banners, and cheering thousands. There would be no exultant yells to herald a good play, only simple quiet personal satisfaction, with an adversary ever on guard to take advantage of every misstep, every weakness, and every error in judgment.

We were fortunate in serving under a man who had played in more big games of this kind than any other man in the world. No other man in history had ever attempted the drift ice of the Polar Sea even twice. Once was convincing, and enough! Commander Peary repeatedly had returned to the attack. We could profit by his mistakes. He told us why he had failed. Admonition followed admonition, until we realized that anything might happen.

We were a serious five men as we gathered in Captain Bob's igd-loo late that evening, not because of impending hard work, extreme cold, frozen hands, faces, feet, open leads, thin ice, easterly drift, and a multitude of other things, but because each one realized that he was a link in the chain, a link upon which Commander Peary depended, and if that link snapped…

We all wanted him to win, as he deserved to do. Henson or anyone of his white assistants would have followed him straight to Siberia, had he wished it. We were to give him our best, perhaps our hands, our feet, or even our lives, as one did. Peary never knew how loyal we were.

We talked and reminisced of school and college days; wondered where we would meet on the Polar Sea, and whether we would all meet and return. A song of some kind seemed fitting. We sang all we knew, ending with one of the best:

Amici usque ad aras
Deep graven on each heart,
Shall be found unwavering true
When we from life depart.

✳

OUT OVER THE SEA ICE

On February 28th, a clear cloudless Sunday, with a temperature of fifty below zero, the Borup and Bartlett units started for the Polar Sea – the first change in the very carefully prearranged plan of attack. Two Eskimos were out of the game, one with a frosted heel and the other with a swollen knee. There were no substitutes. Their loads of five hundred pounds each must be carried. We were further handicapped at the very start by the death of six dogs from throat distemper. Because of this depletion in the ranks and a consequent shortage in the total amount of food needed by the men and dogs of the expedition, Commander Peary decided to have Borup accompany Bartlett for a few days and then return to land for additional loads.

No water could be seen from the summit of Cape Columbia. Everything seemed favorable. Commander declared conditions were vastly different and much improved over what they were in 1906. The next day, March 1st, the whole expedition, twenty-four men, nineteen sledges, and one hundred and thirty-three dogs, was on the move following the winding trail. Since the general movement of the sea ice was from west to east along the northern shores of Grant Land and Greenland, Commander Peary laid his course a little west of true north to counteract an easterly drift.

In his 'North Pole' our leader commented on the weather conditions that first morning as follows:

After breakfast, with the first glimmer of daylight, we got outside the igd-loo and looked about. The wind was whistling wildly around the eastern end of Independence Bluff; and the ice fields to the north, as well as all the lower part of the land, were invisible in that gray haze which every experienced Arctic traveler knows means vicious wind. A party less perfectly clothed than we were would have found conditions very trying that morning. Some parties would have considered the weather impossible for traveling, and would have gone back to their igd-loos.

Accustomed and hardened as we were to traveling through the winter night, and trained by the best man in the world in that particular line of work, no one gave a moment's consideration to drift, wind, or cold. Every man of the expedition had experienced conditions much more trying and much more severe.

With such a large party, with so many sledges and dogs, minor accidents are inevitable, especially in view of the fact that the sledges were carrying maximum loads and were encountering the hardest stretch of traveling of the whole trip – the area of the Polar Sea which adjoins the ice foot. This is an area generally of rough ice, for here an almost resistless force, millions of tons of ice driven on by wind, current, and tide, meets the wide thick collar of an immovable body, the land. The result is a crushing and piling up of immense ice blocks, between which and over which the dogs with their heavily loaded sledges must be driven.

Early in the game we who were in the rear met Kai-o-ta, one of Marvin's division, returning to land. His sledge was smashed beyond repair, and rather than attempt the impossible, he was heading for the land to obtain one of our spare ones left at Cape Columbia. Within an hour Kood-look-to was following his trail with upstanders ripped off and one side of the sledge split from stem to stern. The Polar Sea was not giving up its eon-old secrets without a struggle. We must expect that when attempting to do what man had failed to do for centuries.

According to Commander Peary's judgment, on this first march we covered about ten miles by twilight. The sun was still below the horizon during the twenty-four hours; there were no stars; astronomical observations were impossible.

Our snow igd-loos were up in an hour. The dogs were given their one pound of frozen pemmican each, and were sound asleep in a few minutes, round balls of fur in the snow, with their bushy tails a coverlet for eyes and nose. A few deft strokes with the snow knife fashioned a snow door for the entrance, and this was sealed with loose snow as tightly as any block in the structure. A peephole over the door to watch the dogs and a four-inch ventilating hole in the roof completed our shelter.

The six ounces of alcohol were poured into the aluminum cup of our stove, but it refused to burn. A lighted match went out as if it had been put into a cup of water. The Eskimos were plainly worried. It always did burn, why not now? An evil spirit must be in the igd-loo. Immediately Commander dispelled all fears by tearing up bits of paper and placing them upon the surface of the alcohol which refused to evaporate in such a low temperature. The heat from the burning paper completed the work, and in nine minutes we had hot tea.

March 2d is down as a hard day. My sledge was bottom up three times, once in a deep hole in rough ice. When that happens the dogs are a picture. They seem to take a special delight in sitting on the edge of the bank, cocking their heads, wagging their tails, rolling in the snow, and congratulating themselves that their work is done for the time being. And it is; there is nothing they can do. The sledge must be righted and pushed or lifted to the top of the bank, or the bank cut away with a pick-axe and a road made for traction. What could I have done if I had had a thousand pounds or more on my sledge?

About four o'clock I sighted the sledges ahead all assembled near a large pressure ridge and knew the delay was something more than rest. The hold-up was due to open water, a menace that always confronts one on the Polar Sea. There were great cracks in the ice field, ever opening and shutting, and extending until lost in the maze of pressure ridges, rubble ice, and snow hillocks. Jaws of a gigantic trap of incalculable power, the leads are utterly impossible to navigate.

The lead speaks decisively, 'Thus far and no farther.' It is a far more effective barrier than a pressure ridge, which can always be negotiated in time and with work. But if there is open water, why not use boats? If boats could be used profitably and economically, Commander Peary would have included them in his equipment. Consider our gross weight, with twenty-four men, one hundred and thirty-three dogs, nineteen sledges, and more than five tons of supplies and equipment. This was not a canvas canoe job. By the time a sufficiently substantial boat to do the job could be loaded, the lead might close. At fifty below zero she would become a mass of ice in one crossing. Any kind of boat would be a distinct handicap, a hindrance and a nuisance on sea ice such as that found between Grant Land and the Pole.

I am perfectly well aware of the fact that Nansen and Johansen on their retreat southward in the summer of 1896 used kayaks, that Captain Cagni of the Duke of the Abruzzi expedition used light canvas boats, but their problems were far different from ours.

In summer in comparatively warm temperatures, it is the custom of the Smith Sound native to place sealskins under and around their sledges, thus converting them into crude boats. Wide water cracks are sometimes crossed in this way. Such a method would be impracticable in the low temperatures of early spring, for the covering could be used but once. A sealskin dipped into the sea and then exposed to a temperature of forty and fifty below zero becomes like a sheet of metal. It can never be refolded, rolled, packed, or unpacked without breaking.

After such an experience with leads as Commander Peary had in 1906, he would certainly seriously consider a solution of the problem. Happily, he found one which proved to be entirely practical. He knew that on the trip out the temperatures would be low, and that all leads would either close within a few days or freeze over in eight hours or so with consequent less delay than by waiting for boat transport. His plans for crossing the leads concerned, therefore, only his retreat or return when, with the advancing season, there would be increased motion of the pans and far less freezing of open water. Each of his men, therefore, was equipped with a water-tight sealskin bag, really the whole skin of a little ringed seal, which could be inflated with the breath and then plugged tightly. This is an essential part of the Eskimo equipment for walrus-hunting. Their name for it is Awa-taq. If, on his return from the North, a lead were encountered, a raft could be made of two sledges to ensure stability, floats placed underneath, and away they would go for the opposite shore, using sledge crossbars, snowshoes, or a dozen other things for paddles. Thus Peary secured all the safety of a good boat at the cost of a weight of two pounds.

From an ice pinnacle, on the afternoon of the fourth of March, Commander Peary surveyed the lead which blocked us. After a careful investigation he gave orders to camp and await more favorable conditions.

Knowledge of the continental shelf is of value to geographers, as it indicates the real extent of land masses into the ocean. To establish this fact, in relation to the most northern point of all North America, it was Commander Peary's purpose to run a line of soundings northward whenever the opportunity presented itself. We were equipped with two reels of one thousand fathoms each of specially made piano wire, of a diameter of .028 of an inch, with a total weight of approximately sixty pounds. The three sounding leads, with an automatic clamshell mouth for biting out samples of the bottom, weighed fourteen pounds each, making the total weight of the outfit one hundred and three pounds.

With open water before us and a part of the day left, here was our first opportunity to use this apparatus. Hitching in the dogs, Marvin and I drove to the edge of the lead, about half a mile distant. Our sounding lead reached bottom at ninety-six fathoms, or five hundred and seventy-six feet. In attempting to lift the lead through the hole in the thin ice, I broke through and lay on my side in the water clutching the back of the sledge. With Marvin's help I was out in a few seconds.

The thermometer stood at forty below zero, and Marvin suggested that to prevent freezing, I walk or run back rather than ride. With my rapidly stiffening clothes this was somewhat difficult, but I finally made it. Commander was ready with my emergency bag of spare clothing. Within a few seconds he had stripped off both boots and had placed my now freezing feet up under his red flannel shirt against his bare breast. Such was the manner of the man.

The next morning, Wednesday, March 3d, I awoke Commander Peary at five o'clock at his request, in order to get an early start in an endeavor to make up the distance lost on Tuesday. A distant sound almost as of wind through the treetops could be heard plainly through the ventilating hole of the igd-loo. The lead was 'rafting'; that is, as it closed, the newly formed ice was being crushed to atoms, while broken sections were emerging bodily to the surface of the old ice, increasing its thickness tremendously. We were watching Nature building some of the many floebergs and small icebergs of the Polar Sea. For a long time the source of these bergs was a moot question, as there are no real tidewater glaciers throughout the whole periphery.

Pressure ridges reach a height of sixty feet and more, a chaotic intermingling of rubble ice piled in endless confusion. In a short time this is apparently a solid body, for, as is well known, when two blocks of ice are pressed together they become welded into one, even though hot water be poured over them. In time the interstices of the mass are filled with wind-blown snows, the rough edges are softened by spring and summer suns, and the whole mass takes on the form of a presentable small berg, born of the ocean, not of the land.

The new ice of the lead was so thin that we all crossed it on the run, a wave of ice attending every sledge. We failed to find the trail where it should have been on the opposite shore. Was the broken end to the right or the left? was the question. There was no way of telling, but it had to be found. We learned to our surprise that we had left the main pack and were now on a large pan separated from the main field by newly formed ice. Kai-o-ta was sent west over the bending surface, while Oo-tah went east on what seemed to us a vain quest.

In the meantime, the Eskimos had rapidly constructed a snow shelter and were now busily at work repairing two broken sledges. In a remarkably short time Kai-o-ta was seen mounted on the very top of a pressure ridge vigorously waving both arms. This was the prearranged signal that he had found the captain's trail far to the west. Our dogs were soon in action and carefully stepping over what appeared to be a sheet of rubber. It seemed incredible that it could possibly bear the weight of the dogs, sledges, and men, but it did. No fresh-water ice would ever buckle like that.

Now we were on the trail again and headed northward. Late that afternoon a keen-eyed Eskimo detected among the multitude of footprints in the snow a few pointing the other way. They all began to jabber and point, and the problem was quickly solved. Borup and three Eskimos were on their way back to Cape Columbia with the expectation of meeting the main party and receiving final instructions from Commander as to what to bring to us on the sea ice. By the faulting of the trail we had missed connections.

Immediately Commander ordered Marvin and old Kai-o-ta, an exceptionally good trail-finder, to throw off their loads and hurry backward along the trail to overtake the party. Because of the badly faulted trail and open water, they did not reach land until the evening of the second day, when they found Borup and the three Eskimos preparing to start forward again with full loads.

The Eskimos, however, were not a bit enthusiastic over what lay in store for them on the Polar Sea. They declared that with everything adrift, as it apparently was, it would be impossible to find Peary again. Borup and Marvin jollied them along, gave them a small drink each, to cheer them up, and, finally, all started back with three-quarter loads, the most important part of which was alcohol which the main party needed for the stoves.

Thursday, March 4th, said, 'You have gone far enough.' After working through several bad spots where sledge and dogs required constant attention and considerable pushing, the main party arrived at an abandoned igd-loo which showed obvious signs of recent use. We were rapidly overtaking the advance party. Early in the day black spots had been plainly visible against the white of the stretching field – spots which proved to be Bartlett and his men encamped at the edge of open water. And beyond was the so-called dreaded 'Big Lead' that must ever be reckoned with and conquered when in one of its mildest moods. Rather than take the risk of having the main party severed from the supporting party in the rear, the very thing which had happened in 1906, Commander Peary decided to remain here and go on with united forces.

Visions of rest and repair days were dispelled at five the next morning by Commander's voice at my igd-loo door asking me if I wanted to take a little journey back along the trail to pick up the provisions left by Borup and his three Eskimos.

With fast dogs and empty sledges we galloped back along the beaten trail toward the distant hills of Cape Columbia which showed like rounded white mounds above the ice horizon. We were living in a topsy-turvy world. Nothing was real save our dogs and sledges. A mound of ice apparently five or more miles ahead proved to be only a hundred yards distant. An empty tin on the trail looked like a distant dog team. A dropped mitten was some huge animal. Marvin related that, when on the northern shore of Grant Land in 1906, he carefully stalked a caribou, which suddenly spread its wings and flew away; it was an Arctic owl. A few years ago I was lost in a driving snowstorm and was about to dig into a snowbank for the night. Suddenly I descried three hundred yards distant two snow-covered sledges and sleeping dogs lying in the snow beside them. I jumped to the top of my loaded sledge, waved both arms vigorously, and yelled at the top of my voice. There was no response nor the slightest motion. Upon investigation I found a bit of stained snow about a hundred feet from where I stood.

The literature of the Arctic is full of such incidents. Here is a good illustration of the fact that we estimate distance by the size of a known object, and estimate the size of an object by a known distance. When these facts are lacking, our imagination runs riot.

Finally we reached the igd-loo, loaded up and headed back for our camp at the Big Lead. I felt absolutely fit, and I unwisely told my Eskimos to go on without me. Strapping on my snowshoes, I plodded on at certainly three miles an hour for six hours, reaching camp at 10 P.M., a solitary twilight walk out over a real sea of ice. Fortunately, there were no leads, no faulted trails, no blinding drift, no wind, any one of which I now know would have negatived my return.

Afterward I learned that Commander Peary had told my Eskimos what he thought of them for leaving a tenderfoot alone under such conditions – with not even a snow knife to build a shelter, no food, no matches, no spare boots which are vitally essential if one breaks through a lead. There was no sleep for him until I arrived, and then he told me a few things, but in a kindly and helpful way. The gist of his whole admonition was, 'Never let your Eskimos get away from you.'

Saturday, March 6th, was repair day in camp. I was wearing Commander's spare bearskin pants while mine were being relined with red flannel. The condition of the Big Lead, smoking in places like a steaming kettle, tempted us on; but it was imperative that Borup and Marvin and their Eskimos, who were in the rear with the much-needed fuel, should overtake the main party. Commander Peary nervously paced from igd-loo to igd-loo, first looking south, then to the north. Ahead was his goal; behind his men and supplies. Could he sever connection and succeed without them?

This enforced delay, the sight of the Big Lead, and the very apparent rapid movement of the ice, played havoc with the nerves of the Eskimos. They had an opportunity to compare notes and past experiences, and were plainly panicky. Some remembered their terrible experience of two years before. Some complained of lame shoulders, sore chests, frosted feet, of the fact that they had wives and children dependent upon them. Some were positive that they would never return. Others declared that we were drifting eastward and would never again reach Cape Columbia. A Field Day on the ice at fifty-nine below zero was a new experience for all of us! But it removed their thoughts, for a time at least, from the real and imaginary dangers of the Polar Sea.

How we watched that southern horizon, that white stretch for an unfamiliar object which would indicate that something was coming! How I sympathized with Peary as he paced, paced, back and forth. He was fifty-three years old; this was probably the last attempt of his life, and he was held up in good weather!

Sunday, March 7th, was an eventful day for my little division. The successful functioning of our alcohol stoves depended upon a good draught from the alcohol aluminum cup through the perforated bottom of a cylinder filled with cracked ice. A mixture of snow and ice blocked the 'chimney' so effectively that there was imperfect combustion, with the result that the igd-loo was filled with poisonous gas.

As we sat there on the edge of the snow bed awaiting our breakfast of hot tea, biscuit, and pemmican, my two Eskimos quietly tipped back on the bed platform, as we often did to rest from the labors of the day. But I suddenly discovered that they were both unconscious. They began to mutter and work their arms and legs. I kicked out the snow door and patiently awaited results. Frequent attempts at shaking and propping them up only resulted in an inanimate slump.

Within a few minutes I heard Commander's step and his query as to how I had spent the night. I replied that I was all right, but that both my natives had passed out! The quick popping of his head up through the igd-loo hole and the expression on his deeply lined, red, weather-beaten face would have been truly laughable if it had not been for the seriousness of the whole situation. It needed but an experience of this kind to become known generally for the Eskimos, highly wrought up as they were already by the fear of the Evil Spirits of the Polar Sea, to forget loyalty and leave in a body.

A groan from Tau-ching-wah caused a quick withdrawal of Commander's head to see if the coast was clear. It would never do for the Eskimos to hear that. I did my best to suppress the noise and hold the men down, while Commander stood on guard until they regained consciousness. When I reached the conclusion that their minds were receptive to a degree, I endeavored to make them believe that they had been asleep. How well I succeeded was shown by the fact that when I lighted the stove for supper they both dived for the door. Evidently one of the many devils was in the Peary stove.

A bad headache and a ringing in the ears were my only ill-effects from the occurrence. I wonder what would have happened if I had become unconscious.

In the fear that the disgruntled and the quitters might so influence the better men that the whole expedition might become disorganized, Commander Peary held court that night in his igd-loo. One by one the natives were called in and questioned, and, finally, the verdict and the drastic sentence! Two of the Eskimos were seen to be untangling their traces and hitching in their dogs.

How I pitied poor old Panikpa! In the past he had been one of Peary's best men. He had been loyal; had been through that fearful experience in 1906; had staggered homeward starving, with all dogs gone. He had done his best, as I knew, for he had traveled with me the past two days, suffering from a bad shoulder, and realized that he could not go far. Poo-ad-loo-na, brother of the now famous Oo-tah and smiling Eging-wa, deserved to be sent home. He was a quitter and a trouble-maker, as was, in fact, Oo-tah himself, Peary's 'iron man,' who professed to be an Angekok.

One could not help but sympathize with those two silent figures as they drove away in the half-light over the drift ice of the Polar Sea with a tin can for a lamp and a little food to sustain them until they reached land. Worse still, they had their orders not to stop at the ship, but to take their wives and children and leave immediately for home, some three hundred miles south. That they reached it in due time, living entirely on the country, is proof of the resourcefulness of a Smith Sound native.

March 9th, 10th, and 11th were days of impatient watching and waiting, with the lead opening and closing. Precious time was slipping away and with it opportunity for advance. Food was being eaten, fuel consumed, and not a mile was added to our credit. Commander Peary was worried. If he waited too long for the supporting party in the rear, which might never reach him, there was danger of his not gaining land on the return journey because of open water.

On the afternoon of the tenth we had our orders to build a conspicuous cairn of pemmican tins on the highest pinnacle of ice in the vicinity. That evening Commander wrote to Marvin:

4th camp, March 11, 1909. Have waited here 6 days. Can wait no longer. We are short of fuel. Push on with all possible speed to overtake us. Shall leave note at each camp. When near us rush light sledge and note of information ahead to overhaul us.

Expect send back Dr. and Eskimos 3 to 5 marches from here. He should meet you and give you information.

We go straight across the lead (E.S.E.)

There has been no lateral motion of the ice during 7 days. Only open and shut. *Do not camp here. Cross the Lead.* Feed full rations and speed your dogs.

It is *vital* you overtake us and give us fuel.

Leaving at 9 A.M., Thursday, March 11.

PEARY

P.S. On possibility you arrive too late to follow us, have asked Captain to take general material from your bags.

CHAPTER 18

✳

FROZEN FEET

With dogs fully rested and men ready to go, we were away with a jump and covered at least twelve miles over a fairly good surface, with the exception of a few bad places, rough ice and holes. They gave us a little trouble and plenty of hard work which left us with underclothing wringing wet, too wet for low temperatures. We had to shiver and shake and hug ourselves pretty well all night. We had a constant desire to get under something. It didn't seem a bit like 'retiring for the night' to drink a cup of tea and tip back on a snow bed.

There is no denying the fact that the white men suffered. As one said, 'A hell all right!' All were frostbitten. There were black patches on every face. The rims of our ears were black, where in desperation we had shoved back our hoods to cool our sweating heads and necks. A dull pain across the forehead generally brought us to our senses and caused us to cover up. The tips of our fingers and toes were horny, cracked, and bleeding. Our working coat, the sheepskin kool-e-tah, was a mass of ice about the face and around the bottom as a result of the condensation of the breath and the escape of warm moisture-laden air from the body. To get out of that sodden half-frozen garment and stand for a moment exposed to a wind at fifty degrees below zero, while putting on a dry deerskin coat for sleeping, was heavenly compared to the trying job in the morning of pulling the warm coat over the head and exchanging it for a mass of ice, snow, and wool, which absolutely refused to open up and conform to the shape of the day before.

To ensure warmth the diameter of the neck of a hooded coat is the diameter of the head. When that neck is frozen the head refuses to go up through into place. There is nothing to be done but pull and struggle with freezing fingers, and then to be patient for a few minutes until the heat of the head thaws and softens the aperture. Such an experience is the exception, yet I have seen it happen many and many a time on the trail, if the coat collar is the least bit small. And when it does, it always creates a laugh, and a good deal of banter from the rest of the party. Shut up, as one is in furs, it is a trifle difficult to reply.

Much of the suffering on such a trip is due to lack of knowledge and lack of experience. Commander Peary, Matt Henson, and their Eskimos never suffered as did Captain Bartlett, Ross Marvin, Goodsell, Borup, and myself. They knew how to wear their clothes! It is with reluctance that I include personal suffering in this narrative. It should be endured and nothing said. Any man detests a whine, but he does want information and he does want truth. 'Oh, that's nothing!' 'A joy ride!' 'Nothing to it!' can be interpreted in two ways, either as grit, endurance, physical stamina, plain guts, or as a despicable form of boasting, deception, and untruth.

As a matter of fact it cannot be stated too emphatically that a trip over the Polar Sea is not a holiday. When I saw so strong a man as Bob Bartlett break down and want his mother as we shivered and shook together on a snow bed in the Far North, his underclothing wringing wet, his clothing a mass of ice, his face scarred with frost, his fingers hard, horny, and cracked, his body chafed to sores by walking, plodding endlessly on, I am certain that all should know that Commander Peary's leaves of absence from the United States Navy for a long period of years were not for the purpose of 'having a good time up North.' It was something much deeper than a vagrancy complex that caused him to go all through this himself many, many times, and through even far more than anything we had to undergo.

On March 12th, I went on ahead with the advance party to break trail. To keep a fairly accurate course toward the Pole, it was our custom to place the compass in the snow, well away from any local attraction such as metal on sledges or equipment, and sight due north allowing for a westerly variation of the compass of one hundred and twelve degrees. We then worked for several hours toward the most conspicuous 'landmark' such as a peculiarly shaped knob of ice which happened to be on the course.

On reaching our objective, the compass was again resorted to for a new course. No astronomical observations for latitude and longitude were taken, for the simple reason that up to this time the sun had reached an altitude of only about one degree and a half above the horizon. Under such conditions accurate observations are impossible and absolutely useless. An observation with the sun at this altitude results in an error of some twenty miles, due to mean refraction alone, when the thermometer registers fifty degrees above zero. When the temperature is minus fifty degrees, no one knows what the error is, but it is enormously increased. One of Peary's naïve critics has suggested that he should have postponed his departure until the sun was sufficiently high for accurate observations to be taken all the way to the Pole. But Peary knew better; he realized that every day the sun was above the horizon increased the possibilities of open leads and open water.

On March 12th we covered approximately sixteen miles. We estimated the distance by the character of the sledging surface, by the delays caused by rough ice, holes, open leads, by the time of travel, and by the mean of the distance traveled, based upon the judgment of each assistant. We were navigating simply and solely by dead reckoning. Sledgemeters were out of the question; they would not have stood the strain for an hour. We were on the rough frozen ice of the Polar Sea, not on the ice of the Greenland Ice Cap or the land ice toward the South Pole.

Saturday, March 13th, was a hard day, with deep cracks to cross, and the character of the ice was such that picks were used for hours hewing out a road. With the temperature at fifty-nine below, this was far from fun. One dog was killed by falling into a crack and being crushed by a rapidly oncoming sledge. A number of the dogs had already been killed by the Eskimos and several abandoned on the trail as unfit for work.

In the meantime many were the looks backward along the trail. Where were Marvin and Borup was the one question. So much depended on them! Possibly the success or failure of the whole expedition was packed upon their sledges somewhere between us and Cape Columbia. Possibly they were on the wrong side of a wide smoking lead of water which refused to freeze or close. These were anxious days for us all.

At last, one day as we were building our snow house at the end of the march, Eging-wa, standing on its very top, sighted a ball of low-lying mist on the ice, which he knew to be the condensation of the breath of a dog team. This was one of the most dramatic moments of the whole trip. The Eskimos yelled and clambered for vantage points. Commander, usually so calm and reserved, was visibly agitated. Here at the very crisis of the struggle, reinforcements were coming – the much-needed fuel for our hot tea. As he once said to me at the Big Lead, 'I don't know how long a man can work and live at fifty and sixty below without a hot drink. We may find out. It's got to be done.'

As the one team drew nearer and nearer and emerged from the mist, speculation was rife as to who he was. We rushed back along the trail and recognized Sig-loo. He was smiling, but stiff with cold, and plainly tired, very tired. Commander took the emergency flask of 'Three Star' brandy from his warm breast where he always carried it, and used it for a good purpose. A note from Marvin informed Commander that he and Borup with their Eskimos had been held up by open water; that they had reached the Big Lead the day after we left, and that they were one march behind us. Good news indeed!

This man Sig-loo deserves more than a passing notice. Handsome in appearance, with his long wavy jet-black hair covering his square-set shoulders, stocky, well-built, modest, he was the quietest man on the expedition. As I have already told, he was one of the Clark starvation party in 1906, which, blown by wind far to the east, landed on the northern shore of Greenland. They had eaten their dogs, had even boiled their whips and the webbing from their snowshoes. When their wobbly tracks were discovered, they were *walking away from home* and thought they had reached the land west of Cape Columbia. Sig-loo was found in the hills hunting Arctic hare with a bow and arrow improvised from a snowshoe, his hopes resting largely on the arrow tip which he had fashioned from a spoon.

Yet, after this ordeal, now without a particle of food on his sledge, his only equipment a snow knife, he had volunteered to go on alone, after double-marching with Marvin and Borup, and overtake the main party. This boy had covered a distance of fifty-seven geographical miles, or, of actual travel, *seventy-four miles* over the sea ice with only four hours of sleep, following eighteen hours of hard work with loaded sledges!

Naturally the advocates of the five- and six-mile-a-day theory (Nansen's average on the Polar Sea was six miles a day) will doubt this feat as they have Commander Peary's forced marches from the Pole. Any man who has not *driven good dogs* does not know, and has a right to be a 'Doubting Thomas.'

Sunday, March 14th, was a day of rest and a day of sorrow for me. With frozen toes and holes in both heels badly maturated, I was of little use to the expedition, and would be simply a drag if I were unable to keep up with the sledge. No man wants to be that. With the words, 'MacMillan, you go back in the morning where you can have those feet attended to,' the bottom seemed to drop out of the Polar Sea. It was the harder to bear because the day before Commander Peary had selected for me one of our very best dog teams, one which he said would take me with him very close to the Pole.

Both Borup and Marvin were to return to land within a few days, while Bartlett, Henson, and I were to go on. But had I gone on and broken down when he really needed me, it would have been far more serious for me than frozen feet.

Dr. Goodsell and his Eskimos left for home in the morning with the worn-out and crippled dogs and with one-half enough food to reach land, which meant that they must double their outward marches, and, if held up by water, eat their dogs. All the supporting parties left with the same understanding and under the same conditions. All Arctic travelers know that outward marches with heavy loads and unbroken trails are doubled and often trebled with light sledges when homeward bound.

The next day I bade good-bye to the men, a final good-bye to Marvin, poor fellow, and then walked over to see my dogs, knowing full well that I should never see them together again and doubting that I should see any one of them. Only two of them returned to the ship. After working

The four Eskimos who went with Peary to the Pole

together so long and watching them every minute of the day, and feeding them at night after work well done, there was bound to be a certain feeling of affection and pity when one dwelt upon the possibilities of their future.

The point from which Goodsell and I turned back was in latitude 84° 29′. It should have been obvious to the Spirits of the North then, and to Peary's critics later, that something was being done which was different in every way from what any expedition had done before. Favorable conditions, superb organization, a new system, whatever the reason, Goodsell, a man too heavy for sledge work, and I, a novice in northern work, had reached farther north than had been attained by most expeditions. In fact our latitude had only been surpassed by two – Nansen and Cagni's – other than those of Peary. And we left behind us other men, well supplied to continue on. Borup went on to 85° 23′; Marvin reached 86° 38′, surpassing all the Farthest Norths except Peary's, and Bob Bartlett reached 87° 47′, just missing the 88th parallel of latitude. Yes, things were different this time.

Musk-ox meat for men and dogs

✳

BACK TO THE ROOSEVELT

In spite of our poor dogs my two Eskimos and I covered the two marches in one and overtook the doctor. Although he had been only one day ahead of us, there had been a tremendous change in the ice. The trail had faulted and rafted to a height of thirty and forty feet. At one place it disappeared beneath a pressure ridge, and did not reappear as we fully expected it would on the other side. One would judge that a whole outfit was still beneath the ice. The footprints of the dogs were finally discovered on an upright piece of ice well up toward the top of a pressure ridge. The road had been lifted bodily to a height of forty feet! Driving to the west we knitted together the broken ends of the trail, one purpose, and a most important one, of the different supporting and returning parties. The express would be along later, and the track must be well marked and kept clear.

A few of the cracks in the sea ice revealed its height above the water to be between four and five feet, which would indicate a total thickness of the sea ice at this point to be between thirty and forty feet. When the cracks were too wide, we bridged them with the sledge and walked the dogs across. We relieved the doctor of Arklio, who was so ill that he could hardly walk.

As Borup said, when he overtook the main party, 'That march from No. 4 camp to No. 5 was a hummer!' It certainly was. We couldn't double and were compelled to put up for the night at No. 4. It was so cold that all the Eskimos wanted to sleep together in a ball. Eight of us in an eight-foot bed were too many for comfort.

On March 17th we doubled easily and finished before sunset. It seemed strange to have sunlight, brighter and stronger and longer every day. It felt good on our scab-covered faces. Under its rays we knew that they would heal quickly. Ethnologists and anthropologists have easily explained the whys and wherefores, the customs and habits of strange people, but no one has ever enlightened us as to why the Eskimos are not sun worshipers, which would be the most natural religion for them.

A dog's life! One of our females gave birth to five puppies that evening. It was forty below zero. Four were found frozen as hard as rocks in the morning. She had done her duty and her best. We found one alive, curled up between her warm thighs, carefully covered with her warm chin and bushy tail.

On the eighteenth we stretched out for land, with an early start, as we knew that the nearer the land the worse the trail, due to the immense pressure of the great shifting mass of ice. It was far worse than when we came out, the trail being intersected by numerous leads of open water, the same which had blocked Marvin and Borup. Fourteen hours is a long day, but it is fairly common in Arctic work. The last half-mile leading to the ice foot just west of Cape Columbia was the worst bit of ice of the whole trip; not only was the ice rough, but there were holes full of deep snow into which we wallowed thigh deep. If anyone had been going the other way, he would have been utterly discouraged at the very start.

A change of food awaited us at the 'MacMillan Hotel,' as George called my winter home. Here we found plenty of cocoa, condensed milk, and butter, and a note from George. I read and re-read the last two or three sentences: 'Everything has gone to hell. My Eskimos are talking of quitting and of hiking back for the ship. If they do, I shall go back alone just as soon as I can get across the lead.'

What courage! He had been sent back for oil. Peary needed it. So he was going back alone.

When I had left the main party, Commander Peary, remembering his experience of 1906 and not knowing just where he might be forced to land on his return from the Polar Sea, had requested me, if I could possibly do so, to place a cache of supplies on Ward Hunt Island, some thirty-five miles west of Cape Columbia. We rested our dogs on the nineteenth, dried our clothing and boots, and, in general, prepared for the trip.

The next morning Dr. Goodsell left for the ship, taking with him two Eskimos, both ill and unable to travel. We reached the island on the second day and left there a cache consisting of fifty pounds of biscuit, forty pounds of man pemmican, forty pounds of dog pemmican, five tins of condensed milk, one can of tea, one small stove, three gallons of alcohol, three of kerosene, and a sledge. That cache has been there for twenty-five years untouched, unseen, but it may be of help to someone some day. That someone will land there by plane. The trip will never again be made by dog team.

One physical characteristic of this section deserves more than a passing notice and is difficult to explain. I have never seen this peculiar feature in any other part of the Arctic during my twenty thousand miles of sledging. Twice a day the tide rises and falls, and when it falls in low temperatures, as it does all through the winter night, it leaves a wetted surface which becomes glazed with ice, a fractional part of an inch thick. Upon the fall of each successive tide, this coating increases in thickness, until it is at the height of the highest tide, a solid wall of ice extending from high to low water mark. This is called the 'ice foot'; and serves as an excellent highway of travel along the shores of every Arctic land. It is not caused by snowfall, and is not the accumulation of snow banks at the water's edge, as is stated in many books which purport to deal with the North. The natural line between this, which is firmly attached to the bottom, and the floating sea ice, is known as the 'tidal crack.'

From Cape Hecla 65° W. to Ward Hunt Island 75° W., the northern shores of Grant Land grade off so imperceptibly into the sea that it is impossible to distinguish between ice foot and floating sea ice. For hours we never knew whether we were on land or sea, owing to the fact that the broad ice foot consists of a series of long gentle waves parallel with the coast-lines, greatly resembling an ocean swell, without crack or break of any description, hard blue ice, which I can readily believe is as perpetual as the Ice Cap of Greenland. It is a question whether these are caused by tremendous pressure exerted on the ice foot by the ice of the Polar Sea, or weather they are ice-covered terminal moraines of centuries ago.

We were back again at Camp Crane on the night of the twenty-second, and left for the ship on the morning of the twenty-third, camping at Camp Colan that night, thirty-five miles away. Up at four-thirty on the morning of the twenty-forth, we had to face a disagreeable cold wind and drift all the way to Porter Bay, where we found the doctor. He was traveling slowly, owing to the disabled condition of his men. That night I was aroused at midnight to a banquet fresh from the hills – a large Arctic hare, the first fresh meat we had enjoyed in three months.

Game was evidently increasing, for the next day we sighted both Arctic hare and ptarmigan, fresh meat which our Eskimos evidently craved, as was apparent by their blazing away without order or judgment. Finally, Kai-o-ta brought down a hare with a long shot. The heart and liver were eaten at once, warm and bloody as it was, by the Eskimos who were ill.

We arrived aboard the *Roosevelt* on March 25th, having covered the one hundred miles in three days; good traveling for rather poor dogs at the end of six weeks of sledging.

A week later, two of Borup's men arrived bringing me a letter from him telling me that he had followed me to land five days after I left the main party. He was held up at the Big Lead for twelve hours, but reached the land from 85° 23′ N. in seven marches. He had gone west to Cape Fanshawe Martin to put down another cache of supplies for the Peary division. He arrived at the ship on April 11th.

At this point I want to emphasize the care with which Commander Peary instructed his subordinate parties, especially in the matter of navigation. The orders which he left for Borup and Marvin at the Big Lead were carefully framed as to direction after careful consideration of the variations of the compass. In his later instructions to me he was equally careful to give me the compass variation at Cape Jesup. This point is of importance in view of the claims which have been made that Peary neither was a navigator nor took pains to be accurate in his calculations. And this entire subject of compass variation deserves consideration in view of the general lack of information as to its importance in Polar work.

When we were at Cape Columbia we were about seven hundred and eighty-seven miles north of the Magnetic Pole. The compass needle does not point due north; in certain localities it does not point today where it pointed last year; sometimes it even points downward toward the earth; at other places it points to nowhere at all; it may be absolutely dead and swing with the ship.

How often one hears the quotation, 'as true as the needle toward the Pole!' When Barton Booth wrote that some two hundred years ago little was known about compass variation. The North Magnetic Pole was not discovered until 1830.

If a man knows how much the needle points away from the true north, the compass is as good as gold. If a man knows that his watch is ten minutes slow, he does not throw it away. He can calculate the correct time. When I pitched my tent in 1916 near Ellef and Amund Ringnes Island, my compass needle was pointing south! If my course was north, I went south by compass. If my course was east, I went west.

Everyone knows the common horseshoe magnet and its properties. As this plaything attracts needles, nails, or iron filings, so the earth attracts the steel needle of the compass or any magnetized needle freely suspended, and gives it determinate direction. Just how or why it does this, no one knows. Just what this inherent force is, scientists have not learned even after patient years of study and research. The earth acts like a giant magnet and is one, so far as we know, with the two poles of every magnet, the North Magnetic Pole and the South Magnetic Pole, which are not to be confused with the poles of rotation, Peary's North Pole and Amundsen's South Pole, the 'ends of the earth.'

The North Pole, known as the North Geographical Pole, is at 90° North Latitude, or ninety degrees from the equator. The North Magnetic

Pole is in about seventy degrees North Latitude, and 97° 30′ West Longitude; in Canada, in a territory known as Boothia Felix Peninsula, northwest of Hudson Bay. The South Magnetic Pole is an almost corresponding distance from the South Geographical Pole.

Although they knew nothing of the magnetic properties of the earth, the Chinese used the magnetic needle as a guide in overland journeys as early as the second century. Probably the magnetic needle was introduced into Europe by the Arabs who had commercial intercourse with the Chinese. We do not know when it was first used at sea as a guide for the mariner, probably as a 'needle rubbed with the ugly brown loadstone; stuck in a straw and laid upon water'; but it was possibly in the twelfth century. But here is the important point – it was believed then that the needle maintained a constant direction and that direction was north.

Columbus, on September 13, 1492, was the first navigator to note a change in its direction as the ship sailed westward. Compass variation was not clearly recognized until Button's voyage in 1612. Purchas, in writing of Button, states, 'This seemed strange that in this voyage, as he searched many leagues East and West he found the variation of the compass to rise and fall in admirable proportion, as if the true magnetical pole might be discovered.' In other words, the needle varies in its direction according to its location, its northern end, so called, endeavoring to point toward that spot in Boothia Felix Peninsula, known as the North Magnetic Pole.

Variation of the compass is the angle between true north and the angle which the needle maintains. Accurate navigation is possible only when this angle is known. This fact explains the reason for the valuable work of the Carnegie Institution in studying throughout the world this mysterious force which varies moment to moment.

Equally important is the fact that as one travels northward or southward from the Magnetic Equator, practically midway between the two Magnetic Poles, a freely suspended magnetic needle dips or tips downward and continues to do so increasingly as one approaches the horizontal. The force which pulls the end of the needle downward is known as the vertical intensity. At Refuge Harbor, in 1924, for instance, this dip was 85° 47'.

As a ship sails northward along the Atlantic Coast to Labrador and Greenland, the westerly variation of the compass increases rapidly. In the year 1930, at New York, it was 11°; at Boston, 15° 15'; Portland, 17°; Halifax, 23°; Sydney, 26° 35'; Battle Harbor, 34° 15'; Hopedale, 38° 25'; Nain, 39°; Holstenborg, Greenland, 55°; Disko, Greenland, 59°; Etah, 103°; Cape Columbia, 112°.

During the past few years the Press has stated repeatedly that the magnetic compass is useless at the North Pole, and that is why the earth induction compass is used. The magnetic compass – and by that I mean the ordinary ship's compass – is as valuable to the navigator at the North Pole as it is in any part of the Atlantic or the Pacific.

Of course Commander Peary knew all these facts about compass variations. As I have shown, he used them himself, and was, as always in everything concerning his men, exceedingly careful that his assistants should be fully informed. Peary was as careful in all matters of navigation as he was in the infinite detail of equipment and ice transportation.

CHAPTER 20

TO CAPE MORRIS JESUP

On April 17th I saw two lone Eskimos sledging slowly toward the *Roosevelt* from the northwest. I feared that something was wrong, and I hastened along the ice foot to meet them. They proved to be Kood-look-to and In-yu-gee-to.

Kood-look-to, with tears in his eyes, looked down at the ice, and said, 'Marvin gone. Young ice. I told him look out.'

As Borup joined me, Kood-look-to again tried to explain, in his half English, half Eskimo, how Marvin was lost. It was a terrible blow to us all, closely associated as we had been since the time we left Sydney. Ross was a quiet, unassuming fellow who had endeared himself to us all. Whenever the thought came to us that he was out there somewhere in the water, there was an almost irresistible impulse to go, go, go, until we reached him.

Both the Eskimos were deeply moved. Marvin was a favorite with them both; Kood-look-to especially idolized him. He had been entrusted to their care by Peary-ark-sush. They had lost him and could not get over it. In the calmer moments they told us the story.

Marvin, with these two boys, had left the main party five days after the Borup division. Marvin had no dog team of his own. When riding with Eskimos, it is always our custom, upon breaking camp in the morning, to walk ahead on the trail, leaving instructions with our traveling companions to pack up everything, load sledge and follow. In this way we relieve the dogs of our weight for several hours. If the going is heavy, we often keep ahead of the dogs all day. If it comes on to blow, which generally means drift, or if we encounter difficulties in the way of rough ice and open water, we drop back to our sledges.

Just beyond the Big Lead there was a bad spot, numberless small leads, a regular network. When we returned, we crossed two of these on wide-spread hands and knees, distributing our weight upon four points, instead of two. Here, Marvin undoubtedly met his fate. He walked on alone, the boys told me. He encountered a newly frozen lead. Should he await his Eskimos and cross with them, or should he go on alone? He tried it with his foot; it supported his weight, but cracked. It was cold standing at the edge of the lead. Warm with walking, he would soon become chilled. He would try it alone. He had crossed on thin ice before.

When Kood-look-to and In-yu-gee-to, or Harrigan as we called him, arrived sometime later, the thin ice of the lead was broken into small pieces, and in the middle of it, just projecting above the surface of the water, was a bulging bit of fur, which they recognized as the back of Marvin's caribou-skin coat. He had tried, broken through, struggled until numb with cold, and had died there alone. The air imprisoned in the boots and beneath the impervious body clothing was keeping the body afloat.

In the North, when a man dies, he is believed to pass to another world and continue his work; therefore, he must have his equipment with him. The Eskimos were deeply alarmed and afraid of the Evil Spirits. They immediately unpacked the sledge, selected Marvin's personal things, and pushed them out over the ice to a spot as near the body as possible. Then they ran back from the edge of the lead, quickly constructed a snow house, crawled in and blocked the door. In the morning the body had disappeared. They packed up and hurried toward land.

This is the story they told us when they reached the ship, the one told to me repeatedly with greater detail when traveling later with Kood-look-to for a thousand miles and more; to Bartlett, to Peary, and to Henson, an expert in the Eskimo language. It never varied with time or place. We all believed it implicitly.

After nineteen years a different story was brought out of the North, so astounding in its inaccuracy as to facts – though probably given in perfect sincerity – that it is hardly worth a moment's serious consideration. When one knows Kood-look-to as I have for over twenty years, and when one knows In-yu-gee-to, or 'Harrigan,' whom I have known as long, and reads that Kood-look-to shoots his best friend, Marvin, whom he loved and respected, in order to save the life of 'Harrigan,' whom he has always despised and hated, it is time for the professional psychologist to handle the problem.

With the thought that probably Marvin had written orders from Peary for both Borup and myself, we looked through what little remained of his equipment. There were no orders, but, fortunately, his observations for latitude were intact. He had reached 86° 38', thus breaking Nansen's record of 86° 14'. His last camp, where he bade good-bye to Peary and Bartlett, was two hundred and thirty-two miles from the Pole.

It had been Commander's original plan for Marvin and me, after our return to the ship, to sledge to the northern end of Greenland, the most northern point of land in the world, and there to make a line of soundings northward, take a series of tidal observations, and deposit food supplies the whole length of the coast at appropriate intervals. The movement of the sea ice from west to east might force the Commander to land on the Greenland coast as he had had to do in 1906. I did not know whether Marvin had had the final instructions from Peary with him. If he had, they were probably lost with the other things left as near the body as possible. But with or without orders, I felt that I should carry out Commander's verbal instructions of a few weeks before. If he or Captain Bartlett and their parties were driven to the east and should land and not find food, the result would be serious.

I suggested to Borup that he accompany me, and no one could have been more delighted at the mere thought of it. Spring of the year, bright sunlight, big black cliffs, dark fiords, the long white trail – one can never forget them. That night we figured with pencil and paper the distance, some six hundred miles, and calculated the amount of food, dogs, sledges, and men necessary for the successful completion of the work.

Our plan called for six sledges loaded with six hundred pounds each. The country can always furnish a certain amount of food, and at this time of year many sections can furnish it all, if one can afford the time in hunting. Generally one's objective is at such a distance that, in order to reach it and return before the breaking up of the ice in June, the rate of travel does not admit of any delay. To ensure good work, an experienced man will provide full rations, if possible, and accept what crosses the trail as additional, for both men and dogs are always hungry.

Our expedition of five Eskimos, Borup, and myself, six sledges and forty-eight dogs left the *Roosevelt* on April 19th, Lexington Day at home, probably warm and delightful, but with us twenty-five degrees below zero. Our visions of a spring ramble were ruthlessly shattered that first day. We had more trouble within sight of the ship than we had had on the main trip.

As the tide and southward-flowing current swings out of the Polar Sea into Robeson Channel their load of drift ice is too large for the hole. As a natural result, it is forced against the shore and even up the cliffs well above high-water mark, a tremendous mass of irregularly shaped ice blocks of various sizes. It requires skill, patience, strength, and a few other qualities to drive a six-hundred-pound sledge over such a road.

There was certainly chaos between Cape Rawson and Black Cape, where the coast is exceptionally bold; at times, seven men were needed on one sledge. Even then, in spite of our best efforts, some turned three and four somersaults into the bottom of deep holes. At last we resorted to ropes and gently lowered the sledges to a level strip of ice foot, which afforded us a good highway to our camping place near Black Cape, where we considered it warm enough – twenty-five degrees below zero – to pitch a tent. Good going on the twentieth brought us easily to Lincoln Bay and to a cache of tea, sugar, oil, and biscuit. The milk and pemmican listed as being there were missing. Did some party eat more than its ration, or did Panikpa and Poo-ad-loo-na, bound south, help themselves?

A survey of the channel from the top of the hill looked favorable. We should have an easy crossing. On the twenty-first we reeled off twenty-five miles and went into camp on the ice of Repulse Harbor, so named by Captain Hall in 1871 'in commemoration of his defeats.' The sun was so high now that a constant use of snow glasses was necessary to prevent snow blindness.

The man who has not gone North, imagining as he does a white covering of snow with every storm, is perplexed as to how we are able to follow one another's trails. At this camp we picked up Marvin's sledge trail made three months before! The impression of the steel runners of a heavily loaded sledge in a drift of snow compacted by a strong wind persists for a long time. Because of an absence of heavy rains during the summer season, any deep track in the ground remains for years. In 1875 the *Alert* wintered at Floeberg Beach, a short distance astern of where the *Roosevelt* now lay. The tracks left by a push cart were plainly visible in 1909, *thirty-four years later.*

With heavy sledges and rough ice, a smash-up can be expected at any minute. Each sledge is a link in the chain, and when a link snaps it generally results in a complete hold-up until it is repaired. We were a bit too near the ship for it to be entirely safe to leave an Eskimo alone on the trail. We decided to camp and repair after only five hours of travel.

The time was not wholly lost. We needed every bit of rest for the struggle the next day by the infamous Black Horn Cliffs. Their blackness may be due, one might imagine, to the curses hurled at them by all who have traveled in this vicinity. Sheer out of the water and washed by current and tide, they stand as a mighty bulwark against the attack of the Polar Sea, which seems ever trying to push the shore back into the hills. The most impressive demonstration of power I have ever witnessed was on the edge of this sea, when I watched a huge floeberg being forced bodily out of the water upon the shore, plowing an enormous furrow in the beach. Hardly perceptible, its movement was fascinating, and as certain and regular as the hand of a clock.

I had heard and read much of the difficulties of the Black Horn Cliffs, so called 'in consequence of a remarkable black rock like a horn projecting from one part.' Commander had had his troubles and dangers here nine years before, as his report testifies.

From a scenic point of view, the cliffs are magnificent. They are an almost sheer precipice of black rock, four miles in extent, with a face which reflects back with startling clearness every word uttered, every snap of the whip, every yelp of a dog. But any esthetic feeling or scientific curiosity was completely forgotten after one look at what was truly frightful going.

I could now better appreciate the statement of Beaumont of the Nares Expedition, 'The chaos amongst the floebergs was something indescribable and the traveling the worst that could possibly be imagined.'

Three of the sledges used good judgment, and swung wide from land, while the rest of us pushed, yelled, and swore, at times up to our necks in tidal cracks. It was a wonder that every sledge was not smashed. And to add to our difficulties, it snowed all day, so limiting our view of what was ahead that we simply groped and swung our picks, only knowing that there is an end to everything!

That night we camped in Hand Bay. It was here that James H. Hand, able seaman of the *Alert*, gave out, dying twenty-eight days later in Polaris Bay. And it was here that Lockwood, of the Greely Expedition, found the following pathetic record of Beaumont:

Repulse Harbor Dépôt, June 13, 1876. – Three of us have returned from my camp, half a mile south, to fetch the remainder of the provisions. D— has failed altogether this morning. Jones is worse and can't last more than two or three days. Craig is nearly helpless. Therefore we can't hope to reach Polaris Bay without assistance. Two men can't do it. So will go as far as we can and live as long as we can. God help us!
L.A. BEAUMONT

Whether to take the sea or ice foot is always the question when traveling along this shore. The ice foot can furnish good going, especially after a full moon, when tides are high and gush up through tidal cracks and overflow everything. The surface snow absorbs the water like a sponge and becomes frozen into an excellent highway, our hope and our resort when in difficulty on the sea ice. And the ice foot can be abominable, covered as it sometimes is with deep snow, and hard, slippery snow banks, with the consequent danger of slipping off into the sea.

On the twenty-fourth three of us stuck to the land and fairly flew along the ice foot. Borup and three Eskimos tried the sea ice and, from the heights above our camp near Marvin's tidal igd-loo of the winter, we could see them slowly fighting their way northward. They made land a mile beyond us late in the day, whereupon we broke camp and joined them. They were glad to see us, as we brought along five ptarmigan and an Arctic hare, a beauty weighing about eight pounds.

How fair a face! is descriptive of our view that day as we stood on the highest land at Cape Bryant and looked across at John Murray Island. There was a smoothness in the scene which gave us renewed hope and encouragement after our struggles of the past three days. We left the ice foot with a dash and plunged into a breaking surface, the kind which leaves one leg up and one down, then two up and two down. It was slump, walk ten feet, and break.

Luckily the surface was strong enough to support our dogs and, in general, our sledges, although at times they went down to the crossbars. Under these conditions eighteen miles in ten hours was not a discouraging day's work. We had our snowshoes, thank God, and were having a picnic compared with what Beaumont and his men had gone through thirty-three years before.

We were now beyond the British record of 1876. Inside of us was Rief Island, where Beaumont stated he left a record on May 22d, and the Dragon Point mentioned in his report – 'This was the place where I had settled to build a cairn, and leave a chart and record.' Time would not permit us to visit it. Rasmussen found both records eight years later. It was not physical stamina or youth or powers of endurance – they were probably the better men – but dogs and snowshoes alone must receive the credit for our doing in *eight days* what they did in *thirty-nine*.

Hard work does not kill, but monotony does. Change, ceaseless change, is the plan of Nature, and it should be that of man. The happening of even little things on the trail, a bit of banter, a cake of chocolate, a biscuit extracted with difficulty through a crack in the box, a dog fight, a dropped mitten, changes surprisingly one's attitude toward the work in hand and toward the world. And with the glad cry of 'Musk-oxen!' one is transported to Elysian Fields.

It couldn't be true! They must be rocks, we told old Kai-o-ta, as we reached for our binoculars and scanned the hills. He grinned, and added, 'Watch them, and you will see them move.' Sure enough, our distant black dots on a sloping hillside were changing positions. There could be but one conclusion – something alive.

We hear much of animals in the North, such as the white polar bear, white wolf, white caribou, white fox, white ptarmigan, white hare, white ermine, white lemming, white owl, white baby seal, white gyrfalcon having their color for purposes of protection, as a hunting asset. But here is an animal, one of the most northern in the world, that is black in color, and there is a good reason. *Musk-oxen do not live on a white surface, they graze on dark windswept areas,* which are common enough in the North even in the winter. With hills and plains covered with boulders, it takes an experienced eye to detect the difference. Only a change in relative position is a positive identification. The grayish-white patch on the back of the musk-ox adds to the deception. The result is that the animal looks exactly like a boulder with its top sprinkled with snow.

A tired horse turning for the barn is analogous to a tired Eskimo running for red meat, and so it was this day. For a few seconds there were more things in the air than there were on the sledges. Loads were dumped, and away the Eskimos flew, each man holding a long knife in his hand to cut the traces when the danger zone was reached. A full dog team going pell-mell into a herd of musk-oxen, sledge and all, can be easily wiped out in a few moments. Bound to the sledge and with the traces wound around horns and legs, the dogs have little chance of escape.

Bang! Bang! With a shot apiece just behind the curve of the horns, not in the heavily matted hair of the body, we had five bulls and a cow. The pot boiled late that night, giving us additional stamina and energy for the next day.

Our supporting party had now done its work, so three Eskimos went back on the morrow, leaving four of us with full loads. We missed the Eskimos by noon, for we were compelled to double-bank. Throwing off part of our loads, advancing for a distance, returning with empty sledge, and again advancing over the old trail, was trying work and productive of poor results. Fourteen hours between breakfast and supper create many things besides an appetite.

Fifteen hours on the twenty-ninth brought us through soft going to Cape Frederick, that will-o'-the-wisp which we had been confident we could reach in three. Again we had been deceived in distance and in the size of the hills. Rather than struggle on with a heavy load, Kood-look-to preferred to double-bank, which necessitated starting back after his load when he had eaten his supper. In the morning he had not returned, and I wondered. There was a pretty Eskimo girl at the ship. He was to be married in the fall. 'In the spring the young man's fancy —' yes, possibly he had. Borup and Kai-o-ta harnessed up and started back to overtake the runaway. They met him coming, looking a little sheepish.

Tired out at the end of a strenuous day, he had fallen asleep on his sledge. With no incentive to go on, his dogs took advantage of the lull, and decided to make up some lost sleep of their own. Kood-look-to awoke, whipped the dogs on, and snuggled down for another nap. When all was quiet, the dogs again showed good judgment. It was a slow trip, but both sides seemed somewhat rested. It was well they were.

John Murray Island looks innocent on the map, but John can never propitiate us for the sins of that day. Diabolical was the only word for it. Deep snow, tidal cracks, rough ice, delayed and tormented us all day – a very short day. We simply gave up and camped, tired out, and there and then decided to lighten our sledges by establishing our first cache. We eased our consciences somewhat by hoping that it might help Peary or be of some service to us later, if we surveyed Chipp Inlet, which Commander had promised we should do. I was glad to learn that three gallons of oil and forty-eight pounds of pemmican were later found and appreciated by that able Danish explorer, Knud Rasmussen, undoubtedly our best authority on the life and customs of the Eskimo.

> We are back again in the tent at eleven o'clock [he wrote], gourmandizing to our heart's content on Peary's pemmican. This Polar pemmican, in contrast to the sort with which we are acquainted, has a wonderful addition of lots of raisins and sugar kneaded into meat and fat, so that it has the consistency almost of a sweetmeat; at any rate, no marzipan cake could have tasted better.

Bear tracks near Cape Britannia, the day before, were encouraging. Possibly fresh meat would make up for the amount of food cached and left behind on the trail.

On Saturday, May 1st, there was a decided improvement in the going. We were over the hump, so to speak, and could stretch out for the Cape, which we did, leaving Elison Island at three A.M., and traveling for ten hours to Cape Payer, a really striking spot scenically, as is, in fact, this whole coast. A continuation of good going on the second brought us to Cape Wykander, which proved to be an island and not as delineated on the map. We were now making up for lost time and learning that all south-western shores were deep with snow; all ends of capes were smooth ice; all fiords were rolling blue-top ice covered with an increasing amount of snow as we approached the opposite shore, an obvious result of the prevailing southwest winds. But this was not so obvious at Cape Hummock, which is well named, and which seemed to be the exception. My journal reads,

> Today at Hummock Cape, the ice was jammed up against the shore leaving no ice foot at all, but a frightful jagged mass through which we were obliged to work our way as best we could. Have also had a variety in the way of open leads, some of which we were able to cross, others to go around.

Picks were our salvation. But in spite of leveled roads and the greatest care, two of our four sledges were badly smashed. Rough ice, hard work, and broken sledges were forgotten as we rounded the Cape and looked on toward Lockwood Island, a beautiful bit of scenery with its high, precipitous cliffs inlaid with a great white glacier.

That night we camped beyond the world's record of Lockwood and Brainard of the Greely Expedition. With a latitude of 83° 24' 30", they had wrested the prize from the English, who had held it for more than three centuries! Their feelings at the time and upon such an important occasion are shown in Sergeant Brainard's field notes:

> We have reached a higher latitude than ever reached by mortal man, and on a land farther north than was supposed by many to exist. We unfurled the glorious Stars and Stripes to the exhilarating northern breeze with an exultation impossible to describe.

From now on we were following the footsteps of one man only – Peary, who had traveled this coast nine years before.

Before breaking camp on the morning of the fifth, we walked back along the shore to visit the cairn constructed by Lockwood and Brainard. We had discovered it the day before, as we fairly swept along the face of the island. We found it to be about forty feet above sea level. Knowing that Commander Peary had removed the record, we were careful not to demolish the cairn by searching for the copy, which should be placed in every cairn upon the removal of the original.

To the north of us lay Cape Washington, the most northern point these men saw, and one which they had hoped to reach. Their successful efforts were referred to as follows by Greely in his 'Three Years of Arctic Service':

For three centuries England had held the honours of the farthest north. Now Lockwood, profiting by their labors and experiences, surpassed their efforts of three centuries by land and ocean. And with Lockwood's name should be associated that of his inseparable sledge companion Brainard, without whose efficient aid and restless energy, as Lockwood said, the work could not have been accomplished. So, with proper pride, they looked that day from the vantage-ground of the farthest north [Lockwood Island] to the desolate Cape which until surpassed in coming ages, may well bear the grand name of Washington.

Happy as boys out of school, with good dogs, plenty of food on sledge and on the hills – fresh Arctic hare every day – we were now romping along northward, riding on our sledges whenever we cared to do so. The snow-covered hills and deep unexplored fiords were simply magnificent, Hunt's Fiord especially so. How they tempted us to leave the trail that we might claim something for our own!

The ice pile at Cape Washington was worth coming all the miles to see. We were awe-stricken at the evidence of such tremendous power. Nature must laugh in her sleeve when she sees man's pride, a tiny wooden ship, headed boldly up toward the Polar Sea.

Finding Peary's cairn at Cape Washington

Thursday, May 6th, brought a change. Commander often said, 'When things are going too well, look out! The Devil is only sleeping.' We ate our breakfasts to the tune of a howling wind and bad drift. We were well ahead of schedule time, so we could afford to be patient, although days spent in camp, sleeping and eating, are the black days on the calendar. Naturally, we talked of the boys out on the ice, and wondered where they were, and if Commander would return. We were confident he would, and, we hoped, with colors flying. How we scanned the Polar Sea as we sledged along the coast! It was possible that we should meet him here; if we did, he and his men would be well fed, for we were caching food all along the line.

A MacMillan-Borup camp in North Greenland

A second day was too much. We must do something. Why not open Charlie's box? It was true that it was not to be opened until we reached the Cape, but he would forgive us; we could easily reach it by tomorrow.

Borup and I both had our guess as to the contents. The one great topic of conversation with George was something to eat, and he nearly had apoplexy when I suggested it might be reindeer steaks, which I knew was his favorite dish.

'Reindeer!' he exclaimed almost reverently.

But it turned out to be two loaves of Charlie's best bread, a lump of delicious butter, and a large tin of cocoa! Buttered toast and cocoa put us to sleep for a few hours, and then what was to come next? In spite of wind and drift, why not go on? Tent life was intolerable.

With men and dogs fully rested, we sledged on for fourteen hours with gradually clearing weather and one new adventure. Rather than round one point, we decided to cross over the back of a glacier. The only real glacier that we had ever been on was the one at Cape York, which seemed as solid as Mother Earth itself. Imagine our surprise when great sections dropped with a muffled report from beneath our feet, causing us to catch our breath and wonder just how far it could drop. When two of my dogs disappeared completely, I crept to the hole rather gingerly. I could hear them whining, and, after a few minutes of shading my eyes, I could see them far below me. A lasso improvised from the sledge lashing brought them up choking for breath, but they were soon wagging their tails and ready to go on. The ice foot and sea ice seemed more friendly than usual for the rest of the day.

Our Eskimos were tremendously impressed by our notebooks, and wondered how we could put down our thoughts on paper, as we did at the end of each day. Kood-look-to wanted a book to do as the white man did. There is many an object in many a museum of less interest than that diary. He did learn to make a few letters, and was waiting for an opportunity to convince us that he had profited by our instructions.

As we neared Cape Morris Jesup, I noticed a large spot of blood-stained snow, and, naturally, I was somewhat concerned over what might have happened – dog, man, or animal was the question. One track alone led back to the hills, the footprints of a man! Whatever he had brought out, he had had it on his back. As I turned away I caught the letters 'R M E A M' marked in the snow, evidently with the stock of a whip.

Upon arriving at camp, as Borup and I generally did in the rear, Kood-look-to's first question was, 'Did you see that letter I wrote you?'

'Yes: I replied.

'What did it say?' he inquired eagerly.

I reflected for a moment. There was too much blood for a ptarmigan. But it was so small that he had brought it down from the hills and skinned it in a few minutes, or we should have overtaken him. An Arctic hare?

'Yes, I read the letter. It said, "Kood-look-to has killed an Arctic hare."'

'Nearly right,' he replied, and added, 'You made one mistake, Kai-o-ta has killed an Arctic hare.'

I complimented him upon the rapidity with which he was learning to read and write.

✳

PEARY BACK FROM THE POLE

We had reached our objective, the most northern point of land in the world, Cape Morris Jesup, three hundred and eighty miles from the Pole. But we were not alone; there were musk-ox tracks at the very point, within a few feet of the shore itself. To find musk-oxen, herbivorous animals, as far north as land goes, and to learn that they remain there during the long cold winter night and find subsistence, are two almost unbelievable facts. However, such is the case, which verifies the assertion that we find an abundance of vegetation in the Far North, and that there is really but little snowfall.

Our Eskimos bolted their supper and ran, ran to kill, the natural instinct of a savage, although they had food on their sledges.

We were about ready for bed when there was a snapping of whips, and, to our astonishment, four sledges dashed in from the south. We rubbed our sleepy eyes and looked again – they were two of our supporting party and two from the ship! They had followed close behind us for two hundred miles endeavoring to overtake us.

They had brought the following letter from Commander Peary:

S.S. Roosevelt, April 28, '09

My Dear MacMillan:
Arrived on board yesterday. Northern trip entirely satisfactory. No need of Greenland dépôts.

Captain came on board the twenty-fourth. Concentrate all your energies on tidal observations and line of soundings north from Cape Jesup, and use intended dépôt supplies for this purpose.

A week to ten days' tidal observations, and soundings ten miles apart, up to the 85th parallel, will be satisfactory. I regard this work as second in importance only to the northern work from which I have just returned, and the Morris Jesup work will strengthen and emphasize the other.

You will probably find the edge of the iglacial fringe at Cape Jesup about 83° 40' to 83° 45', so that eighty miles, the distance of your return camp from Columbia, will take you to the 85th parallel. Take two men and two sledges with you well loaded on the ice.

Should you encounter the big lead (that is, conditions similar to those in our fifth march from Columbia), do not go beyond it; the season is too late, young ice will not form rapidly. Push things and get back to Jesup before the full moon of June the third which will open up things again. Am sending you horizon and pocket sextant for latitude observations at your farthest point. Variation at Cape Jesup sixty-five west (65° W.) so that your compass course will be N.E. by E. ¾ E. or N. 65° E. for true north. Am also sending you deep-sea thermometer, pocket aneroid, maximum and minimum thermometers, also tide books. These and the sextant and horizon are packed in a box by themselves.

Should you need either of the two men who bring this, We-shark-ob-see has been longest idle at the ship.

Send back my gray Angel-o-blaho dog, which I believe is in Borup's team, and substitute best dogs of those bringing this letter.

If you still need supplies at Cape Bryant, send back memorandum and full instructions. Marvin's death a great shock to me and a great loss to the Expedition, to the future and to me personally. If your inclinations are that way, you must figure on filling his place in the coming Antarctic work, and should regard all your present work as schooling and training for that.

Remember me to Borup, and say to him that if his inclinations are that way, and his plans for the immediate future permit, there will be work for him in the great National Antarctic Expedition, which, if I live five years longer, will as certainly place the Stars and Stripes on the South Pole.

Never mind about any survey work. Concentrate all on Jesup, and bear constantly in mind, as noted above, that I regard good tidal observations from here second in importance only to the main northern work of the Expedition.

You should be back much earlier than the first of July. In 1900 I left Conger April 11th, in not as good shape as you have started. Did not get away from Cape Bryant till May 1st, was out on the ice five days, then made three marches to the southeast from Cape Jesup and was back at Conger midnight, June 9th.

Am anxious to have you back earliest possible date, not only on account of open water in channel, but for the tidal observations at Fort Conger. As noted above, you should have two Esquimaux with you on the ice and Borup should have two with him at Cape Jesup taking the observations. If we put a boat on the Greenland side it will be at Cape Sumner.

PEARY

Of course you will bring back the line and leads, the latter especially. You will find the lances effective for cutting out a cake of ice to serve as a ferry boat.

The first two sentences were the most important part of this letter, although its whole tone and spirit were one of success. There was enough here to let us infer that he had reached the Pole, and yet he had kept his promise to the loyal men of the Peary Arctic Club that they should be the first to know. We yelled our heads off for a few minutes, and then almost laughed them off at the expression on the faces of the Eskimos. They didn't know and couldn't imagine what it was all about. Happy wasn't the word for us. Peary had won, after years of persisting, fighting, attacking, ever returning to the attack! No man deserved success more, and no man ever suffered more in obtaining it.

S. S. "Roosevelt."
Apl., 28th. 09.

My dear Mc William:—
            Arrived on board
yesterday. Northern trip
entirely satisfactory. No need
of Greenland depots.
            Captain came on board
twenty fourth. Concentrate all
your energies on tidal observations
and line of soundings North
from Cape Jesup, And use
intended depot supplies for this
purpose.
            A week to ten days
tidal observations, And soundings
ten miles apart up to the

7.

As noted above You should
have two Eskimos with You
on the ice And Borup should
have two with him at Cape
Jesup taking the observations
        If You put a boat
on the Greenland side it
will be at Cape Jesup.

                Peary

        Of Course You will bring
back the pins And leads
the latter especially.
        You will find the lancer
effective for cutting out a
cake of ice to serve as a
ferry boat.

                P.

Peary's letter to MacMillan written on his return from the dash to the Pole
(Beginning and ending only)

In our calmer moments, I snatched time to read the following note from Bob:

MY DEAR MAC:

I reached the ship on the twenty-fourth and the land six days earlier.

My God! Isn't it too bad about Marvin! His poor mother! How she will feel it! God alone knows how that woman worked to help Marvin through college, and now Finis.

The Commander reached the ship yesterday, and this morning I am getting things ready for you. I hope everything will meet with your approval. I had a few bags made. That was all the material I could scrape up, nine in all. I guess you will not take many casts.

I will send you a paper with the sounding line marks on it for reference. This is the two thousand fathom one (2000). Now, old boy, I can't thank you half enough for your kind treatment, and after Borup left I got on fine, ate like a horse, and was never better in all my life and reached ship in splendid condition. But it was drive her, boy, drive her.

Kind regards to Borup. The Doc has not begun operations on the M—. Patients require all his attention. Com. has him working today weighing and measuring returning huskies and dogs.

Sincerely,

R.A. BARTLETT

On our return to the ship we learned that Bob had reached to a distance within one hundred and thirty-three miles of the Pole; that following Marvin's departure, he had taken all observations for Commander Peary. When Bob left our leader, he left him stripped for action. There were comparatively few miles to go, and the sledging surface was good. He had five of the picked men of the whole expedition, all expert dog-drivers. He had forty of his best dogs of the one hundred and thirty-three, all tough, seasoned veterans of the trail. The weak and the amateurs had been left behind. With that equipment Peary was bound to reach the Pole, and even go beyond it if he would.

Another item of interest in Commander's letter was his reference to the South Pole trip. Often, as we occupied the same igd-loo on the Polar Sea, he had told me of his plans for the future. Often he had said:

MacMillan, when this end is done, we'll tackle the other end. That is a much simpler proposition. It can easily be done with dogs.

A definite announcement that Borup and I were both to go south and, in the meantime, were to prepare for Antarctic work, was also convincing proof, if any was needed, that this 'end is done.' That our work thus far was satisfactory was a cause for general rejoicing. George had declared that he would never go back to the Altoona Machine Shops, and I had vowed that I would never go back to teaching.

So our tongues wagged on, there at the edge of the Polar Sea, sitting on musk-ox skins within a little brown tent over which were flying the flags of Bowdoin and Yale, our respective colleges. We were recalled to real life by an Eskimo head in the doorway announcing that our own two men, Kood-look-to and Kai-o-ta, were coming. When they reached within hailing distance, there was a rapid fire of questions and answers, which might as well have been Chinese, so far as Borup and I knew. But the exclamations certainly meant something. They had killed sixteen musk-oxen! Tenderloins, hearts, and tongues for us, good meat for our hard-working dogs! Pemmican is good, but no man would ever consider it as a satisfactory substitute for fresh meat, especially musk-ox meat.

Our four visitors were aroused to action by this announcement. Since there are no musk-oxen in the vicinity of their own homes, this was a rare sport for most of them, a new experience to relate to their friends when gathered on the bed platform in their igd-loo far to the south. Within a few hours they were back with seven more musk-oxen. They had hardly left camp when they met two oxen walking along the shore toward our camp, evidently to call upon the new arrivals, the first to disturb the quietness of their lives for nine years, almost to a day. Later, five more of the animals were added to the game list.

In this place man can live on the country, simply by annexing himself to a friendly herd of musk-oxen, which will furnish him with skins for clothing and shelter, tallow for his lamp for cooking, and meat for sustenance. And there are more of the animals than will ever be used. The wolf, not man, is their real enemy. In a herd of ten musk-oxen I have found four mothers with milk in the distended udders, but only one calf. The wolves had exacted their toll.

With our tent now smelling like a cow barn with its thick floor covering of fresh musk-ox skins, we went back to more serious things and talked of the work in hand. Our instructions read, 'You should have two Eskimos with you on the ice and Borup should have two with him at Jesup taking the observations.' We-shark-ob-see and Awah-ting-wa volunteered at once to remain with us. Kar-ko and In-yu-gee-to would return to the ship with full loads of meat and skins.

No time was to be wasted if I was to reach the eighty-fifth parallel so late in the year. From the hills I could see lanes of water extending like the threads of a gigantic spider web until lost in a maze of rough ice.

Kood-look-to, Kai-o-ta, and I were away at six-fifteen on Sunday, May 9th. All went well for five miles, and then we encountered the largest pressure ridge I have ever seen directly across our path. I knew now why Commander considered the route from Cape Morris Jesup to the Pole impracticable, and why he chose the Cape Columbia section as the strategic point of attack.

With only one pick-axe between us, I had considered that George would certainly need it in establishing a tidal station. I could not forget my attempts to penetrate the sea ice in the preceding November. Against his protests I insisted that the ice lance could do our work on the sea. This was expecting too much of an ice lance. We should never get anywhere. I dispatched Kood-look-to back to the land with a note to George instructing him to send me everything he had. He did, and came with it next day. He had reached 85° North Latitude off Cape Columbia, so his account of his visit, in 'A Tenderfoot with Peary,' is of great value as a basis for comparison:

I arrived about one A.M., May 10th, and found that Mac was facing a fearful proposition, for worse ice I'd never seen. It looked as impassable as a cancelled stamp would be at Tiffany's, so I told him to take the pick and I'd try and sink the tide hole with a lance; if he waited till that was done, he'd have to lose a day anyhow, possibly more. Meanwhile, the wind had increased so we could see but a few yards in the drift, so the night was spent there. On occasions like this we used to fall back on the motto of the Tegetoff, 'This, too, O King, will pass away.' At eight A.M. it let up and we said good-bye. I hated to see him going out and me not with him, being very much worried as to where he'd bring up if a good, lively easterly wind should think him *de trop* – to hell and gone out in the East Greenland Sea – so I told him for God's sake to take care of himself, and that in the event of a prolonged gale I'd hike east and south, making caches for him.

By this time it was blowing and drifting to such an extent that to advance simply meant further trouble. I spent the day in reconnoitering. Rather than go over, it might be better to go around. Borup remained with me and watched for an opportunity to make the land. By eight o'clock in the evening, the weather looked favorable enough again to tackle the job, although it was still snowing. A copy of my entries in my journal for May 11th to 14th, written on the spot, gives some idea of the difficulties encountered off the northern point of Greenland at that time of year:

We left our camp inside the pressure ridge last night about eight o'clock and marched till four this morning. It has snowed all night and continues to do so. I thought I knew something about the ice of the Polar Sea, but previous to this trip it has been comparatively child's play to work through it. Here off this cape it is simply frightful, hardly a spot flat enough to pitch a tent, jammed up into one great conglomerate mass, and falling snow concealing holes and crevices to perfection. I have stumbled and fallen forward and backward, wrenching arms and legs and bruising my body in numberless places. At times wading through snow up to my waist and have been in holes over my head.

The first komatik [sledge] as it struck into the rough ice from the glacial fringe, went completely out of sight in the soft snow. The next turned completely over smashing both upstanders. This was decidedly encouraging! While Kai-o-to was doing some repairing, Kood-look-to and I went on ahead road making. In an hour or so we started on again. We are hemmed in tonight on all sides by high walls of ice. How to get out and where to head for will be a question for us in the morning. Still snowing.

Wednesday, May 12th. I could hardly believe my eyes this morning. After traveling for five hours through terrible going, rubble ice, holes and soft snow, we came to what the Innuit called 'Nu-ka-pa-teer seeko' – young ice. It seemed too good to be true. When we had reached the end of it, I decided to pitch tupik so as to take a sounding. Found the depth of water to be ninety-one fathoms. Temperature of water 29°.

Can see more young ice ahead so will not take sight today, but will push on for all we are worth.

Thursday, May 13th. After a bit of rough going we found another stretch of young ice which gave us a long run to the north. At two o'clock this morning we came to what looks like the Big Lead. It is a quarter of a mile wide in some places, extending S. W. just as far as I can see and also east. I got across this morning in one place where the lead was jammed together, but it would be almost impossible for dogs and komatik to do so. Will camp here tonight and take meridian altitude tomorrow noon. If the lead freezes over we shall cross. For the last half mile we have struggled to get through. A part of the way I crawled on hands and knees, it was so much easier than stumbling and falling over the sharp points of ice.

Depth of water here same as before, 91 fathoms.

Friday, May 14th. Decided to try to get across the lead by drawing the komatik back and forth with very light load over thin ice with a rope, I crossing over the high pressure ridge. But the lead had widened during the night leaving open water down through the middle of it; so we were compelled to give it up and try to cross above.

We broke camp and followed the lead magnetic north for two or three hours. Here we became entangled in a regular network branching in all directions. To advance was no longer possible. Decided to give it up as the open water did not seem to freeze a particle.

Meridian sight gave me 84° 15′ 5″ as the site of our last camp. By following a N. 65° W. course for two or three hours we probably made another couple of miles north.

Started back at once stopping here at the last of the young ice for another sounding. Got 56 fathoms here, which I judge to be 12 miles out. Will sleep for a few hours, then push on for land.

We reached the land after plugging along all Friday night and until late Saturday, to find Borup gone from the old camp site. A brief note telling me of his trials and failure to find water ended with 'tidal observation station located about one and a half miles east.'

I found him there, on half rations of biscuit, oil, and milk, but with plenty of meat, and very, very lonesome. I broke the ice in our home-made teapot, a five-gallon oil tin cut in half, and drank long and deep of ice-cold tea, and then settled back in comfort to hear his story. His experience had been but a repetition of my own at Cape Columbia. After digging down through eight feet of solid ice (with a lance) and expecting water to gush up at any minute, they struck land. George said, 'We both collapsed right there and then. Our hands were so sore and mittens so stiff that we gave it up for the day.'

The next day, with renewed courage and in a different locality, they resumed operations. At seven feet they both had reason to believe that the salt-water geyser was ready to spout. Ah-wa-ting-wa was in the hole with one eye on every blow of the lance and the other on a rope held by Borup which was dangling within reach. When the final blow opened the hole, the Eskimo, excited and partly blinded by spray, was at first unable to find the rope. He yelled like a loon, which so added to Borup's keen sense of the humorous that he lacked the strength to pull the poor fellow out. In fact, George declared, he was laughing so hard that he nearly fell in on top of the Eskimo!

When the station was finally in operation, the thing didn't act reasonably. When I reached him, Borup was about ready to give it up and go south to Cape Washington. There are, of course, two high tides in twenty-four hours. George was recording faithfully *one* high and *two* low. He wanted to know where in H — the other high one was, and how it got by the Cape without calling in!

Considering that the mean range of the tide was only .52 of a foot, one can imagine how exasperating the results were of ten-minute readings on a neap tide! They certainly were to poor George, who hated detail and who looked longingly toward the brown patches on the great white hills, for there, he knew, were musk-oxen for his .33 special. He did love to hunt!

Our tide books were so ruled that after recording height, time, maximum, minimum, mean, barometer, thermometer, one page remained for 'Remarks.' Proud of the results, which I hoped would be a credit to the expedition and a distinct contribution to science, I had carefully covered the book with heavy wrapping paper to record everything exactly and neatly, since the book was to be returned to the Coast and Geodetic Survey at Washington. After struggling through six hours of painstaking work, I handed over the precious volume to George. Imagine my consternation on relieving him to find written under 'Remarks' and with an *indelible* pencil,

I do not know whether this God damn tide is going up or down.

At the time it didn't strike me as a bit funny. I strode back to the tent with a martial air, but the only satisfaction I ever got was, 'Mac, that was the page for "Remarks" and that's where I put them.'

Dear old George! There was never a better! Gone now, fighting for his life in the quiet waters of Long Island Sound. Chock full of grit, loyal, true – we all loved him.

Our sixteen days at Cape Morris Jesup were anything but strenuous. It was simply read, rest, sleep, eat, and sit at the tidal hole recording, recording, at times half asleep in the warm spring sun. Our hardest work was to prevent our Eskimos from slaughtering more musk-oxen than we could possibly use for food. Finally, I took their rifles away from them. They were somewhat peeved and wanted to go home. Old Kai-o-ta drove in quietly that night with a big bull lashed down on his sledge!

'How in the world did he ever get that?' we exclaimed in amazement. He had strapped his hunting knife to the end of his whipstock, converting it into a harpoon, which he always regained after each throw by retaining the end of a rawhide line attached to it. But judging from the torn condition of the skin, I knew that his dogs had played an important and cruel part in the kill. Without the dogs, it seems an impossible feat, although Lieutenant Wyatt Rawson of the Nares Expedition actually stabbed a musk-ox with his knife.

Taking the hint from Kai-o-ta, the Eskimos came in with four more musk-oxen on the nineteenth; they had harpooned them with the ice lance. It was a sight to see them gathered under the lee of a windbreak of musk-ox skins, cracking open the large bones and eating the raw marrow, a habit of nearly all primitive peoples.

Commander Peary's cairn of 1900 was plainly visible on the crest of a small hill to the east of the camp. We omitted observations for a few hours to visit this, the most northern cairn in the world. It contained two records had we but known it, one enclosed in a tin tube in his own handwriting and the other a minimum thermometer which had recorded for nine years the lowest temperature at that point – a most valuable piece of information. We knew nothing about this, and were astonished at seeing one of our Eskimos, after digging into one side of the cairn, holding a wooden thermometer case *upside down!* Instantly I snatched it away, but I was too late. The indicator had started back and was now at forty-two below zero, which, as we knew, was far too warm for that place in the middle of the Arctic night or in the bitter cold days of February.

We reset the thermometer, and carefully replaced it to await the explorer in the future.

The written record was as follows:

May 13, 1900 – 5 A.M.
Have just reached here from Etah via Ft. Conger. Left Etah March 4th. Left Conger April 15th. Have with me my man Henson, an Eskimo, Ahngmalokto, 16 dogs and three sledges; all in fair condition. Proceed today due north over sea ice. Fine weather. I am doing this work under the auspices of and with funds furnished by the Peary Arctic Club of New York City.

The membership of this club comprises: Morris K. Jesup, Henry W. Cannon, Herbert L. Bridgman, John H. Flagler, E.O. Benedict, Frederick E. Hyde, E.W. Bliss, H.H. Sands, J.M. Constable, C.F. Wyckoff, E.G. Wyckoff, Chas. P. Daly, Henry Parish, A.A. Raven, E.B. Thomas, and others.

R.E. PEARY, Civil Engineer, U.S.N.

With this record were two others:

May 17. Have returned to this point. Reached 83° 50′ N. Lat. due north of here. Stopped by extremely rough ice, intersected by water cracks. Water sky to the north. Am now going east along the coast. Fine weather.

May 26th. Have again returned to this place. Reached point on East Coast about N. Lat. 83°. Open water all along the coast a few miles off. No land seen to north or east. Last seven days continuous fogs, wind and snow. Is now snowing with strong westerly wind. Temperature 20° F. Ten musk-oxen killed east of here. Expect start for Conger tomorrow.

It is unfortunate that Commander was compelled to enclose such an important record in a tin tube. It was rusty and badly pitted and would have been gone in a few years. We wrapped it carefully with black adhesive tape to resist corrosion and possibly prolong its preservation for a number of years.

It was some satisfaction for me to note that I had surpassed Commander's record of 83° 50′ on the Polar Sea north of Cape Jesup, and had been stopped by the same 'extremely rough ice, intersected by water cracks.'

Our observations were now completed and bench mark established. We placed the following record under a cairn erected near-by:

Cape Morris Jesup

May 23rd, 1909

To whom it may concern:

Acting under orders of Lieut. R.E. Peary, U.S.N., Commanding North Polar Expedition of Peary Arctic Club, we left the *Roosevelt* at Cape Sheridan on April 19th in company with five Esquimaux for the purpose of making a cache of supplies at Cape Morris Jesup for the support of the northern party, to take soundings on the Polar Sea as far as the 85th parallel and to take tidal observations for a period of ten days.

Last sounding at 84° 15' depth of water 91 fathoms. This morning at 1.00 A.M. we completed our tidal observations. Tidal gauge situated from this bench mark 1133 feet 4 in., bearing N. 43° 30' E. in 16 ft. 4 in. of water. Mean range of tides for a period .52 of a foot. Will leave for Str. *Roosevelt* today.

D.B. MACMILLAN

GEORGE BORUP

Assistants to Com. Peary

With sledges packed and ready for home, Borup insisted on appropriate ceremonies at the tidal hole in commemoration of the last and eagerly-looked-forward-to observation. What our Eskimos thought of the Yale and Bowdoin yells, which they had practiced assiduously for several days with Borup as cheer leader, was left to our imaginations. And by what manner of quaint erudition some anthropologist of the future may deduce that there is certainly some racial affinity between the Eskimos and the Latin race, when he sees old Kai-o-ta take his stand, bow to his imaginary audience, and solemnly repeat the first six lines of Virgil's Æneid: 'Arma virumque cano Troiae qui primus ab oris,' etc., may be left as a puzzle to brother scientists!

CHAPTER 22

米

WHAT CAN BE DONE WITH DOGS

On Sunday, May 25, 1909, at two-thirty-five in the morning, we left the Cape to its loneliness, feeling as if we could conquer the world, with every muscle rested and ready to go. Strapping on our snowshoes, we disdained dogs and sledges and waved for them to go on. Who couldn't walk the thirty-five miles to Cape Washington? Why, of course we could! Nothing to it! We fairly romped for the first ten, slowed down at fifteen, and sat down at twenty! We were tired.

Back to back to support each other, we recalled amusing incidents of the past year. But nothing was funny enough or interesting enough to keep us awake. Just when we slumped, or fell over into the snow, we never knew. An hour or so later we awoke with the cold and with a start and remembered that we had an appointment with two Eskimos ten miles down the line. We buckled on our snowshoes and plodded on over the back of a treacherous glacier, finding numerous intersecting cracks to cross, some of which necessitated détours.

As we plodded down the white slope toward the sea ice, we could see Cape Washington faintly outlined in the blue haze, and regretted our ambition to camp there at the end of the first day's march. As we rounded a stretch of rough ice, we were highly elated to see the tent pitched on the ice foot just to the east of Cape Cannon. Our Eskimos had shown excellent judgment in waiting for us.

Two weeks of eating and sleeping had contributed nothing in the way of stamina. We were obviously out of condition. We jollied each other to sleep, I with my feet high in the air against the tent pole, to avoid cramps, and Borup with his bearskin pants down to his knees trying to cool off!

Monday, May 24th, was one of those beautiful northern days which persist in memory with the bright sunshine, blue sky, glittering ice fields, and a temperature of plus twenty-three. A short march brought us to Cape Washington and to the Peary cairn which, we knew, contained records. We located them by removing a few stones from one side of the cairn:

C. Washington, May 29, 1900.
Arrive here today on our way to Ft. Conger. Passed here on my way north May 10. Have rounded north end of Greenland and gone down to East Coast to about N. Lat. 83°. Reached a point on the ice north of the land in N. L. 83° 50′.

    Ten musk-oxen and one bear killed east of here. Continuous fog, snow and wind since the 20th. Am traveling now in deep snow. All well.
R.E. PEARY
Civil Engineer, U.S.N.

May 29th, 1900.
This copy of the record left by Lieut. J.B. Lockwood and Sergt. D.L. Brainard, U.S.A., in cairn on Lockwood I., southwest of here May 16th, 1882, is today placed by me in this cairn on the farthest land seen by them as a tribute to two brave men, one of whom gave his life for his Arctic work.
R.E. PEARY, U.S.N.

Soft snow on the twenty-fifth did not prevent our covering the distance of thirty-three miles to Lockwood Island, where we again visited the cairn, but we failed to find any kind of record. Gradually we were increasing our distance on this homeward stretch. Forty miles on the twenty-sixth and another forty on the twenty-seventh brought us to Cape Salor, passing on the way Cape Newmayer, where we found the site of Commander Peary's camp of 1906 when he landed here, starving, after breaking Nansen's record of Farthest North of 86° 14'. The record now was 87° 6'. We found evidence that the party was in extreme circumstances, for in the ashes were the steel shoes of a sledge, and, scattered about the fire, the bones of a hare, which were the last traces of one of the most thrilling adventures of Peary's thrilling life. I have suggested this incident earlier in my narrative, but Peary's own words on the story are too important to be passed over.

Commander had often told me that he considered that this was the nearest he had ever come to death. 'It was the first and only time in all my Arctic work that I felt doubtful of the outcome.' Cut off from home by the Big Lead, 'the Styx,' which was now two miles in width, their lives depended upon its closing or freezing. They cooked some of their dogs; they burned one of their sledges for fuel. Then the day came. The lead was covered with ice, but was it strong enough to support the weight of a man? It was their only chance. They strapped on their snowshoes. Now come the exact words as he related it to me:

> I told the men that it was each man for himself; that to help each other meant death for all. I was the heaviest. I knew I would probably go first. I took off my deerskin coat, rolled it into a bundle and dragged it on a string behind me. We started, walking wide and some fifty feet apart. I did not dare to lift my feet. I glided one slowly past the other. There were undulations from every man. Twice my toes broke through the ice. 'This is the finish,' I said to myself. I heard a cry. 'God help him, which one is it?' I muttered as I continued on. I reached the edge of the ice and looked along the line. Every man was there! As we looked over that film of ice we could see a dark crack cutting our bridge. We had crossed just in time.

We were all dreading the soft snows of Keltie Gulf. Rather than retrace our old steps and, with the possibility of improved going farther from land, we kept nearer to Beaumont Island as Lockwood and Brainard had done twenty-seven years before.

Kood-look-to objected to our short march of ten hours on the twenty-eighth, but not to the sixty miles on the twenty-ninth! He was glad to get into camp at Cape Bryant and have his tea after seventeen hours of walking, running, riding at intervals, and pushing on his sledge.

We had learned our lesson at Black Horn Cliffs on the upward trip. Now we swung far out from land away from the jam of ice and passed by very easily. We would have undoubtedly attempted a crossing to Grant Land had the air been clear of snow and mist. As it was, we could not see the west side of Robeson Channel. We, therefore, headed for Repulse Harbor, where we found an enormous cairn, so large that I at once attributed its construction to Hall. His enthusiasm and love for the work would prompt him to spend hours on just such a structure.

Upon second thoughts I realized that Hall did not land from his ship in August, 1871, nor did he succeed in reaching Repulse Harbor by sledge before he died on November 7th. His farthest north was Cape Brevoort, fourteen miles south. So this cairn was undoubtedly the Repulse Harbor Dépôt of the Nares Expedition. Knowing that Lockwood had removed the record years ago, I was much surprised to find a tightly corked bottle hidden beneath the rocks. We could read through the glass a part of the record and recognized the well-known handwriting of Commander Peary. Since we were his assistants, we had decided, naturally enough, not to remove any records of his which we might find. It would be far better that someone else should find them and thereby furnish proof to verify his claims.

Eight years later Rasmussen found and removed this record. It read:

Am passing here on my way to Ft. Conger. I left Etah March 4th and Conger April 15th. Reached Lockwood's farthest May 8th; the northern extremity of the Greenland archipelago on May 13th; a point on the sea-ice north of that N. Lat. 83° 50′ May 16th; and a point down the east coast about North Lat. 83° May 21st. There followed over a week of fog, wind and snow, this made the traveling very heavy and the return slow. This is my 16th march from my farthest and 9th from Lockwood's farthest. Yesterday passed Black Horn Cliffs with much difficulty over loose ice. There is open water now off this point and a lane of open water this side of C. Brevoort extending clear across the channel. Have with me my man Matthew Henson, one Eskimo, 16 dogs and 2 sledges, all in fair condition.

This sledge journey is part of a program of Arctic work undertaken by me under the auspices of and with funds furnished by the Peary Arctic Club of New York City.

R.E. PEARY, U.S.N.

Supper was over and we were just on the point of falling asleep, when we heard strange voices. Nothing will awaken a man more quickly after hearing the familiar tones of one's own party for many weeks. We all squeezed through the door at once to meet a supporting party consisting of Big Coadey, acting bo'sun of the *Roosevelt*, and two Eskimos, Ah-lettah and Karko, bringing biscuit, oil, and pemmican. Food was the last thing we needed. But Commander was taking no chances; he was always solicitous in the care of his men.

Now came the latest news from the ship. The Eskimos must have talked all night, if our sunlight sleeping periods could be called night, for we heard them when we dozed off and heard them again when we awoke. We often pitched no tent, but simply lay on our sledges at the end of the day's journey, and slept the hours away in the bright sunshine.

Thick weather – snow – on the thirty-first compelled us to resort to the compass for the most direct route across Robeson Channel to Black Cape, twenty-one miles away. When we arrived there, our Eskimos wanted to camp, as we had traveled twenty-five miles in all. We told them that they might if they wanted to, but that we were determined to reach the ship that night; she was only eight miles beyond. As we looked back along the trail, we saw them following. The comfort of the ship also appealed to them.

Dogs versus men – it was always the same story. That day we had covered *ten* of the marches of the Nares Expedition. Commander met us at the rail with 'Well! Well! you've beaten my old record all to pieces!' We had reached Cape Morris Jesup in eighteen marches and had returned to the ship in eight.

To quote Commander Peary:

Even when compared with the journey of Lockwood and Brainard from Conger to Lockwood Island, using southern Greenland dogs and driver, the journey of MacMillan and Borup along the same coast from Cape Sheridan to Cape Morris Jesup is instructive. Lockwood and Brainard were twenty-five marches from Conger to Lockwood Island and sixteen marches on the return.

MacMillan and Borup went from Cape Sheridan (nearly the same distance as Conger) to Cape Jesup, forty miles beyond Lockwood Island, in much less time, and on the return covered the distance in eight marches averaging thirty-four miles per march.

My reason for recording these facts, personal as they are, is to enlighten certain critics as to what can be done with dogs, with by no means empty sledges.

✳

GREELY'S OLD CAMP AT FORT CONGER

One night in our stuffy little stateroom was enough for us both. We both wanted to get away in the morning and Commander Peary had promised us that we should.

We congratulated him upon reaching the Pole. He thanked us, smiled, and added: 'When I get home, I can tell you all about it. We may meet a ship at Etah. She might reach home ahead of us.'

The thought that the crew of another ship might first bear to civilization the important announcement that Peary had reached the Pole was not pleasant to anyone on board.

And yet we all knew the facts. They were there flat on the deck for all to read – a wooden cross with the following inscriptions upon its four arms:

Cape Morris K. Jesup, May 16, 1900, 275 miles
Cape Columbia, June 6, 1906
Cape Thomas Hubbard, July 1, 1906, 225 miles
North Pole, April 6, 1909, 413 miles

This was a list of the important points of the Far North which Peary had reached, the time of visit, and the airline distance of each from Cape Columbia, the first 'Air Ship Sign Post' ever erected.

Attached to the crossed arms was a record framed and under glass, an absolutely definite announcement signed by Peary.

PEARY ARCTIC CLUB NORTH POLE
EXPEDITION, 1908

S.S. *Roosevelt,*
   June 12th, 1909
This monument marks the point of departure and return of the sledge expedition of the Peary Arctic Club, which in the spring of 1909 attained the North Pole.

   The members of the expedition taking part in the sledge work were Peary, Bartlett, Goodsell, Marvin[1], MacMillan, Borup, Henson.

   The various sledge divisions left here February 28th and March 1st, and returned from March 18th to April 23rd.

   The Club's steamer *Roosevelt* wintered at C. Sheridan, 73 miles east of here.

          R.E. PEARY, U.S.N.

1 Drowned April 10th, returning from
  86° 38′ North Lat.

Commander R.E. Peary, U.S.N.
   Comdg. Expedition
Captain R.A. Bartlett, Master of
   Roosevelt
Chief Engr. George A. Wardwell
Surgeon J.W. Goodsell
Prof. Ross G. Marvin, Assistant
Prof. D.B. MacMillan, Assistant
George Borup, Assistant
M.A. Henson, Assistant
Charles Percy, Steward
Mate Thomas Gushue
Bosun John Connors
Seaman John Coady
   ″   John Barnes
   ″   Dennis Murphy
   ″   George Percy
2nd Engr. Banks Scott
Fireman James Bently
   ″   Patrick Joyce
   ″   Patrick Skeans
   ″   John Wiseman

How many, many times I have had to answer the question, 'Why didn't Commander Peary tell someone that he had reached the Pole before he heard of Cook's announcement?' Could anything be more plain or emphatic than this inscription?

Borup was instructed to sledge the beacon to Cape Columbia, and to erect it at the very point of our departure from land. Undoubtedly it is still there today unless it has been destroyed by bears, for no one has visited the spot since Borup left it on June 23, 1909.

My instructions were to go to Fort Conger, the headquarters of the Lady Franklin Expedition of 1881–84, in latitude 81° 40′ N., which was some sixty miles to the south by dog team. I was to make a series of tidal observations to supplement those taken by Greely. My traveling companions were to be Kood-look-to, who had just returned with me from Cape Morris Jesup, and Jack Barnes, my tidal assistant of the winter at Cape Columbia.

Since it was late in the season, we had to make plans for the possible abandonment of everything – equipment, sledges, dogs – in the event of the ice breaking up and open water preventing travel. I knew that there were places which would demand three men on one sledge, so I concluded to take one team of ten dogs rather than two of five each. We had orders to shoot four dogs for food on reaching Conger.

We left the *Roosevelt* at five-thirty in the afternoon of June 8th, as we preferred night travel at this time of year – not so warm, not so hard on the eyes, not so soft under foot. Within seven hours we were in camp at Lincoln Bay, discussing snow-white owls and long-tailed ducks, both of which we had seen on the way. Summer had returned and with it the looked-for bird life of the North.

Wednesday, the ninth, was a great day. Within fifteen minutes of leaving camp, both Jack and I broke through the ice, now melting beneath the rays of a warm sun. Once out of the water, we scrambled madly for shore, where Kood-look-to, with better judgment, was driving the dog team.

At Cape Frederick VII there was no ice foot! There was a high steep bank of snow, its surface now compact and glazed by the sun, and, below, the water filled with sludge. We studied the situation for a few minutes. Kood-look-to thought that he could do it. 'All right, let's try,' I suggested.

I looked with distrust at the one narrow groove which he was cutting in the surface of the sloping bank. That was for one runner of the sledge, he explained – an old Eskimo practice. Kood-look-to led the march ahead of the trembling dogs, which by now were beginning to crouch and dig in their toe-nails. I was designated to handle the sledge. Jack was the supporting party, at the moment quite inactive, but looking decidedly worried. In the opinion of this sailor the end of a yardarm on a stormy night was obviously a far more comfortable place.

We were halfway across when the runner jumped the groove and the whole outfit began to slide toward the brink. In trying to control it, I made matters worse by losing my feet on the slippery ice. Jack nearly had a fit, and Kood-look-to became so excited that I thought he would bleed at the nose. The one thing happened which alone could save the situation – the sledge rolled over on its side and was stopped by the friction of the load acting as a brake.

For a few seconds I didn't dare to move. The dogs were flat on their stomachs whining and clawing at the ice in an attempt to regain their former place on the bank. Gingerly, we removed the lashings and the goods, piece by piece, until the komatik was unloaded and everything was removed to a safe place around the end of the Cape.

Here there was a real summer scene – a large pool of water in which were a black guillemot, eight brant geese, and a flock of old-squaws, forerunners of the great influx of Arctic bird life.

The bit of pleasure here was succeeded by a lot of hard work beyond. A one-runner track was in ill favor for the rest of the day. We resorted to ropes on the front and rear end of the sledge to prevent rolling over and sliding, two of us walking above on the rocky talus slope, while the third managed the dogs.

When the ice foot became impassable, we slipped the dogs from the bridle, pointed the sledge down toward the improved channel ice and let her go, as we had been used to doing on the Polar Sea. With her strong reinforced knockabout bow she bounded over the rough blocks as handsomely as a good boat bounds over a rough sea – and landed right side up! Another triumph for the Peary komatik!

As we approached Cape Beechey, we descried a black dot in the distance. There was no mistaking what it was – a seal sunning himself on the surface of the ice, the first one of the season for us, and, as always, a most welcome sight. Kood-look-to did his best. He wriggled and crawled, lifted his head repeatedly as a seal lifts his, waved his hand, a pretended flipper, and moved his foot in circles, lying flat on his side. The seal, ever on the watch for bear, was suspicious of this thing ever getting nearer. He was gone in the twinkling of an eye and with him our promised meal of seal flippers.

Now came a strange and unfamiliar sound. I listened a few moments and wondered what it could possibly be. Was it the wind, or the sound of moving ice? Suddenly we made out a white mark on the cliff, the spray of falling water. Instinctively we turned toward this unfamiliar sound, this unfailing sign of summer, and pitched our little brown tent as near to the stream as possible, that we might listen to the lull of its music as we dropped into dreams of budding trees, of green grass, of long summer holidays.

Thursday, June 10th, brought to me the realization of a wish of my boyhood. I was at Fort Conger! No boy could read Greely's 'Three Years of Arctic Service,' pathetic as it is in parts, without yearning to see the North. As I snowshoed around the end of Distant Cape, every point was as familiar as if I had lived here. There was Bellot Island, Proteus Point, Archer Fiord, and – a man standing near the house. Who in the world could it be? Could it possibly be – yes, it must be Dr. Goodsell. He had left ship several weeks before for Lake Hazen for trout and fossils, and must be returning by way of Conger. And so it proved to be – brown, hearty, and glad to see us, but deeply pained and worried because his Eskimos persisted, in unguarded moments, in lightening their sledges by throwing away his precious rocks, declaring that there were plenty near the ship! No one is right in his mind who carries rocks around in his pockets, or so their philosophy seems to run.

We had a new dish on our menu that evening in the large red-meated trout. Every part of our anatomy must have been surprised, for we had had no fresh fish for a year. It is strange to think of trout – which we in New England associate with running brooks and streams winding down through green meadows – as living almost at the top of the world beneath a sheet of ice eight and ten feet in thickness. Their short annual visit to the sea must be their only pleasure in life.

Since there are so many kinds of trout that the best authorities are not agreed as to their classifications, the term 'trout' is most indefinite. We speak of our New England brook trout; but this is really a species of charr, known to science as the *Salvelinus fontinalis*. Undoubtedly these fish from Lake Hazen are a charr of some kind, but they were not included in the list of specimens brought back by the Nares Expedition and examined by Albert Gunther. The *Salmo arcturus, alipes,* and *naresi* are all much smaller and were obtained by us later in small lakes.

It was with the deepest interest that we examined the remains of what was a home for the twenty-five men who landed here in August, 1881. The ends of the building were gone; the kitchen alone remained with its large cooking range in an excellent state of preservation. To my surprise there were three small houses to which Lieutenant Greely never referred in his narrative, and for which I was entirely unable to account. Later, I learned that these had been built by Peary and his Eskimos in 1900–02, when he made Fort Conger his base for his attack on the Pole.

But visiting Eskimos could never have removed the multitude of things found there by Commander Peary when, on January 6, 1899, he stumbled in through that door, unopened for sixteen years. The grounds and houses were littered with a heterogeneous mixture of a little of everything from blue and white striped Indian clubs to a volume of Bishop Brooks's sermons; from a really good pair of skates to a large two-wheeled pushcart.

And there was food in large airtight tin cases, tea, coffee, hominy, and what? Very plainly we could read the labels – Canned Potatoes! Potatoes with our trout, why not? Potatoes brought into the Arctic twenty-eight years before! I had never dreamed that potatoes were canned so long ago as that. The first can revealed its contents as rhubarb! And so did the second and the third and the fourth. They were all rhubarb. Some factory girl had made a mistake in labeling.

But the rhubarb wasn't wasted. There was a certain tempting tang about it which kept the spoon busy in spite of its long years of confinement. Members of the medical profession have since informed me that we were taking chances. In the North a man can eat anything and seemingly forget it!

Everything in the Greely camp was so absorbing that it was hard to get to work upon the main object of our little expedition – a series of tidal observations. A good crack in the ice directly in front of the house would serve as our tidal hole. The water was nine feet deep, a convenient depth. A long iron rod driven firmly into the mud bottom, to which we lashed a graduated board, made an excellent gauge. With such facilities at hand we managed to begin work the day of our arrival.

When off duty and between observations, we continued to explore and delve into everything. There were boxes of stuffed birds, boxes of geological specimens, sections of petrified trees, fossils, Eskimo skulls, and photographic plates. There were yards of blue army cloth, and full regalia in which Kood-look-to proudly arrayed himself and paraded for days with a martial air. With epaulettes, long swallow tails, and a visored cap of the vintage of 1861, he was anything but a frightful warrior.

Mingled with moments of pleasure were hours of silence, of pity, sympathy, pathos. How unfortunate that they had left a good home, well stocked with food, in a region where game was plentiful, to die at Cape Sabine! But they had obeyed their orders.

How unfortunate, and I may add how stupid, that the War Department did not foresee the possibility of the loss of the relieving vessel north of Littleton Island, and this in spite of the difficulties encountered by the *Neptune* the year before. She had failed to reach within one hundred and fifty miles of the Greely station.

There can be but one reasonable explanation of their attitude and of their action. In 1881 the *Proteus* had reached easily the site of the station; therefore, *she could do it again!* If there is one place in the world where conditions are uncertain and vary from year to year, that place is the Arctic.

One man alone, Louis V. Carziac, a clerk in the office of the Chief Signal Officer at Washington, should receive credit for providing for this very contingency. The fate of the nineteen men who died hung upon an enclosure designated as 'Memorandum 4.' Known to be unofficial and considered of little importance, it was thrown into the waste-paper basket.

MacMillan (left) and Jack Barnes at Fort Conger
Headquarters of the Greely expedition of 1881–1884

Kood-look-to, the 'game-getter,' at Fort Conger

The *Proteus* was crushed some thirty-five miles north of Littleton Island. Greely and his men, retreating southward, and daily looking for the relief ship, were abandoned to their fate.

A careful study and comparison of Lieutenant Garlington's orders with 'Memorandum 4' is of the utmost importance in realizing the completeness of the disaster. I quote them in full:

War Department
Office of The Chief Signal Officer
Washington City, June 4, 1883

Lieut. E. A. Garlington,
Commanding relief vessel to Lady Franklin Bay:

Sir: You are aware of the necessity of reaching Lieutenant A.W. Greely and his party with the expedition of this year. This necessity cannot be overestimated, as Lieutenant Greely's supplies will be exhausted during the coming fall, and unless the relief ship can reach him he will be forced, with his party, to retreat southward by land before the winter sets in.

Such a retreat will involve hardship and the probable abandonment of much valuable public property, with possible loss of important records and life.

For these and other reasons which will occur to you no effort must be spared to push the vessel through to Lady Franklin Bay.

In the event of being obstructed by ice in Smith Sound or Kennedy Channel, you are advised to try to find a passage through along the west coast, which, besides being usually the most practicable, will afford better advantages for sighting and communicating with any party sent out by Lieutenant Greely. To make communication surer, your party must be able to readily send and receive messages by flag or heliograph, and other means, and the necessary articles should be kept in readiness for instant use when communication is possible.

Should the vessel be unable to get through the ice to Lady Franklin Bay or to reach the west coast at points above Cape Sabine, it will be of great importance that Lieutenant Greely should know of the efforts being made to relieve him and of the plans for doing so. You will endeavor, therefore, to convey such intelligence and omit no means of informing him or any of his party of the situation. Should any landings be made at prominent points on either coast during the efforts to get through the ice, you will leave a short record of the facts, with such information as it is desirable to convey, so deposited and marked as to render it discoverable by parties traveling southward. If such landings be made at points where caches of provisions are located, you will, if possible, examine them and replace any damaged articles of food, leaving, of course, a record of your action.

If it should become clearly apparent that the vessel cannot be pushed through, you will retreat from your advanced position and land your party and stores at or near Lifeboat Cove, discharge the relief vessel, with orders to return to St. John's, N.F., and prepare for remaining with your party until relieved next year. As soon as possible after landing, or in case your vessel becomes unavoidably frozen up in the ice-pack, you will endeavor to communicate with Lieutenant Greely by taking personal charge of a party of the most experienced and hardy men, equipped for sledging, carrying such stores as is practicable to Cape Sabine, whence a smaller party, more lightly equipped, still headed by yourself, will push as far north as possible, or until Lieutenant Greely's party is met. In this and other matters you will follow the instructions of Lieutenant Greely, dated August 17th, 1881, a printed copy of which is furnished you herewith. (Enclosure '1')

The men not employed in these expeditions will lose no time in preparing the house for the whole party, and in securing the stores preparatory to the arrival of Lieutenant Greely.

You will be furnished two observers and an outfit of scientific apparatus, and will be guided in their use by instructions herewith. The character and amount of meteorological and other scientific work to be accomplished by your party is enumerated in enclosed memoranda marked, B, C, D, E.

In addition to the medical officer, enlisted men taken from this city, you will employ three hardy ice-men at St. John's, who have already been selected by the U.S. consul there under my direction, and in Greenland such Esquimaux as you may require.

It is important that a careful and complete record of events should be made, and in case your party does not return this year that a full report be sent by the vessel on her return to St. John's. Each member of your party will be required to keep a private diary, which will be open to the inspection of the Chief Signal Officer only in case it should be necessary. Whenever a junction is effected with Lieutenant Greely, you will report to him with your party for duty.

Should any important records or instruments have been left behind by Lieutenant Greely in his retreat, they may be recovered by the steamer to be sent in 1884.

It is believed that with the stores and supplies sent last year, which are at St. John's, N.F., and at Greenland ports, a list of which is furnished (enclosure '3'), and which you will gather on your way northward, together with the provisions and articles supplied for this year, everything needful will have been furnished for safety and success. I believe and expect that you will zealously endeavor to effect the object of the expedition, which is to succeed in relieving your comrades, since upon your efforts their lives may depend, and you cannot overestimate the gravity of the work entrusted to your charge.

A ship of the United States Navy, the *Yantic*, will accompany you as far as Littleton Island, rendering you such aid as may become necessary and as may be determined by the captain of that ship and yourself, when on the spot.

With my best wishes for your success and the safe return of the united party, I am, very respectfully, your obedient servant,

W.B. HAZEN
Brig. and Bvt. Maj. Gen'l,
Chief Signal Officer, U.S.A.

With the above instructions, Lieutenant Garlington discovered the following, not signed or dated. Later, at the court of inquiry, it was marked 'Memorandum 4,' a plan quite different in its essential points:

The naval tender to join the *Proteus* at St. John's, N.F., and to proceed with her to the neighborhood of Littleton Island.

The *Proteus* to land her stores, except supplies for more northerly dépôts, at Littleton Island, on her way North. If she succeeds in reaching Lady Franklin Bay, to pick up the stores, excepting the house and dépôts, if possible, on her return. The naval tender will await the return of the *Proteus* at the neighborhood of Littleton Island, and, on her return, steam to the south in her company, until she reaches the southern limits of the ice-pack, when the vessels may separate. Should the *Proteus* be crushed in the ice, her crew will retire on Littleton Island, and the tender will bring to St. John's, N.F., the officers and crew of the *Proteus*. The rest of the party to remain at Littleton Island. But should the ice render it dangerous for the tender to remain in the neighborhood of Littleton Island, until the *Proteus* returns or her crew and the expeditionary force succeed in reaching there, the tender may go back to the south, leaving full particulars at Littleton Island.

Signals by flags, heliograph, and guns should be preconcerted, and communication by this means should be maintained between the two vessels as long as possible after they have separated by the passage north of the *Proteus*.

Nothing in the northward movement must be allowed to retard the progress of the *Proteus*. It is of the utmost importance that she take advantage of every lead to get to Lady Franklin Bay.

Lieutenant Garlington was informed by the Chief Signal Officer that this 'was not part of his orders.'

One other light should be thrown on the screen in order to understand fully just how and why this tragedy of the Arctic. The *Yantic* was detailed to proceed north in company with the *Proteus*, to keep with her if possible and to render aid in every way. If separated, each ship was to call at Cape York, the southeast Cary Island, Pandora Harbor, and Littleton Island.

After the disaster to the *Proteus*, the only hope for the rescue of Greely and his men was to get into communication with the *Yantic* as quickly as possible. Naturally, the lines of retreat for the open boats proceeding southward would be via these points. The shipwrecked men called at Littleton, then Pandora Harbor, then debated as to the wisdom of going out to the Cary Islands. They decided *not* to do so and went on to Cape York. *The Yantic arrived at the Cary Islands that day.* She went on to Pandora Harbor and Littleton Island, found a record of the disaster, and rushed back down the coast. She missed the boat crew at Cape York, missed them again at Upernavik. When, finally, the crew of the *Proteus* climbed over the rail of the *Yantic* at Disko on August 31st, the season for ice navigation in the Far North was practically over. The Fates had played their cards well. Greely and his men were left to their fate.

I knew the story of poor Kislingbury, second in command of Greely's forces, who, within a week of his arrival at Conger, resigned his commission, hastily packed his personal effects, and ran for the shore to miss the returning ship by a few minutes. With the anchor at the cathead, they waved good-bye as he waved for them to send a boat. I picked up a book from the ground, a schoolbook upon the fly-leaf of which was written: 'To my dear Father. From your affectionate son, Harry Kislingbury. May God be with you and return you safely to us.' The father was to die at Cape Sabine.

Strange are the avenues of thought when sledging permits moments of reflection! Mental pictures not recalled for years. Varied and multiple duties are so dominant at home that all else is dwarfed. In the North it is a common experience to recall childhood days, early school days, and early friendships. As I rippled the pages of a notebook I found in the pocket of an old coat, I stopped. There were three lines. I could well understand the sentiment which prompted them:

'Past, Present, and Future
Dost thou remember long ago
Those school days that we loved so well?'

Only two lines of his past! His present was hope of relief. His future was to end two hundred miles south.

I turned back the cover of a trunk and read the stencil, 'Charles H. Bush.'

As I knew that there was no man of that name in the Greely party, I wondered. A year later I knew the answer. There was a man by the name of Charles B. Henry, the largest and apparently the strongest man in the party. During those trying days at Cape Sabine, he was twice detected stealing food from his dying companions. Twice he was pardoned by Lieutenant Greely and gave his word that it would not happen again. A third time he was guilty of the same offense, and was ordered to be shot.

The three men designated to do the work drew straws as to who should be the executioner. They kept their word that the secret should never be divulged, and it never has been. His body was thrown into the ice. The relief ship arrived at Cape Sabine six days later to find only seven living out of twenty-five. When the bodies of the dead, tightly sealed in metallic coffins, were delivered at the Portsmouth Navy Yard, in August, 1884, there was one unclaimed, that of Charles B. Henry. For some time the country tried to solve the mystery. It was finally discovered that Charles Henry Bush, to conceal his identity, had enlisted as Charles B. Henry. He was a fugitive from justice under a charge of murder. A strange working of Fate! Here was his trunk now, nine degrees from the Pole. He had fled almost to the ends of the earth.

＊

CHAPTER 24

BACK TO THE ROOSEVELT AGAIN

Dr. Goodsell left us on June 11th bound for the ship, his eyes upon his box of trilobites, coral, and other evidence that at one time the North had a warm climate, with tropical seas. Here as elsewhere mountain chains were ocean beds, and the ocean beds of today will become grass and forest-clad and rock-strewn hills.

Life at Conger was happy for us. Seals were sunning themselves on the ice, and now and then bobbing up in the tidal hole, curious to know why the iron rod, and what we were doing. Jack, a born Newfoundlander and true to form, insisted on having his national dish at least every other day – seal flippers. This we varied with the delicious meat of the Arctic hare, which we easily obtained on the slopes of the hills. Lemmings were plenty and a source of constant amusement with their comic little ways of standing on their hind legs, clicking their teeth, and pawing the air with their front feet. Disposed at first to resist, to struggle and to fight, within a few hours they snuggled in our hands and pockets, their beady little eyes smiling with contentment.

Kood-look-to was so quiet that I wondered what he was doing, for generally he was playing with a crude windmill, which was buzzing along merrily from the ridgepole of our shack. His interest in this waned completely when he discovered the expedition anemometer, four brass cups attached to rods crossed at right angles – a real white man's windmill. It buzzed merrily for the remainder of the time.

Then he discovered a bronze propeller, and I wondered what he would make of that. He built a tripod of three long iron pipes, suspended the propeller from the apex with a length of wire, and made the hills ring, pounding away with a hammer to his heart's content. It made an excellent bell – a dinner gong.

I crept quietly to his tent one day, peeped through, and was astonished. Four unresisting lemmings had been fitted with tiny harnesses and were drawing a tiny wooden sledge across the floor! What he hoped to prove or demonstrate I could not learn from his sheepish grin. And so on and so on, day after day, his naturally curious mind was always busy.

By now the birds were increasing rapidly. There were new arrivals every day. The mingled cries of the long-tailed ducks (old-squaws) were heard from every pool, not so wild as the cry of the loon, not so musical as that of the Canada goose, but always commanding.

Jack, busy with tidal work, was a bit envious of Kood-look-to's success in bringing in food for our table, today a seal, tomorrow a hare, and the next day ducks. His hands itched for a gun to show us what he could do. Pencil and paper work did not appeal to him.

One day while Jack was sleeping, Kood-look-to arrived with a bag of game. I carried three of the ducks to the edge of the pool, set them on the ice and tied their heads back with a string, and left them, lifelike and perfectly contented with their surroundings.

When Jack awoke, Kood-look-to beckoned him to the doorway and, in a hushed voice, whispered, 'Metit' (ducks), pointing to the pool. Here was Jack's chance. He borrowed my rifle and was away, creeping around the corner of the building, stealing along in the shelter of the rough ice of the tidal crack, and out over the harbor ice, taking advantage of every hummock. Kood-look-to, peering around the corner of the building, was bursting with laughter.

At last Jack arrived at a vantage-point and settled down in the snow for a steady shot. He poked the muzzle of his rifle up over a piece of ice, took a long careful aim and fired. The ducks were unconcerned; they were still there! He crawled a bit closer and fired again – with the same result. Had he killed two or did the .22 calibre fail to reach them? In desperation he crawled up to within twenty yards and fired again. They must all be dead! He jumped to his feet and ran to pick them up. When he was stopped within ten feet by a water crack in the ice, he looked long and earnestly at his quarry and then, quickly, toward the house. He had discovered the string. We had the ducks for dinner the next day, and congratulated Jack upon his skill as a hunter. It was not one of Jack's happy days. He had made a new discovery. On the day of our arrival he had found a gold ring, the very thing he wanted. He was engaged to be married in the fall. She would be pleased with it. Today his finger was green beneath the band!

Kood-look-to brought me something new, a strange-looking thing – a telephone mouthpiece.

'Yes, we talk through that, Kood-look-to; it is attached to a wire which goes over the tops of the poles far, far off in the distance. Let me see, yes, I could talk from here to Etah.'

Naturally enough, he was interested and wanted to know more about it. We found a long piece of wire, and I tried to show him how the line was built, explaining that there were bottles on the top of each pole. With an 'in-nulle-ark-too-e-erk-tunga' (I am going to bed), I left him with the wire and the mouthpiece.

When I awoke six hours later and stepped to the door, the MacMillan-Barnes-Kood-look-to expedition was equipped with a telephone line. He had made poles by splitting boards, had driven them into the ground with his hatchet, and had stretched the wire, twisting it around the top of each pole, for a distance of two hundred feet. Holding his lips to the mouthpiece, he yelled something in Eskimo, dropped it, then ran for dear life down the line, grabbed the end of the wire, and stuck it in his ear! At breakfast, with a positiveness which was almost convincing, he declared that he didn't believe it. It wasn't possible. There wasn't even a hole in the wire.

The Bench Mark of the Lady Franklin Bay Expedition could not be found, search high, search low. It is strange what became of the 'brick pier set in cement' with the 'XX on its south side (true).'

On the 24th, we built another, the top of which was 25 feet, 9.25 inches above the zero of our tidal gauge, and 22 feet 7.3 inches above the mean range of tide. I hope that it will be permanent enough to enable the next observer to make comparisons. The real value of such observations is that they aid the scientist in determining the oscillation of the earth's crust in a particular locality.

In the cairn built over and around our Bench Mark, I placed the following record:

Lady Franklin Bay
Fort Conger, June 25, 1909
To whom it may concern:
This iron stake has served as our Bench Mark for tidal observations through a period of fifteen days. Its top was 25 feet 9¼ inches above the zero of tide gauge, or 22 feet 7.3 inches above the mean range of tide.
    Arrived here June 10th. Shall leave today for Str. *Roosevelt* at Cape Sheridan.
DONALD B. MACMILLAN
JACK BARNES
KOOD-LOOK-TO

We left this place reluctantly. Birds were in the air, seals in the water, and musk-oxen back among the hills. One could live here indefinitely without supporting parties or relief ships, without even resorting to the soapstone seal-oil lamp of the Eskimos. The tenderloins of the musk-ox could be broiled over a hot coal fire. Only a short distance from the house was a seam of coal from twenty-five to thirty feet in thickness. A vast bed of coal within four hundred and forty miles of the North Pole!

H.W. Fielden, the naturalist of the Nares Expedition, wrote of it as follows:

The Grinnell Land lignite indicates a thick peat moss, with probably a small lake, with water lilies on the surface and taxodias on the banks, with pines, firs, spruce, elms, and hazel bushes on the neighboring hills. Further research of vegetable remains, and possibly those of vertebrate fauna, as well as of the insects that probably tenanted the forest; but at present the elytrum of a beetle (*Carabites feildenianus, Hr.*) attests their former presence.

If lands formerly extended to the Pole, they were probably covered with these Arctic forests.

At eight in the evening of June 26th, we left Conger, Jack and I going overland to St. Patrick's Bay by way of North Valley, and Kood-look-to with a load of trunks, a 'steamer' for his sweetheart and a Saratoga for himself, around Proteus Point, Distant Cape, and Cape Murchison, with the understanding that we were to wait for each other off Cartmel Point. I had forgotten my instructions, 'Never let your Eskimos get away from you.'

The pass between the hills was a surprisingly short cut to St. Patrick's Bay, but the descent to the sea ice demanded caution, for the loose rocks of the talus slope slid repeatedly beneath our feet, threatening to carry us down more quickly than we cared to go. In attempting to cross the shore lead, I came within an ace of taking a complete bath. The edge of the ice broke off as I jumped across. When we arrived at Cartmel Point there was not a sign of the Eskimo. After waiting for an hour I began to fear that something had happened to the baggage train. It was a long way back. We snuggled down in the rocks and went to sleep. Why worry?

An hour later we could see a black dot far out on the ice of Robeson Channel, evidently hunting for better going. From the highest point we waved our arms and noted his change of course toward the shore. Kood-look-to must have seen the signal; so we moved on for a mile. To our disgust on looking back we saw him mounted on the summit of a small berg, making signals toward Cartmel Point. As yet he had no idea where we were. Between us lay deep snow, slush, and pools of water.

Hours later we found him; we were wet to our waists and completely 'all in,' and he was smiling, his face glistening with perspiration. His huge wardrobe trunk was gone – he had jettisoned cargo to save the ship – but the girl's small steamer trunk, which he later painted pink, was still on board, lashed firmly to the crossbars of his sledge.

I could now understand Commander Peary's injunction, 'Be prepared to abandon everything.' It was plainly too late in the year for work with dog teams. The entries in my journal under the dates of June 27–29 give a true picture of the difficulties encountered in late spring sledging.

June 27th. Had fine going today up to Cape Frederick VII. Here Kood-look-to shot a seal and here our trouble began. To avoid the open water of Lincoln Bay we kept out in the middle of the channel, our objective point being Black Cape. When opposite the bay we encountered a lead extending nearly across the channel. Doubling back we attempted to make the land but were prevented doing so by a shore lead stretching far below Cape Frederick VII.

Once on the land the disagreeable features of summer sledging began to be in evidence, water and slush and steep rocky hillsides. The komatik upset twice in five minutes. A long stretch of rocks and water drove us into camp.

June 28th. A day of interesting incidents. On arriving at Cape Frederick VII we found the ice foot entirely gone, the snow had melted, leaving a sloping, slippery point terminating in a steep drop into the sea. Looking it over we decided to try it. With all three guiding the komatik we crept slowly along until on the very point when the whole thing started to slide. The upsetting of the sledge was the only thing which saved it, the load presenting more friction to the slippery ice than the iron runners. When trying to right the sledge I slipped again, but just managed to grasp the tail of a snowshoe.

This over, we struck out across Lincoln Bay, threading our way among the leads and endeavoring to avoid rotten ice. In crossing a hole the bottom fell out, the komatik upset hanging on the edge by one runner, and Jack hanging to the upstanders up to his waist in water not daring to let go for it meant a swim and not daring to climb for he would sink the komatik. Of course the dogs stopped just when they shouldn't and for a moment it looked serious. Pulling, tugging, yelling and whipping the dogs we succeeded in yanking the sledge out of the water. Here we waited for Jack to change his clothes.

To cross Shelter River we were obliged to unload again and ford the stream carrying everything on our heads. A little beyond Cape Union the deep water of the ice foot compelled us to camp.

The sledding is wicked. At Lincoln Bay Kood-look-to left his Conger trunk containing a large number of Conger souvenirs, hoping that there may be an opportunity to get them again if the *Roosevelt* is driven in here for shelter.

At this camp I shall leave my kamik-pucks, four seal skins, sheepskin kooletah, and lantern box.

June 29th. Troubles were heaped upon us today. It has been unload, pack and load again all day long until we were about played out. Yet, at times, it has been interesting and exciting. Below Black Cape Kood-look-to got discouraged and wanted to leave everything, packed his bag and was on the point of starting for the ship. I shamed him by saying I would take the dogs and komatik to the ship.

Time and again we were obliged to let the dogs all loose and lower the komatik over a wall of ice or rocks with ropes. Once we attempted to cross a pool of water by wading in boldly hoping that its depth would not increase. Kood-look-to broke in to his waist filling his bearskin pants with slush; the komatik sank deeper and deeper. We were wallowing up to mid-thigh and the dogs were nearly submerged. The sledge refused to move either way but was determined to stay there and go down.

Pounding the dogs with everything at hand we finally drove or swam them around back of the sledge and shifted the traces to that end. Here the dogs secured a better footing and drew it to land.

It was now tote again and so it continued all the way to the ship.

George got in last night from Cape Columbia; came in a week ago from Clements Markham Inlet with a young musk-ox, but it lived only a day or so.

✳

WILD LIFE OF THE ARCTIC

All was activity and bustle on board ship. We were going home! The smell of tar and paint and new rope was in the air. The sailors looked happy.

One day of unpacking, a bath, a drying of wet clothes, and then came an assignment to bird work, in which I was interested. We were particularly fortunate in finding two nests of the knot (*Calidris canutus*), one nest discovered by Mr. Scott, our second engineer, and the other by one of the Eskimos. The eggs of this bird had never been found previously. Our experience showed the obvious reason. As the bird is one of the family of snipes, sandpipers, curlew, and plover, and, consequently, a shore bird, we had been hunting for its eggs along the shore. The first nest was at least two miles back among the hills, the second about one mile. A second reason was that the back of the bird, a rufous brown, lightly streaked with black and white, blends beautifully with the nesting-place – a case of almost perfect protective coloration. In addition, the bird wisely refuses to leave the nest and eggs until it is certain that it is about to be stepped on or seized. Borup photographed one of the birds on the nest at a distance of six feet.

On my trip up from Conger I was fortunate in finding a set of eggs of the long-tailed jaeger (*Stercorarius longicaudus*) at Lincoln Bay. As far as I can learn this was the most northerly nesting-place that has ever been discovered. Entirely unaware even of the presence of the bird, I fairly dropped upon hearing the sudden rush of wings a few inches from my head.

The snowy owl (*Nyctea nyctea*) was nesting about two miles from the ship on top of a slight elevation of the bank of a small stream. To our astonishment the nest contained young nearly ready to fly, half-grown, quarter-grown, and eggs. Mrs. Owl must have wisely decided that all of one size in the nest at one time would render her domestic quarters somewhat uncomfortable.

The red-throated loons were breeding at the edges of ponds and on small islands in the ponds. The Arctic terns were laying their eggs on a small sand-spit a mile north of the ship. The old-squaws and brant geese were nesting in the moss a short distance from the edges of pools and the shore of the Polar Sea. Eiders and king eiders were passing and repassing the ship day by day.

One morning a strange bird flying in company with the Arctic tern was visible, a black or slate-colored head and throat, its back a dark pearl gray, the tips of its wings black – I had never seen anything like it. It proved to be Sabine's gull (*Xema sabini*), a bird that winters on the coast of Peru!

The snow bunting (*Plectrophenax nivalis nivalis*) was our most common bird, nesting beneath broken rock and in cracks and crevices hardly admitting the passage of the hand, a precaution against the white and blue fox stealing the eggs. Its mating song is entirely different from the note uttered in the South on a wintry morning. The male was attractive in his nuptial garb.

Along with bird life came the flowers, the purple saxifrage springing to life beneath the snow blanket and ready to blossom at the first ray of sunshine. The Arctic poppy was next. We found it nodding its yellow head wherever we went. The cinquefoil, snow buttercup, sedge, alpine foxtail, moss campion, mountain sandwort, and alpine chickweed were abundant. It would have needed a good botanist and months of work to classify and name them all correctly.

On July 6th the stream issuing from the valley just ahead of the *Roosevelt* was so swollen that four Eskimo women were unable to reach the ship. Laughing at their predicament, their husbands went up to the bank of the stream and threw them their supper. The next day they were not to be seen. They had gone back into the hills to sleep. But everyone was hugging the ship pretty closely. She might sail for the South at any moment.

On the 13th, the *Roosevelt* floated up and out of her cradle with only a narrow strip of ice between her and open water. To our astonishment the propeller was a huge ball of ice, due to the fact that the intense cold of the hold, unoccupied during the winter, was conducted by the propeller shaft to the propeller. Just how to remove the ice was a problem until Captain Bob suggested dynamite. He is the kind of man who would. He chuckled like a small boy ramming dirt and grass into a toy cannon on the morning of the Fourth of July. He fastened a stick to the end of a long pole, connected the wires, pushed the pole down under water as near the propeller as possible, and connected his batteries.

The men on the ice declared the whole ship jumped a foot out of water, but Charlie, the cook, busy with his dinner inside and entirely unaware of what was going to happen, declared that they were a mile under the height. His broken dishes and a broken window in the after cabin testified that Bob's charge was a trifle heavy; but he accomplished his purpose. The propeller would now go around.

We couldn't leave the North without erecting some sort of memorial to Marvin. It was a matter of love for Captain Bob, his roommate, to do this. A cairn and cross stand on the crest of a low hill near our winter quarters. On a brass plate is the inscription:

IN MEMORY
ROSS G. MARVIN
Age 31
Drowned April 10, 1909
45 Miles North of Cape Columbia
Returning from 86° 38′

Its outline against the western sky followed us as we steamed away from Cape Sheridan. We were going South one man the less.

Ever cautious and ever suspicious of the Arctic, Commander Peary ordered every man to have his emergency bag packed, to put on his best fur clothes, and be ready to abandon ship at any minute. If the ship were caught in a squeeze near the Black Cape, where the cliffs drop abruptly into the sea, she might be pressed flat within a short time. When we reached

Cape Rawson, Captain Bob found one-season ice blocking the channel completely; so he tucked the *Roosevelt* into a niche near the shore and waited patiently for us to obtain a collection of flowers in Grant Land.

On the nineteenth the *Roosevelt* steamed down below Black Cliff and on to Cape Union, where we found everything as solid as a concrete road, with no possible chance of getting through. As the ship slowly drifted north with the tide, a sounding was made which showed 277 fathoms, which is more evidence of a strong undercurrent than a deep sea.

Blocked on the twentieth and blocked as effectively on the twenty-first, the novice would have said that we were here for the winter, but Commander and Bob merely smiled at the delays. Life on board was not monotonous; on the contrary. With the sun above the horizon continuously and with fifty Eskimos who apparently never slept, it required strength of character to say, 'I'm going to bed!'

Commander distributed cartridges to the Eskimos, with the result that life was one continuous bang. Before breakfast Eging-wa shot six guillemots – one, strange to say, all black, a freak of nature. A few minutes later he knocked down a herring gull (*Larus argentatus*), our record for its farthest north. In the afternoon we were surprised to secure a fulmar which was far north of its habitat. This bird is an almost constant attendant on whaling and sealing ships, and is familiarly known among sailors as the 'Molly,' 'Mollimoke,' and 'Wooden Wings.' Then came the cry of 'Narwhal!' For the next two hours we were excited spectators of the Eskimos maneuvering in their kayaks. Oo-tah succeeded in getting within a few feet – we held our breaths. He missed! Ah-lettah drew back his arm and – missed! A thousand pounds of fresh meat lost. The Eskimos groaned.

In the meantime we were drifting back and forth with the tide and ice off Cape Union. Someone recalled the fact that twenty-six years before to the day (July 23d) the *Proteus* was crushed and sunk off Cape Sabine.

Kane Basin, Kennedy and Robeson Channels must be a busy thoroughfare for the narwhal, the fabled sea unicorn, for we saw them practically throughout the whole distance, now sunning themselves, their backs just awash, now a tip of the white ivory horn, now a dark spotted back reflecting the sunlight. The narwhals are excessively timid and most wary of the approach of a hunter either on the ice or in his kayak. With an ear no larger than the point of a pencil, it is surprising what sounds they can detect. And yet on the night of the twenty-fourth many were 'playing' about the ship, as a whaler would say. There were three in the open pool to breathe, which they do through a hole in the top of the head. Their progress under such conditions is from pool to pool, and on some of their journeys they must be compelled to hold their breaths for a long time and over a long distance.

If through a change of the wind, the ice should be packed tightly in a certain region, all water leads disappear, and only one small pool remains, then all the narwhals in the vicinity must gather at that hole to preserve their lives. This has often happened in South Greenland waters with the result that astounding and almost incredible stories have been told as to the numbers taken from one hole, all with their heads out of the window, as it were, struggling to catch their breaths.

Upon the present occasion our Eskimos, as is their custom in the early spring, immediately scattered out upon the borders of the neighboring pools with their harpoons, floats, and drags ready. By the yells and rapid running from one open space to another, we knew that someone had hit the mark. The harpooned narwhal had dived, then swam under the ice, and reappeared for breath in another pool. Now we heard the crack of their rifles, which is the usual method of dispatching the wounded animal after it has been harpooned.

Three sledges were sent for the meat, but before they could return the leads had so widened that Captain Bob deemed it advisable to send a whaleboat. Three loads were necessary to transport everything to the ship. A narwhal rarely exceeds twenty feet in length. Its one tusk or horn, which is really a development of one of its upper left canine teeth, protrudes through its upper lip just to the left of the nose; it is spiraled from left to right, and in exceptional cases attains a length of nine feet. With rare exceptions the horn is peculiar to the male alone. On July 25, 1875, near Cape York the Nares Expedition killed a female 'with a well-developed tusk.'

The meat, almost black in color, is decidedly oily in taste, and far more palatable when raw and in a frozen state than when cooked. The Eskimos often dry it by hanging it on the face of a cliff and keep it as a delicacy for visitors during the winter.

Two specimens of the beautiful ivory gull were obtained on the twenty-fifth. Never so common as the glaucous, the herring, or the kittiwake, it is always welcome and always interesting on account of its gentle manners. Without discordant cry to herald its approach, or wheeling, or rush of wings, it is there at your feet as if by magic, perking its head, looking at you, then looking at the meat, as if asking, 'May I help myself?'

By July 26th we had reached Cape Frederick VII, which made an advance of *twenty-five* miles in ten days!

Now the dinner bell was a summons to seal meat, strong, dark, bloody, but nourishing. One was the hooded seal, known to the Dundee whalers as the 'blethernose,' to science as the *Cystophora cristata,* dark bluish-gray in color, fully as large, the Eskimos told me, as the bearded or 'ground' seal, which weighs, when full grown, eight and even nine hundred pounds. Its peculiarity is its hood, a skin bag or excrescence, on the frontal part of the skull, capable of being inflated at will. This happens when the animal is angry and engaged in combat.

'Look out for an old hood' is the common admonition among the men of the sealing fleet. They have been known to seize a club from the hand of a man about to deal a blow, and chew it into bits. I carefully examined the air passage which leads from the back of the throat to the sack and which we readily inflated by inserting and blowing through a rubber tube.

Back and forth we drifted, now off Cape Frederick, now off Cape Union, now abreast of Lincoln Bay. By July 31st we had reached a point between Cape Tyson and Bellot Island, where we tied up to a floe, which was, by actual measurement, three and a quarter miles long.

After a hot bath, I decided that a cold plunge might, as the doctors say, 'close the pores of the skin.' I was about to dive from the rail when Borup yelled, 'Wait for me!'

The Eskimos streamed from their quarters for'ard. There was only one conclusion. The white men had gone piblockto. To jump into ice water bare naked and swim around like a seal was more than they could understand. The one plunge, followed by a swim of some twenty yards, did us no harm whatever.

Another hooded seal on the twenty-fourth measured eight feet eleven inches in length and weighed, exclusive of the blood, six hundred and twenty-four pounds. Little ringed seals (*Phoca hispida*), the common seal of the Smith Sound native, were being killed every day, furnishing an abundance of fresh meat.

We were away at last! When we awoke on the morning of August 4th, the ship was vibrating to the stroke of the pistons and the churn of the propeller. Both boilers were going. Bob was bound South through a lead in a thick snowstorm. On the morning of the fifth the *Roosevelt* passed Cape Durville and later tied up to a floe off Cape Frazer to await a further break-up. On the sixth we were well over on the east side, in fact, only sixteen miles off Cairn Point on the Greenland shore. Before night we were driven rapidly to the west by a strong southeast wind. We saw large numbers of narwhals from time to time in the various leads, but they were inaccessible on account of the character of the intervening ice.

We were free on August 7th, to be welcomed at Cape Sabine by a terrific windstorm. Flying spray swept our decks in sheets. Everything loose was up and off. A boat amidships was lifted by the wind, as it hung in the davits, and then crashed to the deck with a ripped-out eyebolt dangling from the davit block.

Captain Bob changed his course and headed the *Roosevelt* up under the lee of Cocked Hat Island, passing the Greely Starvation Camp, and on into Buchanan Bay, where he tied her up to the edge of the pack, a short distance from the wintering place of the famous *Fram* on Sverdrup's Expedition.

Naturally we expected that Etah was our destination and we were considerably surprised, therefore, to go steaming by gaily on August 8th. Commander Peary was, as usual, considering the welfare of his Eskimos, who had made it possible for him to reach the Pole and to whom he owed so much. From the time when seals begin to appear and to sun themselves on the ice, generally about the first of May, to the latter part of September, the Smith Sound Eskimo is busy caching food for the long winter night, during which little food can be obtained. It is true that now and then a bear is caught by moonlight, an Arctic hare by snare, or a white or blue fox, formerly by stone, but now by steel, trap.

In assisting Commander Peary, our fifty Eskimos, men, women, and children, had lost May, June, and July in the preparations for the coming winter. Although Peary's friends at home were awaiting the important announcement that he had reached the Pole, there was not a doubt in his mind what he should or might do – he must remain in the North, hunt walrus for his people, and leave only when he knew that they were comfortably prepared.

The natives of the expedition were landed according to their choice of location, that they might be established at once in their new winter homes. Other expert hunters, well-known men of former trips, were added as assistants for the work in hand.

Nine days of hunting and excitement landed a huge red pile of nutritious meat on our decks and, later, before the doors of our Eskimo friends. We dreamed of sleeping groups of walrus, of emerging heads and backs, of bobbing black floats, ever pulling, pulling; we dreamed of being shot, for bullets were flying in a haphazard way. Dead tired, we rolled into our bunks on August 10th, with decks covered with blood and meat, a total of thirty walrus that day. It seemed but a few minutes when the breakfast bell rang. I dropped from the top bunk to the floor.

Borup, a hard worker, ever energetic, and consequently, always sleepy, in an imploring voice said, 'Don't get up. We can't hunt today.' I looked out of the opened porthole. It was raining and blowing; the ship was at anchor under the lee of Herbert Island.

Responding to the bell and then getting back into the bunk probably saved my life. I had been sleeping with my back to the wall. I now faced the wall and lay partly on my breast with my left arm across it, the left hand resting on my right shoulder. In that position I dropped asleep.

After breakfast Commander came from his room with a heavy .40–82 Winchester rifle, which I had been using the day before, and about which I had cautioned him as I passed it up over the rail, because the magazine was loaded. Chief Engineer George Wardwell volunteered to remove the cartridges and clean the barrel. Standing at the messroom table with rifle upside down, and lever up, he began to pump the cartridges out of the chamber. Evidently his finger caught the trigger as he closed the lever, and with a bang the bullet was gone!

It passed through a partition, over the head of the sleeping mate, through another partition, and burst through the wood within a few inches of my eye, ripped through my arm between the ulna and radius, came out at the very middle of the wrist, entered my shoulder just above the collar bone, came out through my back, clipped off the side of one finger, passed across the room, dented the wall, and dropped to the floor!

And the Chief didn't even ring a bell – no bones, no arteries, no real damage! Dr. Goodsell soon patched me up with needle, thread, and adhesive plaster, and within a few days I was about deck and, apparently, all right with the exception of my left thumb, which hung down into the palm of the hand, probably owing to a severance of one of the muscles of the lower arm.

CHAPTER 26

✳

DR. COOK AND HIS NORTH POLE

On August 17th we were back in Etah Harbor, meeting there old Panikpa and Poo-ad-loo-na, who had left us on the Polar Sea on that memorable day at the Big Lead. Naturally, we were relieved to know that they, with their wives and children, had made the long distance safely, living entirely upon seals and polar bears. But of far more interest to us was Panikpa's son E-took-a-shoo and his companion Ah-pellah, both companions of Dr. Frederick A. Cook. I shall tell their story in detail farther on.

We sailed from Etah on August 21st, and on the twenty-third we met the little auxiliary schooner *Jeanie,* Captain Samuel Bartlett in command, which had been sent north to us by the Peary Arctic Club with a load of coal. This schooner was also to carry Harry Whitney, the sportsman who had been at Etah for a year, back to Newfoundland, and, if Dr. Frederick Cook could be found and needed passage, he also was to be taken back to civilization.

'Captain Sam' had as passengers a Mr. Fuller of the New York *Herald* and an Eskimo by the name of Mene Wallace. The latter was the last of a party of nine Smith Sound natives whom Commander Peary had taken to New York some twelve or thirteen years before. Mene's parents died in the States, and he was adopted by a Mr. Wallace of the American Museum of Natural History. The boy was educated at private schools and by private tutors, and even enrolled for a time at Hamilton College.

Although of a most primitive race and one of a people living as man lived in the Stone Age, Mene was as intelligent as any boy in his classes, a fact which seems to support many of the statements of Alfred Russel Wallace:

There is no proof of any real advance in character during the whole historical period.

That our mental faculties have increased in power during the last two thousand years is totally unfounded.

There is no proof of continuously increasing intellectual power.

There has been no definite advance of morality from age to age; even the lowest race at each period possessed the same intellectual and moral nature as the higher.

Every man who has visited, has lived with the Smith Sound native, and has studied them agrees with me that they are fully as intelligent as we are. Having for centuries utilized all the natural resources at their command, they were at the height of their civilization at the time of the appearance of the white man, who has furnished them with wood, iron, and firearms, three valuable contributions to their struggle for existence.

Up to a certain point Mene was interested in his studies and was an average, normal boy, but as he grew older, he lacked concentration, due to his failure fully to appreciate the value of an education. He found that there were other things in life more important to him than an 'education,' and much more interesting and much more easily obtained.

He had not entirely forgotten the free, unconventional life of his people, the great snow- and ice-covered hills, the calm blue waters of a northern bay dotted with glistening white icebergs, a heavenly moonlight night with its long snow trail – he wanted to return to his people. And with his people we landed him, a pathetic figure in a way, for he had forgotten his mother tongue, he could not drive dogs, he was unfamiliar with the use of the sledge. Without help from his friends he could not subsist upon the country. Commander Peary supplied him with everything he wanted – a new tent, rifle, ammunition, wood for a new sledge, clothing, and several boxes of food. There we left him surrounded by friends who remembered him as a small boy, and who now envied him in his possession of a new white sweater and a pair of polished russet shoes!

From a home of refinement to a hole in the ground was almost too abrupt a change. After his experiences with the new, he found the old much harder to accept than he had ever imagined. Within seven years he was back in New York working in a Wall Street office, and announcing to reporters that for one million dollars he would tell them who discovered the North Pole!

The Eskimo is inherently a nomad. This predominating trait asserted itself with Mene again and again. To Montreal; where he slept under a freight car; to Maine, to California, to State after State and back again to the primitive. Finally, to a lumber camp in the woods of New Hampshire, where he rests under the trees, a victim of the influenza which raged throughout the world during and after the Great War, and which even reached his own people in the Far North.

From those on board the *Jeanie,* we now learned that Taft was President of the United States; that Henry H. Rogers was dead; that there had been a terrible earthquake; that Harvard had defeated Yale in both football and rowing; that Shackleton had succeeded in reaching within one hundred and eleven miles of the South Pole; and that the Danish Expedition had lost three men by starvation in attempting to map the northeastern shore of Greenland. Borup and I had known that their objective was Cape Morris Jesup, and had looked for their records when we were there in May. However, we failed to find any evidence that they had reached that point.

A call at North Star Bay revealed a new mission station. One phase of civilization had at last reached these people. Half-breed Eskimos from South Greenland, brought up in the faith of the Lutheran Church, and educated at the 'University' of Godthaab, were here to teach their far northern brothers modern Christianity. They were to be educated from one of the most primitive religions on earth, really animism. To them every animate and inanimate thing has a soul within it. The chief religious duty of this faith seems to be the propitiation of the evil spirits, of which there are legions. Now they were to pray to one great good spirit for help and mercy and salvation, and acceptance when all is done. On the whole they would be the cleaner and the happier for the acceptance of the new faith and the forgetting that there is a real devil behind every rock.

On August 25th we arrived at Cape York, where we found two families who informed us that a whaler had called and had left a box of mail among the rocks. Under the direction of the Eskimos we found this within a few minutes.

As we sat there on the hillside reading our letters, the Commander tossed over a letter, with a 'Read that.' It was a note from Captain Adams of the Dundee whaler *Morning*, stating that he had met Dr. Cook in South Greenland and that Cook had told him that he had reached the Pole. This was our first verification of the suspicion that Dr. Cook would claim the Pole.

Turning to the Commander, I asked, 'Do you think he will carry that story home?'

'Absolutely,' he replied.

And now I must relate the history of the Dr. Cook episode, a story utterly discredited and unbelievable now, but which at the time was the sensation of the world, and which made our homecoming an anti-climax to the magnificent achievement of the Commander. We had, as I shall tell, heard of Cook many times on our way north, during our stay there, and on our return to Etah.

Our first word about Cook's activities in the North came at Sydney as we headed north in 1908. Dr. Frederick Cook had been Peary's physician and surgeon on his first trip to North Greenland in 1891. It was he who attended Peary when the latter was carried to his cabin on the *Kite* with a broken leg. 'Thanks to the professional skill of my surgeon, Dr. Cook, and the unwearying and thoughtful care of Mrs. Peary, my complete recovery was rapidly attained,' was what Peary wrote.

Dr. Cook was one of the supporting party which accompanied Peary on his first trip northeast from Red Cliff House over the Greenland Ice

Cap; at the end of one hundred and thirty miles he was the first to volunteer to go on. Peary selected Eivind Astrup of Christiania, Norway, an expert ski runner, as his sole companion! Landgon Gibson and Dr. Cook returned to Red Cliff in McCormick Bay. Later Cook was surgeon on the Belgian Expedition into the Antarctic. It is obvious, therefore, that he had little or no sledging experience and no training in the lessons of the trail.

In 1907, or one year before our departure for the North, Dr. Cook sailed north in the Gloucester fishing schooner *John R. Bradley,* as the guest of Mr. Bradley, a sportsman who was to hunt the big game of the North such as the walrus, polar bear, and musk-ox. Under the skillful pilotage of Captain Moses Bartlett, an uncle of Captain Robert Bartlett, our Captain Bob, the expedition reached a point in North Greenland known to the Eskimos as Anoritok, about sixteen miles north of Etah. This old village site at the entrance to the ice-infested waters of Kane Basin is rarely occupied by the Eskimos, who know that a living here is far more precarious than one in more southern settlements.

But in 1907 it happened that there were several families at Anoritok. With Mr. Bradley's permission, Dr. Cook decided to land with one volunteer, Rudolph Franke, the cook of the schooner, and remain indefinitely. He stated that he might try to reach the North Pole if conditions were favorable. Now this base for polar exploration is six hundred and eighty-five miles in an airline from the objective. By dog team, this journey to the Pole and return, with its many deviations, would total at least eighteen hundred miles. This fact alone should have been sufficient to convince any student of Arctic work of the impracticability and folly of such a route.

There were many other factors of even greater weight. This long journey cannot be undertaken until the return of twilight, in the bitter cold days of February, the worst month of the year for travel, and must be finished at the very latest by the last of June on account of the danger of open water. Men who had followed the history of Arctic exploration knew that

Opposite: Taking on water from the Cape York Glacier

Anoritok, the site of the headquarters of Dr. Frederick Cook

Peary, with all his experience and with the best men of the Smith Sound tribe as his able assistants, had failed from Etah, seven hundred miles from the Pole. He had failed from Cape Sabine, six hundred and seventy-five miles from the Pole. He had failed from Victoria Head, six hundred and sixty miles from the Pole. He had failed from Lady Franklin Bay, five hundred miles from the Pole; and he had failed from Cape Sheridan, four hundred and fifty miles from the Pole. How could any man, even the best Arctic man in the world, with the slightest of equipment, with his base at Anoritok, hope to accomplish with dog team what Commander Peary had absolutely demonstrated again and again to be impossible? And Cook had never even seen the Polar Sea!

Just before we sailed from Sydney, word was received and published that Dr. Cook, being so fortunate as to find a large village of Eskimos well supplied with meat, had engaged the services of Peary's best native help and was to undertake a trip to the Pole. Everyone who knew anything of the Arctic or of the history of Arctic exploration dismissed this report with a smile of incredulity, pigeon-holed with the report that a man had decided to go to the moon!

At North Star Bay, on our way north, we discovered in the tupik of Pee-a-wah-to, a trunk marked 'F.A. Cook, Brooklyn, N.Y.' He had arrived bag and baggage. No one knew just where he was at this time. The Eskimos informed us that he had gone west in the spring with two boys, E-took-a-shoo and Ah-pellah, and had failed to return before the warm rays of the sun had made sledging impossible.

A few days before we left Etah for the North, we were surprised to see approaching a regular American fishing dory. This is so distinctive in type that it can never be mistaken in any part of the world. The oarsman was Franke, the assistant and only white companion to Dr. Cook. He had rowed down the sixteen miles from Anoritok, where he was in charge of Cook's hut and supplies. Down with scurvy and utterly discouraged, he wanted to go home and begged Peary for permission to sail on the *Erik* when she returned to St. John's, Newfoundland.

At first Peary refused to take a man away from a station over which he was in charge, leaving everything to the Eskimos to do with as they saw fit. Franke declared that he would certainly die of scurvy if he remained in the Arctic another winter. This was easily possible, as he did not like seal and walrus meat, and persisted in living entirely on canned goods.

Franke assumed all responsibility, and pleaded to be taken home in the following note:

I was very glad to think I could go home. I was kindly received by Captain and scientific staff of the *Roosevelt*. Please, Mr. Peary, let me now go home with your other vessel, for the whole life I will be thankful to you.

For the received kindness I thank you very much, and if I can be of any service to you, please command about them.

Respectfully yours

RUDOLF FRANKE

As a proof that he had orders to abandon his station, he submitted the following note from Dr. Cook:

While I expect to get back to you by the end of May, still I wish you to be ready to go to Acpanie, the island off North Star Bay, when the whaling steamers come by the 5th of June. And if I am not back start to go home with the whalers. I think, however, we will be back.

Franke sailed southward on the *Erik*. Just what arrangements were made to pay his fare, I do not know.

On our return from our successful explorations in the North, we found at Etah, as I have said, both E-took-a-shoo and Ah-pellah. At last they had returned to Greenland after an absence of nearly a year. The story of their wanderings as given to Matthew Henson, well versed in the language after eighteen years of experience, to Commander Peary, to Captain Bartlett, to us all with the help of pencil, paper, and maps, was the same as told to their parents and to all the tribe. As I well know, they tell the same story today. It has never varied one iota.

With Dr. Cook they left Anoritok in the early spring, accompanied by four Eskimos. They proceeded west to Ellesmere Land, passed north through Eureka Channel to the northern end of Axel Heiberg Island and started out over the Polar Sea. After a short march over the sea ice, they built their snow houses a short distance from land. From this camp the four boys returned to land and then home, leaving Dr. Cook with E-took-a-shoo and Ah-pellah to go on alone. They slept there two nights. Dr.

Cook then took a picture of the igd-loo with flag flying, and then said, 'Now we'll go home.'

They started south. E-took-a-shoo returned to Cape Thomas Hubbard to remove a rifle left there in cache, rejoined his two companions, and then all proceeded southward on the sea ice on a line roughly parallel with the western shores of Axel Heiberg Island. They turned southward to the eastern shores of Amund Ringnes Island, discovering on the way two uncharted islands. *At no time were they ever out of sight of land.*

Thence they moved southward to Jones Sound by the Hell Gate of the Sverdrup Expedition, where they abandoned their dogs, and proceeded on by canvas boat to the northern shores of North Devon, where they established a winter camp at Cape Sparbo. Dr. Cook was disappointed in not being able to reach an English whaler, by which he hoped to return to civilization.

The party succeeded in living through the winter. Game was abundant. In the spring they began their long walk back to Anoritok. They were often hungry, at times nearly starving.

'Dr. Cook pushed the sledge, Ah-pellah and I pulled,' said E-took-a-shoo.

An old seal found under the rocks at Cape Sabine gave them strength to cross Smith Sound in May. Then Cook went south along the coast of Greenland by dog team, with the intention of catching the first steamer for Copenhagen.

Indeed, it was a wonderful trip, and Cook was unfortunate in not receiving honor for what he actually did. The fault was all his own. Tempted to grasp the thousand miles of travel over the Polar Sea, he lost all.

This is the answer to the men who have asked, 'How did Peary know that Dr. Cook had not reached the Pole?' He knew it from the evidence of E-took-a-shoo and Ah-pellah, but he also knew from his own long experience with dog teams, which were Dr. Cook's only means of conveyance.

On Thursday, August 26th, the *Roosevelt* definitely headed for home, her immediate objective being Turnavik on the Labrador Coast where coal awaited us. We arrived there on September 5th, loaded our coal, and sailed at once for 'Smoky,' the wireless station near Indian Harbor. Just before we dropped anchor, there was a knock on our door.

'Come in,' we called.

To our surprise it was Commander Peary. We wondered why; it was unusual for him to visit our 'Chamber of Horrors.' We knew within a few minutes.

'Boys,' he said, 'we are in sight of the first wireless station. Following my own announcements, you may tell your friends that we reached the Pole. Say whatever you wish, but please remember that there is to be no mention of Dr. Cook's name.'

Commander went on to say that we had done our work, and that he – Cook – was no part of that work. This conversation took place previous to our arrival, and up to that time we had heard nothing of Dr. Cook's claim, except the statement in Captain Adams's note.

Upon our arrival at Smoky Tickle, Commander Peary and Captain Bartlett were rowed ashore to send the following messages:

Indian Harbor
via CAPE RAY
Sept. 6, 1909
Mrs. R.E. Peary, South Harpswell, Maine
Have made good at last. I have the old Pole. Am well. Will wire again from Chateau.
BERT

Associated Press
Stars and Stripes nailed the Pole
PEARY

New York Times
I have the Pole. April 6th. Expect arrive Chateau Bay Sept. 7th. Secure control wire for me there and arrange expedite transmission big story.
PEARY

Herbert L. Bridgman
Secretary of the Peary Arctic Club, Brooklyn, N.Y. [In code] Pole
reached. *Roosevelt* safe.
PEARY

After Commander Peary had sent his messages, our own followed.
One I sent my sister read:

Arrived here today with Pole on board.
Have had the best year of my life. Love to all.

And another to Dr. Daniel W. Abercrombie of Worcester Academy:

Top of the earth found at last. Greetings to Faculty and boys.

Within a half-hour after our arrival, the British revenue cutter *Fiona*
came in and from her officers Commander Peary learned that on September 1st, four days before, a message had been received from a man by the
name of Dr. Frederick A. Cook. He claimed to have reached the Pole. The
message had been sent from Lerwick, Shetland Islands, and read:

Reached North Pole April 21, 1908. Discovered land far North.
Return to Copenhagen by steamer *Hans Egede*.
FREDERICK COOK

Geographers, scientists, students of Arctic literature, all had questioned the possibility of ever reaching the Pole, and *two* men, within five
days of each other, were claiming to have done that very thing! Was this a
practical joke?

Immediately the air was surcharged with messages from America and
Europe for confirmation and additional information. The Associated
Press sent an urgent request for an authoritative statement and some com-
ment, however brief, concerning Dr. Cook's claim. Peary's compliance

Commander Peary and Captain Bob Bartlett
At Indian Harbor, Labrador, on the return from the North

with this request was the first big gun in the unfortunate controversy which ensued.

I have nailed the Stars and Stripes to the North Pole. This is authoritative and correct. Cook's story should not be taken too seriously. The two Eskimos who accompanied him say he went no distance north and not out of sight of land. Other members of the tribe corroborate their story.

Another message to Mrs. Peary did not improve matters:

Good morning. Delayed by gale. Don't let Cook story worry you. Have him nailed.

This hurling of a lie angered the American people. Why did he not wait until Dr. Cook had submitted his proofs to some representative body before condemning? How could Peary possibly know that Dr. Cook had not reached the Pole?

On September 8th we dropped anchor in Battle Harbor, and found the station there flooded with radiograms for Commander Peary, all of which I was appointed to deliver to him. I had also to carry all which he might write to the station, look them over carefully for errors, and deliver them to the operator.

Several of the telegrams received on the day of our arrival were from geographical societies in Europe who desired to honor Cook, if honor was due, before he left for America; also many were from newspaper agencies, all with the same request that he give them his honest opinion as to Dr. Cook's claim. Poor Peary! He had emphasized the fact that Dr. Cook's name was not to be mentioned in any of the expedition dispatches. I can see him now walking the after deck in the dark, a silent figure, back and forth. He could have shouldered the burden onto Bartlett, onto Borup, or onto me. We had our honest opinions, but they all wanted *his opinion,* not ours. If any man in the world knew, he did, as to the probability, the possibility of that claim being true.

Commander sent for me to come to his room. He sat in his wicker chair, tapping a pencil on the table.

'MacMillan,' he asked, 'what is a synonym for gold brick?'

'I don't know,' I replied. 'As far as I know there is no word just like it in the English language.'

'It is an ugly word,' he added. 'I don't like to use it. Let's think it over for a while.'

We did and failed, and so he wrote the radiogram which hurt him more than it hurt Cook:

To the Editor of the New York *Times:*

The *Roosevelt* will remain here three or four days coaling and overhauling ship. I expect to arrive at Sydney about September 15.

Do not trouble about Cook's story or attempt to explain any discrepancies in his statements. The affair will settle itself.

He has not been at the Pole on April 21st, 1908, or at any other time. He has simply handed the public a gold brick. These statements are made advisedly and I have proof of them. When he makes a full statement of his journey over his signature to some geographical society or other reputable body, if that statement contains the claim that he has reached the Pole, I shall be in a position to furnish material that may prove distinctly interesting reading for the public.

ROBERT E. PEARY

That radiogram added fuel to the fire. Commander Peary had sold his story to the New York *Times* for four thousand dollars. Dr. Cook sold his to James Gordon Bennett of the New York *Herald* for twenty-four thousand dollars. The latter was syndicated. Where there was one reader of the Peary story, there were a hundred of the Cook narrative.

The latter was difficult to disprove to a public ignorant of the problems of the North. The man in the street argued, 'If one man can do it, why not another?' The more intelligent accepted the opinion of the University of Copenhagen, which in turn accepted without question Dr. Cook's bare statement that he had reached the Pole, and honored him with the degree of LL.D. Within a short time they repudiated their action.

Four years later, in 1913, I traveled west from Etah with E-took-a-shoo. We were following in his footsteps of four years before, Flagler Bay, Ellesmere Land, Bay Fiord, Eureka Sound. Often as he stood and looked long at the rolling white hills, he remarked, 'We camped there'; 'Here we killed musk-oxen.'

All was familiar at the northern end of Axel Heiberg Island. We swung our sledges to the sea ice and headed out northwest over the Polar Sea. That night we built our snow house, some fourteen miles from land. Tea was over – we climbed the nearest pressure ridge to select our route for the next day.

Here was my opportunity. 'E-took-a-shoo,' I asked, 'how much farther did you go with Dr. Cook?'

Carefully he surveyed the horizon, looked back at the white rounded hills of Cape Colgate, at the more abrupt Cape Thomas Hubbard, and answered, 'We passed Doctor Cook's last camp as we came out from land.'

We had gone beyond Dr. Cook's North Pole!

This point was, roughly, five hundred miles south of the true or geographical North Pole. While one might like to be generous in attitude and try to believe that Cook thought he was there, that his observations deceived him, it is obvious that *within sight of land* no one could deceive himself.

At the time of the controversy too much emphasis was placed on the fact that, unfortunately, Dr. Cook's 'observations' had been left in a box at Etah, and that, therefore, it was difficult for him to furnish proof of his achievement. The public was vague on the subject of 'observations,' but jumped to the conclusion that they must be extremely heavy and bulky, or else Dr. Cook, fully realizing the importance of such proof, would certainly have brought them with him when he sledged south along the shore of Greenland to Upernavik.

An observation for latitude on the Polar Sea, or on any other sea, can be placed on a postal card. *And when placed there, or anywhere else, it is absolutely worthless as proof that a man has been there!*

Here is an observation, taken with sextant and artificial horizon, worked out in full, as proof that I was at the North Pole on May 1, 1928:

Meridian Altitude O	May 1, 1928	Sun's S.D.	15' 54"
Observed Altitude O	29° 51' 45"	P & R	− 3' 26"
Index Correction	+ 2' 30"	Temp.	− 28"
2)	29° 54' 15"		+ 12' 00"
	14° 57' 07.5"		

Cor. Ref. Parallax S.D.

& Temp.	+ 12'		
	15° 09' 07.5"	Dec.	14° 56' 12"
	− 90	Corr. +	12' 54"
Z.D.	74° 50' 52.5"		15° 09' 06"
Dec.	15° 09' 06"		
Lat.	89° 59' 58.5"		

This observation places me one hundred and fifty-two feet from the Pole. On that May 1st I was at Bowdoin Harbor, Labrador, in 56° 32' 45" North Latitude, a distance of more than two thousand miles from the Pole!

An astronomical observation for latitude is of the utmost value to the observer, as it proves to him that he has reached a certain spot, *but it is of no value to the world, for it can be easily falsified.*

The final verdict on this point of the subject was spoken by Amundsen, Norway's great explorer. He wrote:

Admiral Peary was the first man ever to reach the North Pole. 'But,' you may ask, 'how do you know he reached it? You have only his word for it... Peary, with his technical knowledge, could easily have faked his records.' Nevertheless, I know that Admiral Peary reached the Pole. What you say about his ability to fake his observations is perfectly true. The answer to any doubt on that score is that Peary was not that kind of a man. The character of the explorer, therefore, is always the best evidence of his claim of achievement.

The Cook-Peary controversy raged on with column after column of statements, contradictions, denials, facts, falsehoods, a welter of words.

Battle Harbor, Labrador, was too far away. The reporters must be on the firing line; they must have a personal interview with Peary. On September 13th the tug *Douglas H. Thomas* emerged out of the rain and mist flying an enormous American flag, and bringing representatives of the Associated Press, Harper and Brothers, and a Mr. Foster of Halifax. This small tug had stolen a march on the big parade, the cable boat *Tyrian*, which came in puffing away on September 16th. Seventeen reporters, five photographers, and one stenographer poured over the rail; the *Roosevelt* heeled to the wave.

We scurried to shelter. They cheered as they came alongside – three boatloads. There was a bargain-counter rush for Commander Peary's door. I can see him now in raincoat and rubber boots with his back against the after cabin, jaw set, serious. He jerked his neck out of his collar, cleared his throat, and said, incisively:

'Gentlemen, I will see you this afternoon at two o'clock in Mr. Croucher's loft – that building there' – pointing with his finger.

They cheered again.

He smiled again and thanked them, and smiled again as the irrepressible Dick Sears pushed through the crowd and handed the Commander a picture of Mrs. Peary, Marie and Robert, taken a few days before on the steps of the Sydney Hotel. He was the only man admitted to the after cabin.

That scene in the old fish loft at Battle Harbor on September 16th was so impressive, so dramatic, and so unique in many ways that the lines of memory etched then will never be erased. It was a whitewashed building with red trimmings, overlooking the narrow 'tickle,' bordered by barren gray hills, their shores white with breaking seas. Worn steps led to the loft, dark as one entered, stained with smoke, dirt, age. There were but two windows, one at the very end, one in the sloping roof. Silhouetted against the former was the well-shaped head and square shoulders of Commander Peary. In front of him and around him, seated on the floor, on barrels, and on nets, the reporters, intent, hanging on every word, for the moment inquisitors, sought to learn the truth. Searching questions, the ready answers, the scratching of pencils, the muffled tones of fishermen in the rear – history was being recorded.

The *Tyrian* sailed during the night freighted with columns and columns of what was accepted as proof by a few that Peary had at last reached the Pole; with columns and columns of what was accepted as convincing evidence by many that Peary was nowhere near it; with damaging statements that he had sent all his men back that he might alone have all the glory; with headline captions that he preferred the company of a negro to that of a white man.

The battle-front moved south from Battle Harbor – not so called because of that – to Sydney, Nova Scotia; the Cook-Peary controversy became the leading topic of the day. Thousands of postal-cards were printed and sent through the mail, containing the one question: 'Are you for Cook or Peary?' Proofs, proofs, proofs, was the incessant call, *something which had never before been demanded of a single Arctic explorer.* The explorer's word had always been accepted without question. In 1607 Henry Hudson came sailing out of the mists of the North with the claim that he had reached the high northern latitude of 81° 30'. Who *knows* that he did? In 1826, Captain W.E. Parry came struggling south over the ice-pack with the claim that he had reached 82° 45'. Who *knows* that he did? In 1876, Commander A.H. Markham turned back toward the northern shores of Grant Land, his men dropping one by one. He claimed that he reached 83° 20'. In 1896, Fridtjof Nansen, the great Norwegian explorer, announced from his hotel in Tromsö, that he had reached 86° 14', a new world's record. In 1901, the Duke of the Abruzzi cabled that his expedition had broken the Norwegian record, that he had reached 86° 34'. In 1926, Byrd sent a radiogram from Spitzbergen that in company with Floyd Bennett he had flown to the North Pole. In 1926, Amundsen announced to the world that the Amundsen-Ellsworth-Nobile Expedition in the *Norge* had succeeded in flying over the Pole. What absolute proof or conclusive evidence did each or any one of the above-mentioned men ever offer to verify or substantiate his claim? *Not one iota.* Each one *said* that he did. His word was accepted. That was enough proof for Geographical and Scientific Societies the world over. Every one of the above records stands and will never be erased.

We steamed south on September 18th. On the nineteenth the sturdy little *Roosevelt* received her first salute from a tramp steamer. She certainly deserved it. At least she had done her work. There was proof of that. Sydney, Nova Scotia, a foreign port, the point of our departure the year before, disregarding all doubts as to this or that, had planned a record-breaking reception which proved to be far more cordial than any received at any home port.

At six in the morning of the twenty-first, we descried through the glasses a large white yacht with the American flag at the fore, a British on the main. By seven-thirty we could see the name *Shellah* and on the bridge Mrs. Peary, Marie, and Robert. A boat was quickly lowered. The last to leave us on our departure almost at this very spot were the first to climb over the rail as we entered port.

Within the next few hours the horizon was fairly dotted with craft of all description – power boats, excursion boats, rowboats, sailing yachts, and canoes – a long line of fluttering flags and cheering people and white jets of steam. A throng of people banked the shores of the harbor; the wharves were black. Peary had arrived! Schools were out, the steel mills were closed, business suspended. The United States consul in tall silk hat climbed the rail beaming with pride at this exceptional opportunity of welcoming a most distinguished man.

Captain Bob edged the *Roosevelt* carefully in to the end of the dock. Ropes whizzed over the heads of the crowd. We were home!

As Commander landed, a delegation of schoolgirls, dressed in white, met him with wreaths. The daughter of Mayor Richardson stepped forward from the group and with a salutatory speech presented him with a huge bouquet of flowers. We were escorted to the Sydney Hotel through a long narrow black line of cheering people. Standing in an open carriage, Commander made his first speech, thanking the reception committee and the people of Sydney for their tribute and for their kindness.

A banquet followed, and then more reporters. The press was calling incessantly for news. Dr. Cook had landed in New York amid great excitement. Triumphal arches were erected in Brooklyn. Bands were playing. Flags were flying. The Pole had been 'Discovered'!

On October 2d, the *Roosevelt* anchored quietly under Sandy Hook. The City of New York was busy with the Hudson-Fulton celebration and had no time for a reception. As an addition to the program the *Roosevelt* was invited to steam up the Hudson to Newburgh. She did – with hardly a salute. Steamer after steamer passed quietly by without a wave of the hand. The shipping paper, the New York Herald, was carrying Cook's story.

By a unanimous vote of the Board of Aldermen, the keys of the City of New York were presented to Dr. Frederick A. Cook. By a vote of the Hudson-Fulton Committee, Commander Robert E. Peary received a Hudson-Fulton Medal, which was presented to a thousand or more visitors to the city!

But reason began to triumph. Peary presented his original observations and notebooks to the National Geographic Society. All were accepted instantly and without question. Cook presented his to the University of Copenhagen. They were rejected. The authorities were astounded to discover that his proofs consisted of a typewritten report of his trip and a set of observations figured out by a Captain Duncan and a Captain Loose of New York. The tide began to turn.

Commander went to his island home off the Maine coast. Dr. Cook went on the lecture platform at three thousand dollars a night, two nights five thousand! Even at this figure, one Western university made a profit by advertising:

Either this man is the greatest explorer the world has ever seen or the biggest liar the world has ever known.

The auditorium was packed!

To one man alone should be given the credit for the first enlightening piece of information, a strong indictment against Cook, which brought the public to a realization of how it had been hoodwinked. This man was George Kennan, the old Siberian traveler, who presented unanswerable arguments in the Outlook of October 2d. This was followed on October 16th by an article on 'Arctic Work and Arctic Food.' The people realized that this man knew something; they sat up and listened. The tide began to run the other way, stronger and stronger, and here the controversy may be dismissed.

One question I have been asked again and again during the past years is, 'Why did Peary select a colored man to accompany him to the Pole rather than one of his white assistants?'

Matthew Henson first went north with Peary in 1891. He was with him on his long trip over the Greenland Ice Cap in 1893. He was with him when he rounded the northern end of Greenland in 1900. He was with him off Cape Hecla in 1902. He was with him when he broke the world's record in 1906. He was the most popular man aboard the ship with the Eskimos. He could talk their language like a native. He made all the sledges which went to the Pole. He made all the stoves. Henson, the colored man, went to the Pole with Peary because he was a better man than any of his white assistants. As Peary himself admitted, 'I can't get along without Henson.'

After his many failures, Commander Peary owed it to himself, his family, and his loyal backers, his country, to take the most effective man, to use the most serviceable. And this he did. And he won!

I have sometimes thought that Commander's worst enemy was the perfection of his system. The work was done too well, almost so well as to be deemed impossible. Now comes a critic who denies that Peary had any system – that all the things he planned and did had been planned and done before by other men. The infinite pains which went into the equipment of the expedition and the care of organization set this final expedition of Commander far apart from any other of which I have read. If his combination of details was not a system, I fail to sense the meaning of the word. Taylor has been credited with inventing a new labor system of laying brick – he used bricks and mortar and men as had his predecessors, but he used them in a different way. The same is equally true of Peary.

That Borup turned back from 85° North Latitude, Marvin from 86° 38', Captain Bartlett from 87° 46' 49", has never been doubted. But that Peary covered the last one hundred and thirty-three miles and returned to land on April 23, 1909, was doubted and is even doubted by some today. Henson stated that after Bartlett left for home, they went on for five long marches. The four Eskimos all declare that they went on for five long arches. That they could double and treble their distances on the return has been demonstrated. We all did it with the cast-off dogs of the expedition.

On the return journey of Peary from the Pole, it was up and on with little sleep. The Eskimos were deeply worried. Commander was anxious over the next full moon, open water, and easterly drift. They were different men when they reached the *Roosevelt*. Their faces, their bodies, their loss of weight, showed plainly the tremendous strain under which they had been. One look was convincing. They had been a long, long way, and had worked-hard and had suffered.

One question more. 'What proof had Peary to offer that he had reached the Pole?' His word.

What reasons had we, his assistants, for believing that he reached the Pole? We had every reason. In the first place, we knew Peary. And in addition:

1. His long experience, 1886–1909, in the North.

2. His system as we studied it in actual operation.

3. A sufficiency of the best sledging dogs in the world, food, men, and equipment.

4. His position on the Polar Sea when Ross Marvin left the main expedition, as shown by his sextant observations.

5. His position on the Polar Sea when Captain Bob Bartlett departed for land, as shown by his published observations. At that time he was only one hundred and thirty-three miles from the Pole. He had thirty-two of the picked dogs out of one hundred and thirty-three. He had four of the picked men out of twenty-five. He had sufficient food not only to reach the Pole, but to go far beyond and return.

6. His own observations, which place him within one mile and a quarter of the exact spot and which we believe were taken honestly. Just how near a man must be to the Pole, in order to claim that he actually reached it, is simply a matter of opinion. Scientists state that ten, fifteen, or even twenty miles is sufficient.

The North Pole is a needle-point, roughly, in the middle of a great mass of moving ice. Today it may be a point on the surface of a pool of water, tomorrow the top of a small iceberg, a pin-point on a pressure ridge, a

Matthew A. Henson
He went with Peary to the Pole

point in the snow. *If the North Pole were in so well known a place as the middle of Boston Common, no man on earth could find it in one set or two sets or three sets of observations.* No portable instrument is sufficiently accurate, nor is any man skillful enough, to locate a needle-point by an observation of the sun, moon, or stars.

Peary was near enough. That is why his great achievement is recorded today in history, geography, in encyclopedia. He will stand for all time as the Discoverer of the North Pole.

THE END

✳

APPENDIX

The following geographical societies have recognized the claims of Peary to the discovery of the North Pole:

London	Antwerp	Lima
Berlin	Vienna	Chicago
Paris	Dresden	New York
Geneva	Madrid	Mexico
Rome	St. Petersburg	Philadelphia
Brussels	Tokio	

The following list of medals, decorations, and gifts, presented to Rear Admiral Robert E. Peary is a testimonial of the recognition of his years of work in the Arctic:

The Elisha Kent Kane Gold Medal for eminent geographical research, awarded by the Geographical Society of Philadelphia, in 1902, to Robert E. Peary, U.S.N.

Gold Medal – presented by the Geographical Society of Geneva to Rear Admiral Robert E. Peary, U.S.N., in 1913, in recognition of his achievements in connection with Arctic exploration.

Gold Medal – awarded by the Royal Geographical Society, London, in 1898, to Robert E. Peary, U.S.N., 'for his service to the science of geography.'

Gold Medal – awarded by the Italian Geographical Society to Robert E. Peary, U.S.N., 'for his expedition to the North Pole in 1909.'

Gold Medal – awarded by the Geographical Society of Philadelphia to Robert E. Peary, U.S.N., 'for the discovery of the North Pole,' in 1909.

The Nachtigal Gold Medal of the Geographical Society of Berlin – awarded in 1910 to Robert E. Peary, U.S.N., 'for his Arctic explorations.'

Gold Medal – awarded to Rear Admiral Robert E. Peary, U.S.N., in 1911, by the Paris Academy of Sports, in recognition of his achievements in attaining the North Pole, April 6, 1909.

Gold Medal – presented by the Geographical Society of Marseilles to Rear Admiral Robert E. Peary, U.S.N., in 1913, in recognition of his achievements in connection with Arctic exploration.

The Cullum Gold Medal of the American Geographical Society, of New York – awarded to Robert E. Peary, U.S.N., 'for his Arctic expedition of 1902 which determined the insularity of Greenland.' First impression and award of this medal.

The Hubbard Gold Medal of the National Geographic Society, Washington – awarded to Robert E. Peary, U.S.N., 'for farthest north in Arctic exploration, 87° 6'.'

Gold Badge of the Saint Andrews Society of Philadelphia – presented to Rear Admiral Robert E. Peary, U.S.N.

Gold Medal – awarded by the Geographical Society of Paris to Robert E. Peary, U.S.N., 'for Arctic Exploration from 1886 to 1902.'

Special Great Gold Medal of the National Geographic Society, Washington – awarded to Robert E. Peary, U.S.N., 'for the discovery of the North Pole, April 6, 1909.'

The Peary Arctic Club Medal of Honor – awarded to Rear Admiral Robert E. Peary, U.S.N., April 6, 1912, on the third anniversary of his discovery of the North Pole, and in recognition of the following achievements made possible by the encouragement and financial assistance of the Peary Arctic Club, namely: The crossing of Greenland, 1892 and 1895; the securing of the Cape York meteorites, July–September, 1897; the determination of the insularity of Greenland, May, 1900; the farthest north, April 21, 1906; and the attainment of the

Pole, April 6, 1909. The five metallic points of the star are from the Ahnighito Meteorite brought from near Cape York by Peary in 1897. This is the first, and, so far, the only award of this medal.

Gold Medal of Kane Lodge F. and A.M. of New York City (Fraternal and Ancient Order of Masons).

Special Great Gold Medal of the Royal Geographical Society, London – awarded in 1910 to Robert E. Peary, U.S.N., 'for Arctic exploration from 1886 to 1909.'

Gold Medal – presented by the City of Paris to Rear Admiral Robert E. Peary, U.S.N., in 1913, in recognition of his achievements in connection with Arctic exploration.

Great Gold Medal of the Explorer's Club of New York City – awarded to Rear Admiral Robert E. Peary, U.S.N., in recognition of his discovery of the North Pole, 1909.

Great Gold Medal of the Paris Geographical Society – awarded to Rear Admiral Robert E. Peary, U.S.N., in recognition of his discovery of the North Pole, 1909.

Silver Medal – awarded by the Royal Scottish Geographical Society, in 1897, to Robert E. Peary, U.S.N., 'for distinguished services in Arctic exploration.'

The Helen Culver Gold Medal of the Geographical Society of Chicago – awarded in 1910 to Robert E. Peary, U.S.N., 'for distinguished services in Arctic Exploration and the discovery of the North Pole on April 6, 1909.'

Bronze Medal commemorating the services of Elisha Kent Kane, Arctic Explorer (1820–1857) – presented to Rear Admiral Robert E. Peary, U.S.N.

Gold Medal – awarded by the Royal Geographical Society in 1910, to Robert E. Peary, U.S.N., 'for north polar expedition in 1908–1909.'

Gold Medal – awarded by the Hungarian Geographical Society in 1910, to Robert E. Peary, U.S.N., 'for north polar expedition.' First impression and award of this medal.

Gold Medal – awarded by the Royal Geographical Society of Antwerp, in 1910, to Robert E. Peary, U.S.N., 'for the discovery of the North Pole.'

The Von Hauer Silver Medal of the Imperial Geographical Society of
Vienna – awarded in 1910 to Robert E. Peary, U.S.N., 'for eminent
services to the science of geography.'

The David Livingstone Gold Medal of the Royal Scottish Geographical
Society – awarded in 1903 to Robert E. Peary, U.S.N., for Arctic exploration.

The Charles P. Daly Gold Medal for geographical research – awarded by
the American Geographical Society of New York in 1902, to Robert E.
Peary, U.S.N.

Gold Medal – presented by the Geographical Society of Normandy to
Rear Admiral Robert E. Peary, U.S.N., in 1913, in recognition of his
achievements in connection with Arctic exploration.

Silver Model of Ship showing type of vessel employed by Arctic navigators of the sixteenth and seventeenth centuries – presented in 1910 by
the Royal Scottish Geographical Society to Robert E. Peary, U.S.N., in
recognition of his achievement in reaching the North Pole in 1909.

Wooden plaque with the following inscription, 'Presented to Commander
Robert E. Peary, C.E., U.S.A., Discoverer of the North Pole, April 6,
1909, by the Canadian Camp of New York City, March 5, 1910.'

Act tendering thanks of Congress to Robert E. Peary. (Painted on silk.)
'Act tendering Thanks of Congress to Robert E. Peary. Be it enacted by
the Senate and House of Representatives of the United States of America in Congress assembled. That the Thanks of Congress be, and the
same are hereby tendered to Robert E. Peary, United States Navy, for
his Arctic Explorations in reaching the North Pole. Approved March
4, 1911. William H. Taft, President, J. S. Sherman, Vice-President.'

Silver Loving Cup – presented by the citizens of Portland and South Portland, Maine, September 23, 1909, to Robert E. Peary, U.S.N., in recognition of his achievement in reaching the North Pole, April 6, 1909.

Silver Loving Cup – presented by Delta Kappa Epsilon Association of
New York City, December 18, 1909, to Robert E. Peary, U.S.N., in
recognition of his achievement in reaching the North Pole, April 6,
1909.

Silver Loving Cup – presented by the City of Bangor, Maine, September 23, 1909, to Robert E. Peary, U.S.N., 'in recognition of his remarkable achievement in placing the flag of the United States at the North Pole, April 6, 1909.'

PHOTOGRAPH CREDITS

INTRODUCTION

1 Photograph by Donald B. MacMillan, Peary-MacMillan Arctic Museum, Bowdoin College, 3000.1.4.

2 Photograph by Donald B. MacMillan, Peary-MacMillan Arctic Museum, Bowdoin College, 3000.2.23.

3 Reproduction of original in the collection of the Peary-MacMillan Arctic Museum, Bowdoin College.

4 Photograph by G.H. Nickerson, Peary-MacMillan Arctic Museum, Bowdoin College, 1994.5.2445.

5 Unidentified photographer, Peary-MacMillan Arctic Museum, Bowdoin College, 1994.5.2345.

6 Unidentified photographer, Peary-MacMillan Arctic Museum, Bowdoin College, 1966.110a.

7 Unidentified photographer, Peary-MacMillan Arctic Museum, Bowdoin College, 1994.5.2888.

8 Unidentified photographer, Peary-MacMillan Arctic Museum, Bowdoin College, 1994.5.2886.

9 Photograph by Maurice Tanquary, Peary-MacMillan Arctic Museum, Bowdoin College, 2006.4.14.

10 Photograph by Donald B. MacMillan, Peary-MacMillan Arctic Museum, Bowdoin College, 3000.33.3045.

11 Photograph by Donald B. MacMillan, Peary-MacMillan Arctic Museum, Bowdoin College, 3000.33.902.

12 Unidentified photographer, Peary-MacMillan Arctic Museum, Bowdoin College, 1994.5.2630.

13 Photograph by Alfred M. Bailey, Peary-MacMillan Arctic Museum, Bowdoin College, 1995.2.212.

14 Unidentified photographer, Peary-MacMillan Arctic Museum, Bowdoin College, 1994.5.2241.

15 Unidentified photographer, Peary-MacMillan Arctic Museum, Bowdoin College, 3000.33.5160.

COLOUR PLATES

1 Photograph by Donald B. MacMillan, Peary-MacMillan Arctic Museum, Bowdoin College, 3000.32.1805.

2 Photograph by Donald B. MacMillan, Peary-MacMillan Arctic Museum, Bowdoin College, 3000.32.954.

3 Photograph by Donald B. MacMillan, Peary-MacMillan Arctic Museum, Bowdoin College, 3000.32.1113.

4 Photograph by Donald B. MacMillan, Peary-MacMillan Arctic Museum, Bowdoin College, 3000.32.59.

5 Photograph by Donald B. MacMillan, Peary-MacMillan Arctic Museum, Bowdoin College, 3000.32.1126.

6 Photograph by Donald B. MacMillan, Peary-MacMillan Arctic Museum, Bowdoin College, 3000.32.1142.

7 Photograph by Donald B. MacMillan, Peary-MacMillan Arctic Museum, Bowdoin College, 3000.32.1821.

8 Photograph by Robert E. Peary or Matthew Henson, Peary-MacMillan Arctic Museum, Bowdoin College, 3000.32.1824.

9 Photograph by Donald B. MacMillan, Peary-MacMillan Arctic Museum, Bowdoin College, 3000.32.12.

10 Photograph by Donald B. MacMillan, Peary-MacMillan Arctic Museum, Bowdoin College, 3000.32.1076.

11 Photograph by Donald B. MacMillan, Peary-MacMillan Arctic Museum, Bowdoin College, 3000.32.1826.

TEXT

Frontispiece. Photograph by A. de Lalancy, from the Peary-MacMillan Arctic Museum collection.

1 Photograph by Donald B. MacMillan, Peary-MacMillan Arctic Museum, Bowdoin College, 3000.33.259.

2 Photograph by Donald B. MacMillan, Peary-MacMillan Arctic Museum, Bowdoin College, 3000.33.143.

3 From a photo-reproduction in the Peary-MacMillan Arctic Museum collection.

4 Photograph by Donald B. MacMillan, Peary-MacMillan Arctic Museum, Bowdoin College, 1994.5.554.

5 From Capt. John Ross, *A voyage of discovery, made under the order of the Admiralty, in His Majesty's ships Isabella and Alexander, for the purpose of exploring Baffin's Bay, and inquiring into the probability of a North-west Passage.* 1819. In the Peary-MacMillan Arctic Museum collection.

6 Photograph by Donald B. MacMillan, Peary-MacMillan Arctic Museum, Bowdoin College, 3000.33.263.

7 Photograph by Donald B. MacMillan, Peary-MacMillan Arctic Museum, Bowdoin College, 3000.1.129.

8 Photograph by Donald B. MacMillan, Peary-MacMillan Arctic Museum, Bowdoin College, 3000.33.275.

9 Photograph by Donald B. MacMillan, Peary-MacMillan Arctic Museum, Bowdoin College, 3000.40.55.

10 Photograph by Donald B. MacMillan, Peary-MacMillan Arctic Museum, Bowdoin College, 3000.33.296.

11 Photograph by Donald B. MacMillan, Peary-MacMillan Arctic Museum, Bowdoin College, 3000.33.1408.

12 Photograph by Donald B. MacMillan, Peary-MacMillan Arctic Museum, Bowdoin College, 3000.1.35.

13 Photograph by Donald B. MacMillan, Peary-MacMillan Arctic Museum, Bowdoin College, 3000.40.26.

14 Photograph by Matthew Henson, Peary-MacMillan Arctic Museum, Bowdoin College, 3000.32.1822.

15 Photograph by Donald B. MacMillan, Peary-MacMillan Arctic Museum, Bowdoin College, 3000.33.293.

INDEX